Power for Abundant Living

Other books by Victor Paul Wierwille

Receiving the Holy Spirit Today
Are the Dead Alive Now?
The Bible Tells Me So
The New, Dynamic Church
The Word's Way
God's Magnified Word
Jesus Christ Is Not God
Jesus Christ Our Passover
Jesus Christ Our Promised Seed

Power
for
Abundant Living

The Accuracy of the Bible

Victor Paul Wierwille

American Christian Press
The Way International
New Knoxville, Ohio 45871

The scripture used throughout this book is quoted from the King James Version unless otherwise noted. All explanatory insertions by the author within a scripture verse are enclosed in brackets. All Greek, Hebrew, and Aramaic words are italicized and transliterated into English.

International Standard Book Number 0-910068-01-1
Library of Congress Catalog Card Number 72-164674
American Christian Press
The Way International
New Knoxville, Ohio 45871
Sixth Impression. Hardbound. 1982
Printed in the United States of America

To my daughter
Karen Ruth Wierwille Martin

CONTENTS

Part IV The New Birth

Part V Power in Christ Jesus

Part I

The Power of Believing

Introduction
The Abundant Life

Jesus' proclamation as recorded in John 10:10 is the foundational Scripture for this book.

> ... I am come that they [believers] might have life, and that they might have *it* more abundantly.

This verse literally changed my life. My wife and I began in the Christian ministry, plodding ahead with the things of God; but somehow we lacked an abundant life. Then one time I was especially alerted when I read from the Word of God that Jesus said He had come to give us life more abundant. I was startled into awareness. As I looked about me at communities where I had served and among the ministers with whom I had worked, the abundant life was frequently not evident. In contrast to these Christian people, I could see that the secular world of non-Christians were manifesting a more abundant life than were members of the Church. Thus I earnestly began to pursue the question, "If Jesus Christ came that men and women might have a *more abundant life*, why is it that the Christian believers do not manifest even an *abundant life?*"

I believe most people would be thankful if they even lived an abundant life; but The Word says Jesus Christ came that we might have life not just abundant, but more abundant. If His Word is not reliable here in John 10:10, how can we trust it anywhere else? But, on the other hand, if Jesus told the truth, if He meant what He said and said what He meant in this declaration, then surely there must be keys, signposts, to guide us to the understanding and the receiving of this life which is more than abundant.

This book, *Power for Abundant Living*, is one way of showing interested people the abundant life which Jesus Christ lived and which He came to make available to believers as it is revealed in the Word of God.

This is a book containing Biblical keys. The contents herein do not teach the Scriptures from Genesis 1:1 to Revelation 22:21; rather, it is designed to set before the reader the basic keys in the Word of God so that Genesis to Revelation will unfold and so that the abundant life which Jesus Christ came to make available will become evident to those who want to appropriate His abundance to their lives.

Chapter One
The Fountain of Living Waters

The first and most basic key for power for abundant living is that *the Bible is the revealed Word and Will of God.* This key is the greatest secret in the world today. It is a secret not because God is keeping it to Himself; it is a secret because people have not believed. Most people do not believe that the Bible is the revealed Word and Will of God. They take out one segment of the Word of God and insert another. But to be logical and consistent, either the entire Bible is the Word of God from Genesis to Revelation or it is not the Word of God anywhere. Knowing that the Word of God is the Will of God is the primary step in our search for power for abundant living.

Jeremiah 2:13 says,

> For my people have committed two evils; they have forsaken me the fountain of living waters, *and* hewed them out cisterns, broken cisterns, that can hold no water.

The Power of Believing

To whom is God talking? He says, "my people." He is not talking to people who are on the outside of His fold; He is talking to those within the fold when He says, "... my people have committed two evils; [first] they have forsaken me the fountain of living waters ...." God is a fountain as opposed to cisterns which belong to people.

A fountain has an unlimited supply of water. When people forsake God who is a fountain, they hew out for themselves cisterns which are man-made and which hold only a limited amount. If the cistern is a fifty-barrel one, fifty barrels is the maximum supply a person can get from it. When people forsake God, the fountain of living waters, they hew out for themselves, not fountains, but cisterns. Furthermore, those cisterns are broken cisterns; always leaking away their limited supply.

I too was like a broken cistern at one time in my life. I too had hewed out for myself a supposedly valid theological system. I had read this, I had read that, I had concluded this, and I had concluded that; but just when I needed power, I didn't have the necessary resources. When I needed the limitless supply of living water, all I had was an empty hole. This dilemma is what brought me to the years of Biblical research; the questing for a solution to my empty cistern spurred my start in the Biblical field.

Have you ever asked yourself or considered what is the greatest sin you can commit? If you asked the residents of your community do you know what they would say? One person would say that the greatest sin is murder; someone else would say that it is adultery; somebody else would say something else. You would come up with a multiplicity of answers as to the greatest sin.

What does the Word of God say concerning this question? Matthew 22 tells us.

> Matthew 22:37,38:
> Jesus said unto him, Thou shalt love the Lord thy God with all thy heart, and with all thy soul, and with all thy mind.
>
> This is the first and great commandment.

If that is the first and great commandment, then what is the first and great sin? By simple logic breaking the first and great commandment of not loving God — of loving something else more than we love God, putting something ahead of God — hewing out our own religious systems, our own ideologies, our own thinking patterns — rather than adhering to the divine revelation of God's wonderful, matchless Word.

The Power of Believing

Look at Hosea 4:6,

> My people are destroyed for lack of knowledge ....

Again God is talking to His people when He says, "My people are destroyed for lack of knowledge ...." This lack of knowledge is not in science, philosophy, newspapers or the latest movies. If God's people are being destroyed today, there is only one reason: a lack of knowledge of the Word of God. This lack of knowledge of the integrity and the greatness of God's Word — that the revealed Word of God is the Will of God — is the reason His people are being destroyed.

Many times people say to me in my classes on Power for Abundant Living, "Dr. Wierwille, you sure get excited about your Biblical research." That is right; why shouldn't I be enthusiastic about the greatness of God's Word with its message of unlimited resources? When I was playing basketball, I was involved and enthusiastic. I became concerned and had tremendous zeal for that sport. Why not have a tremendous zeal for the greatness of God's Word which is much more lasting and rewarding. A man is admired for being a football or basketball fan; but when he dares to get excited about the greatness of God's Word, people think that this Biblical fan has a "screw loose." Surely there must be something wrong with

8

our scale of values. The Word of God is so tremendous, so wonderful, so rich, that when Jesus Christ said He came that we might have life and have it more abundantly, we should naturally respond with excitement. Not only do we need to have a knowledge of the integrity and the accuracy of God's Word, but we must also get the zeal, the enthusiastic believing, the concern that other men and women might know that the Word of God is the Will of God.

Chapter Two
Availability, Receivability, Usability

1

In order to tap the resources of the power of God, one must know first of all *what is* and *what is not* available from God. There are some things that are not available today; and if they are not available, we can pray until we are exhausted and we still will not receive an answer to our prayers. If we want to effectively tap the resources for the more abundant life, we must find out what is available to us, what God has promised us. In the secular world we constantly apply this principle. Take, for instance, this book which you are reading. Could you have gotten it if it were not available? Certainly not. Spiritually the same is true. We must find out from God's Word what is available.

As an example of availability, III John 2 tells us what God desires for us.

Beloved, I wish above all things that thou mayest prosper and be in health, even as thy soul prospereth.

The will of God is that we may prosper. He never meant for the Christian to be poverty-stricken and down-trodden in any segment of his life. He meant for the Christian believer to prosper. Furthermore, God's will for every believer is that we "be in [good] health, even as thy soul prospereth." God never meant for the Christian believer to be sick; sickness is never glorifying to God. He never meant for the Christian believer to be full of frustrations and fears and anxieties. God meant for us to prosper and be in good health. Since the Word of God is the Will of God, prosperity and good health must be available.

Let's check other examples of availability.

Philippians 4:19:
But my God shall supply all your need according to his riches in glory by Christ Jesus.

God's will is to supply all our *need* — it doesn't say *greed*. If God is going to supply all our need according to His riches in glory, a supply to fill it must be available. If the supply is not available, then He cannot fulfill our need.

Look at II Corinthians 9:8.

12

Availability, Receivability, Usability

And God *is* able to make all grace abound toward you; that ye, always having all sufficiency in all *things,* may abound to every good work.

How are we going to have all sufficiency in all things if it is not accessible to us?

Check Romans 8:37, another wonderful record in God's Word telling us some of the things that must be available.

... in all these things we are more than conquerors through him that loved us.

If we are going to be more than conquerors in every situation, it must be possible. How could I be more than a conqueror if the power were not available?

Read Ephesians 3, beginning with verse 16.

That he [God] would grant you, according to the riches of his glory, to be strengthened with might by his Spirit in the inner man.

How am I going to be strengthened with might by His Spirit in the inner man if it is not possible?

13

Ephesians 3:17—19:

That Christ may dwell in your hearts by faith;
that ye, being rooted and grounded in love,

May be able to comprehend with all saints what
is the breadth, and length, and depth, and
height;

And to know the love of Christ, which passeth
knowledge, that ye might be filled with all the
fulness of God.

"That ye might be filled with all the fulness of
God." How am I going to be filled with all the fulness
of God if it is not available?

How am I going to be able to apply the principles
of the Word of God and find out what God wants me
to do if I do not know the promises in His Word? The
first thing that we must find, in our quest to tap the
resources for the more abundant life, is what is available. There are hundreds of different promises in the
Word of God that will enable us to prosper and to be
in good health. One cannot utilize, one cannot operate, any more than those promises he knows. How
many do you know?

There is only one place where we can possibly go
to find out what God has available to us and for us:

14

we must go to the Word of God.

Many times the things that people have said God does, His Word says just the opposite; things that they say He does not do, He declares in His Word that He does. In this book, *Power for Abundant Living*, let's be sure in our Biblical quest for the more abundant life that we first find out what is available so that we as God's people will not be destroyed because we lack knowledge. When we know what is available, then we can learn the other principles that are involved in making our life more abundant so that we can manifest the greatness of the power of God.

2

When I was a young lad, my mother would say to me on Saturday night before I went to town, "Be a good boy." This admonition actually never helped because one cannot make a boy good by telling him to be good. People seldom read the Word of God by being told they have to read it. People never tap the resources of prayer by being told that they ought to pray. I do not tell you that you ought to read the Bible; I teach you *how* to read it. I do not tell you that you ought to pray; I tell you *how* to pray. I do not tell you that you should believe; I teach you *how* to believe.

15

The Power of Believing

It is important that we know *how*. Since birth, we have been taught how to receive material things. If we had not been taught how to receive a material object, this book could be available, but we would not know how to go about taking or receiving it. So it is with the Word of God. Spiritual things may be received on the same basis as we receive this book in the natural or material realm. In this book, not only do we look for what is available from God, but we also discover how to receive that which is available.

For many years I moved among groups in which I constantly heard people preaching sin, condemnation and hellfire, and other negative subjects. These well-meaning ministers were not telling people how to get rid of sin, they were just saying that it was wrong. To tell someone that something is wrong does not help him to overcome it. I learned this lesson the hard way.

In the town of my second congregation lived a man who was an alcoholic. For about two years many of us had prayed that this man would come to church so that he could hear the sermon which I had prepared on the abuses of alcohol. Finally one Sunday morning when I least expected him, he came and sat in the last pew. As I walked to the pulpit having just noticed his presence, I thought, "Well, goodness, here he is this morning." I put aside that morning's sermon and I

16

went into the files of my mind and brought out the sermon I had developed on the misuse and the sin of excessive drinking. I preached with all the strength I had. When I finished, I patted myself on the back for having preached with such zeal against drinking that I thought God would have to move over someone in the spiritual realm and give me a special place in heaven.

I walked from the pulpit to the vestibule of the church where a minister shakes hands with the people as they leave the sanctuary. As this poor alcoholic passed through the handshaking line, he had tears in his eyes. He limply shook my hand and he said, "I came to church this morning to find out *how* to get out of what I am in, but all you did was put me in deeper." He cried, "If you want to know about alcoholism, I can tell you more than you will ever know." That response cut me to the bone. I thought I had preached a tremendous sermon. But this man walked out saying he came to church trusting that maybe I would tell him how to get out of the dilemma he was in; instead I had merely told him less than he already knew.

I quit shaking hands and returned to my office where I knelt in prayer next to my office chair. I hardly ever kneel when I pray, but somehow that morning I dropped next to my chair and I asked God

to forgive me. I promised the Father that if He would
forgive me, as long as I lived I would never preach a
negative sermon, I would never condemn anybody.
Why? I want to teach people how to tap the resources
for the more abundant life, not the less abundant life.

I cannot help what people have been in the past; all
I can do is to teach that what they were in the past
can be forgiven and forgotten and that they can move
on with the greatness of the power of God. This is
why we must not only know *what* is available if
we are going to live the more abundant life, but we
must also know *how* to receive the spiritual things of
God. After we have received from God, in the third
place, we must know what to do with these spiritual
things.

3

First, what is available; second, how to receive; and
third, what to do with it after we have received. For
example, here is this book. It is available and I know
how to receive it; but unless I know what to do with
it after I have it, I still cannot utilize it for the purpose for which it was designed. I knew the book was
available; I knew how to receive it; but then if I used
it as a garden hoe, it would not serve very well, would
it? It is not designed for that. This book was designed
for reading. In the spiritual realm we must know what

to do after we have received what is available. There are people who know what is available and they know how to receive something; but when it comes to knowing what to do with it after they have it, they are entirely at a loss and especially so on the subject of the holy spirit. To find proper usage we must again go to the Word of God.

I believe that the Word of God is the Will of God and that if we are going to know the will of God, we must go back to the Word of God. One cannot listen to the man on the street. He says, "Well, this is God's will." He may be right and he may be wrong. You and I can be accurate and sure only if we go to God's Word. No one can know the will of God without knowing the Word of God. The Bible is the revealed Word of God; this Word of God means what it says and says what it means, and God has a purpose for everything He says, *where* He says it, *why* He says it, *how* He says it, *when* He says it, and *to whom* He says it.

If we are going to tap the resources for the more abundant life, we must not only know what is available, how to receive it, and what to do with it; but we must also get our needs and wants parallel. If our needs are light and our wants are heavy, we are not balanced. If our wants are light and our needs are heavy, we will never get an answer. When we believe,

19

The Power of Believing

we get results in prayer if our needs and our wants are equal.

Look at Matthew 18:19.

> ... If two of you shall agree on earth as touching any thing that they shall ask, it shall be done for them of my Father which is in heaven.

In the Greek text the word "agree" is "symphonized." If the two people agree, they are in harmony; they have their needs and wants parallel because "it shall be done."

John 14:13 is another tremendous truth.

> And whatsoever ye shall ask in my name, that will I do, that the Father may be glorified in the Son.

Whatsoever we ask in Jesus' name, having our needs and wants parallel, He is going to do.

In John 15:16 is another wonderful promise.

> Ye have not chosen me, but I have chosen you, and ordained you, that ye should go and bring forth fruit, and *that* your fruit should remain:

20

that whatsoever ye shall ask of the Father in my name, he may give it you.

If we know what is available, how to receive it, what to do with it, and have our needs and wants parallel, then whatsoever we shall ask shall be done unto us.

There is another promise in I John 5:14.

And this is the confidence that we have in him, that, if we ask any thing according to his will, he heareth us.

If we have our needs and wants parallel, we can ask anything according to His will. How can we know His will without knowing His Word? His Word is His Will.

One more great truth is that God's ability always equals God's willingness. Many people say that God is willing, but He is not able; others say He is able, but not willing. This may be true of men, but not of God. A man may have the ability and lack the willingness, or have the willingness and lack the ability. For instance, let's say I am stranded along the highway with a flat tire and need a jack. You come along that highway, stop and say, "Hello what can I do for you?" And I say, "Well, I need a jack"; but you do not have a

21

jack either. You are willing to help me, but you lack the ability. On the other hand, let's say you would come along the highway and you do have a jack, but you will not let me use it; then you have the ability, but you lack the willingness. This is never true with God. God's ability always equals His willingness — they are always harmonious. What God is able to do, He is willing to do; and what He is willing to do, He is able to do.

Let us look at Romans 4:20 and 21.

He staggered not at the promise of God through unbelief ....

And [But]being fully persuaded that, what he [God]had promised, he was able also to perform.

God's ability always equals God's willingness.

Numbers 23:19 contains a phrase that I want to point out. "God *is* not a man, that he should lie ...." God's promises are always true and dependable.

In Romans 11:29 we read of the permanence of God's gifts.

For the gifts and calling of God *are* without repentance.

When God gives something, these gifts and these callings of God are always without repentance; God does not withdraw or take them away. Whatever God has promised that He will perform, that He will honor when men and women believe God's wonderful, matchless Word.

I want to give one more example to illustrate that God's ability equals His willingness.

Hebrews 11:11:
Through faith also Sara herself received strength to conceive seed, and was delivered of a child when she was past age, because she judged him faithful who had promised.

Sara brought forth this child because of the promises which God had made many years before for "she judged him faithful who had promised." Who had made the promise? God. What God promised He kept when Sara believed. So, too, what God promises in His Word, He will honor when *we* believe.

If we are going to tap the resources for the more abundant life, we have to go to The Word to find out what is available, how to receive, and what to do with it after we have it. We are going to keep our needs and our wants in balance, recognizing that God is not only able but willing to perform every promise set forth in His Word.

Chapter Three
Believing Equals Receiving

In every Scriptural account in the Word of God where a miracle took place or where God did a mighty work, the principles pointed out in the previous chapter were present. The persons involved knew what was available, how to receive what they needed, and what to do with it after they received, and they had their needs and wants coordinated knowing that God's ability equals His willingness to keep His promises. When these keys are understood, we can read any place from Genesis to Revelation and see this pattern.

As an illustration, let's begin with Mark 3:1.

And he [Jesus] entered again into the synagogue; and there was a man there which had a withered hand.

The man had a need. The synagogue was the place where people worshipped, where they were taught, where people of God were to meet and have their needs met.

Verse 2,

> And they [the Pharisees] watched him [Jesus], whether he would heal him on the sabbath day; that they might accuse him.

Why did these so-called religious leaders watch Jesus? Because they wanted to accuse Jesus if He did any healing on the wrong day of the week. These people were surely interested in the man who had the withered hand, were they not? No. They were only interested in whether Jesus acted at the right place, at the right time, and with their blessing. This man with the withered hand was at the place to expect help, but what had he received? Nothing.

Verse 3,

> And he [Jesus] saith unto the man which had the withered hand, Stand forth.

The moment the man stood forth he knew he was separating himself from the onlookers and that he would receive the same criticism they were leveling against Jesus.

Verse 4,

> And he saith unto them, Is it lawful to do good
> on the sabbath days, or to do evil? to save life,
> or to kill? But they [the leaders and the
> Pharisees] held their peace.

Do you know why? The leaders in the synagogue
were not interested in whether the man was delivered
or not; they were interested only in one thing
— exposing Jesus.

Verse 5,

> And when he had looked round about on them
> with [compassion? NO. NO. It says] anger ...

We have always been taught that if a person is a
real Christian the only thing he ever does is love.
Don't you think that Jesus Christ loved? Wasn't He
all love? Yet, Mark 3 records that He looked around
about on those synagogue leaders with anger. Jesus
was really irritated. The idea that Christians and men
of God have to go around patting everybody on the
back all the time is a distorted concept. Sometimes
men of God have to take a stand against those obstruc-

27

ting the power of God. Jesus looked upon them with anger.

Verse 5,

> And when he had looked round about on them with anger, being grieved for the hardness of their hearts, he saith unto the man [with the withered hand], Stretch forth thine hand ....

In an analysis of this section from Mark 3:1–5, the first thing we see is what is available. The command stated what was available. The command was "Stretch forth thine hand." That appeared to be an impossibility because the man's hand was withered; he could not naturally stretch it forth. Yet Jesus said to the man with the withered hand,

> ... Stretch forth thine hand. And he [the man] stretched *it* out ....

The man with the withered hand who had this tremendous need, stretched out his hand. He did the impossible. How? He believed. *Believe* is a verb and a verb shows action. The man believed that what Jesus said was God's will; therefore, he stretched his hand forth. Once you have the promise of God, the "how" of receiving is to believe literally what that promise says. It appeared impossible for the man to stretch

28

out his hand. Yet this man, believing what The Word said or what God said by way of Jesus Christ, stretched it forth.

... and his hand was restored whole as the other.

He did not receive his wholeness first and then stretch forth his hand; it was in the stretching forth that he was made whole. Before one receives any-thing, he must act as though he already has it and then he receives.

Whenever I read this record from Mark 3, it re-minds me of the times I was practicing the principles of the greatness of God's Word in other countries of the world. On one occasion when I was teaching in Jubbulpore, India, a lady who had worked in a mis-sion service for thirty years was delivered by God's power of a number of sicknesses which appeared in-curable. This deliverance caused such a stir in the city of Jubbulpore the morning after the miracle occurred, that when my family and I were ready to board the train and leave Jubbulpore, hundreds of people gathered at the railroad depot. This crowd, which was composed mainly of Hindus, wanted me to lay my hands on them individually because they thought that I must have some special power in my hands since I had laid my hands on the woman the previous day. They felt that if I just laid my hands on

29

them, they too would be delivered. Just before the train on which we were traveling moved out of the depot, a high-caste Hindu, whose paralyzed arm was hanging limp at his side, ran up to our railroad compartment. He said to me, "Will you pray for my arm?" However, he immediately added, "But I do not believe in your Jesus."

What would you have done? I asked him if he believed God would deliver him. He said, "I believe that God will heal me if you pray for me, but I do not believe in your Jesus." So again I asked him, "Do you believe God will set you free?" And he said, "I believe God will heal me, but I do not believe in your Jesus." I laid my hands on him and I prayed that God would set him free in the name of Jesus Christ. When I finished I said to him, "Now lift your arm." He began to put it up and suddenly he thrust up both of his arms. He leaped and shouted with tears streaming down his face. Once he had lifted his arm a little, he realized the miracle. He was totally set free. About then the train began moving and I said, "Praise God; thank God that you were healed in the name of Jesus Christ."

At the next stop a man came to our compartment in the train saying that he was representing his master who wanted to come and meet the man of God. He said his master was so-and-so, a member of Parliament

30

in New Delhi, who was also riding on the train. The member of Parliament then came to our compartment to tell Mrs. Wierwille and me that what he had seen in Jubbulpore was the most tremendous Christian event he had ever witnessed — that a man of God would bless all God's people irrespective of whether they were Christian or Hindu. He offered us the keys to his city and said that any time we wanted to minister in India, the doors of India and the Far East would be open to us to teach the accuracy and the greatness of God's Word.

In Mark 3, as well as in Jubbulpore, both persons had the promise of God; both men believed, and when they believed, they acted; and when they acted, their hand and arm were restored whole. The *how* of receiving is believing. When their needs and wants were in balance, they received. After knowing what is available, how to receive, and what to do, a person then believes and finally acts upon his believing in a positive way.

Look at the power of believing as defined in Ephesians 1:19.

And what *is* the exceeding greatness of his power to us-ward who [do one thing] believe ....

31

The Power of Believing

Ephesians 3:20:
Now unto him that is able to do exceeding abundantly above all that we ask or think, according to the power that worketh in us.

He is not only able to do things *abundantly*, but *exceeding abundantly*. Believe and then receive.

The law of believing is the greatest law in the Word of God. As a matter of fact, it is not only the greatest law in The Word, it is the greatest law in the whole world. Believing works for saint and sinner alike. In Mark 11 this great law of believing is set forth.

Mark 11:12,13:
And on the morrow [this is the last week of Jesus' life here upon earth], when they [Jesus and His twelve apostles] were come from Bethany, he was hungry:

And seeing a fig tree afar off having leaves, he came, if haply [perchance] he might find any thing thereon: and when he came to it, he found nothing but leaves; for the time of figs was not yet.

Jesus went to the fig tree hoping to find something thereon, but "... the time of figs was not *yet*." Do you mean to tell me that Jesus was ignorant? Would I go to an apple tree if it were not time for apples? Do

32

you think that Jesus would go to a fig tree if He knew it was not the right season? What is the situation?

There are two trees in the Bible designated as the people's trees: the coconut palm and the fig tree. It was never stealing to take fruit off either of those trees no matter on whose land the tree stood. If I had a fig tree in my front yard, you could walk over and help yourself to the fruit of the tree anytime because it was a people's tree. In the record of Mark 11, Jesus was coming from Bethany to Jerusalem and He was hungry. That does not mean that He was starving to death. He was hungry as we get hungry for a snack. He wanted a little bit to nibble on, so he saw a fig tree and he walked over hoping to find something. The time of figs was not yet and Jesus knew that. However, as the leaves come out on this species of fig tree, there are little buds which are as sweet as candy. It was not time for the mature, ripe figs; but if the tree did not have any buds, Jesus knew that it would not have any figs later on. Now watch the story develop.

"And Jesus answered and said unto it" — Jesus was speaking to the fig tree. Can you imagine the neighbors looking at Jesus, can you imagine the apostles scratching their heads wondering what Jesus was doing talking to that old fig tree? Let's look at the record.

Verse 14,

> And Jesus answered and said unto it [If you ever want to receive the power of God you have to be specific. He did not beat around the bush; He spoke to the tree.], No man eat fruit of thee hereafter for ever. And his disciples heard *it*.

Jesus and the apostles returned to Bethany that very day.

Verse 20,

> And in the [following] morning, as they passed by, they saw the fig tree dried up from the roots.

The death of a tree is generally noticeable first in the upper leaves, then down the branches, and finally the roots. But this tree died backwards and overnight.

> Mark 11:21,22:
> And Peter calling to remembrance saith unto him, Master, behold, the fig tree which thou cursedst is withered away.

> And Jesus answering saith unto them, Have faith in God.

The "original" text read, "... Have the faith of

God." Observe verse 23 carefully.

> For verily I say unto you, That whosoever shall say unto this mountain, Be thou removed, and be thou cast into the sea; and shall not doubt in his heart, but shall believe that those things which he saith shall come to pass; he shall have whatsoever he saith.

This is the great law in the Word of God. "... Whosoever ..." It does not say Christian or non-Christian; *whosoever* means *whosoever*. "Whosoever shall say unto this mountain, Be thou removed, and ... cast into the sea and shall not doubt ... but shall believe that those things which he saith shall come to pass; he shall have whatsoever he saith." In other words: say it, believe it, and it will come to pass.

Then Jesus reiterated this truth in verse 24.

> Mark 11:24:
> Therefore I say unto you, What things soever ye desire, when ye pray, believe that ye receive *them*, and ye shall have *them*.

The law of believing is the greatest law in the Word of God: whosoever says it, whosoever believes, will act and receive.

35

Chapter Four
Believing: Faith and Fear

There are two types of believing: (1) positive and (2) negative. We either have faith or fear. We must recognize that believing has both a negative and a positive side.

We are what we are today because of our believing. We will be tomorrow where our believing takes us. No one ever rises beyond what he believes and no one can believe more than what he understands. We believe what we believe because of what we have been taught. We think the way we think because of the way we have been led.

Believing is a law. As one believes, he receives. On the negative side, fear is believing; fear is believing in reverse; it produces ill results.

There is basically only one thing that ever defeats the believer, and that is fear. Fear is the believer's only enemy. Fear is sand in the machinery of life.

The Power of Believing

When we have fear, we cannot believe God and have faith. Fear has ruined more Christian lives than any other thing in the world.

If a person is afraid of not being able to hold his job, do you know what will happen? He will lose it. If one is afraid of a disease, he will manifest that disease because the law is that what one believes (in this case, what one believes negatively), he is going to receive. People have a fear of the future; they have a fear of death. Fear always encases, fear always enslaves, fear always binds. This law of negative and positive believing works for both Christian and non-Christian. When we believe, we receive the results of our believing regardless of who or what we are.

The Word of God demonstrates negative believing in the Gospel of John. Isaiah had prophesied, hundreds of years before, that when the true Messiah came there would be one miracle which He would do that had never been done before. This one miracle, opening the eyes of a man who was born blind, would prove He was the Messiah of God. This is the miraculous record in John 9.

John 9:1—8:
And as *Jesus* passed by, he saw a man which was blind from *his* birth.

And his disciples asked him, saying, Master, who did sin, this man, or his parents, that he was born blind?

Jesus answered, Neither hath this man sinned, nor his parents: but that the works of God should be made manifest in him.

I must work the works of him that sent me, while it is day: the night cometh, when no man can work.

As long as I am in the world, I am the light of the world.

When he had thus spoken, he spat on the ground, and made clay of the spittle, and he anointed the eyes of the blind man with the clay,

And said unto him, Go, wash in the pool of Siloam, (which is by interpretation, Sent.) He went his way therefore, and washed, and came seeing.

The neighbours therefore, and they which before had seen him that he was blind, said, Is not this he that sat and begged?

The Power of Believing

Even the neighbors were not sure of what was going on.

John 9:13 and 18:
They brought to the Pharisees [the heads of the temple and the synagogues got involved] him that aforetime was blind.

But the Jews [the Pharisees] did not believe concerning him, that he had been blind, and received his sight, until they called the parents of him that had received his sight.

First the neighbors were involved, then the religious leaders, and next the parents were called in.

John 9:19–23:
And they asked them, saying, Is this your son, who ye say was born blind? how then doth he now see?

His parents answered them and said, We know that this is our son, and that he was born blind:

But by what means he now seeth, we know not; or who hath opened his eyes, we know not: he is of age; ask him: he shall speak for himself.

These *words* spake his parents, because they

feared the Jews: for the Jews had agreed already, that if any man did confess that he was Christ, he should be put out of the synagogue.

Therefore said his parents, He is of age; ask him.

Put yourself in this situation. If you had a son who was born blind and he was healed of his blindness, the least you as a grateful parent could do is to admit, "Yes, Jesus Christ healed him." But these parents did not say this. Why were they not able to be the kind of parents one would have expected? They were inhibited from testifying as would have been fitting because they were full of fear — "for fear of the Jews." Fear enslaved them, fear stopped these parents from being the kind of parents they really should have been. Therefore the parents said, "He is of age; ask him." These Jews had already agreed that if anybody said that Jesus was the Christ, that person would be put out of the synagogue.

This action does not mean much to us today because if a person is thrown out of one church, the church on the next street corner is glad to have him. But it was not that way at the time of Jesus. When a man was ostracized from the synagogue, people would not talk with him; he could not attend the synagogue; he could not buy or sell goods. Do you see why the parents were enslaved by fear of what would happen to them?

These parents were not the only ones in the Bible who manifested fear. In John 20:19 is a record of the disciples.

> Then the same day at evening [This is the day of the resurrection appearance of Jesus.], being the first *day* of the week, when the doors were shut where the disciples were assembled for fear of the Jews, came Jesus and stood in the midst, and saith unto them, Peace *be* unto you.

The disciples were behind closed doors for fear of the Jews. Fear always puts us behind closed doors; it always binds us; it always enslaves us.

Years ago I knew a minister whose wife had passed away leaving him with seven children. About a year later he married another woman who had five children and they lived happily together. About a block and a half away from them lived a woman who had just one son. The woman with the one son was always frustrated, always nervous, always afraid, while this minister and his wife who had twelve children never seemed to worry, to be upset, or to have the least anxiety about their children. When the woman's child started to kindergarten, the mother would walk with him across the street to the next block where the kindergarten was located for fear he might get run over by a car. When he was in the first grade she did the same thing, the second grade, and the third grade. One time the boy's mother called on the minister and said, "I don't understand why I am so nervous and upset all the time. I have just one boy to care for; and you have all these children and nothing ever seems to happen to them. You live without worry." He replied, "This is how we live. My wife and I get the children around the breakfast table; that is the only time we get our whole family together. When they are all seated, I do the praying. I pray like this: 'Lord, here we are all together at breakfast. They are all going out to school and other places today, so I leave them all in your protection and care. Thank you. Amen.' " He believed God would answer his prayers and he relinquished them to the Lord's protection. His children flourished.

About a year later the woman's only son was coming home from school early. Mother had not met him at the street corner. As the boy walked out into the street, he was hit by an automobile and killed. I went to the funeral service of that boy, and guess what the minister preached? "God now has another rose petal in heaven." Imagine that! That the God who created the heavens and the earth should want to kill a little boy because God needed another rose petal in heaven. Do you know what killed that little boy? The fear in the heart and life of that mother. She was so desperately afraid something was going to happen to her little boy that she finally reaped the results of her believing.

What one fears will surely come to pass. It is a law. Have you ever heard about people who set the time of their death? When somebody says, "Well, this time next year I will not be here," if you are a betting man, bet your money; you are going to win. If a person makes up his mind that this time next year he is going to be dead, God would have to change the laws of the universe for the person not to be accommodated.

A number of years ago a man came to see me about his fear. He told me that according to insurance statistics in the United States a traveling salesman is supposed to wreck his automobile every so many thousands of miles. This man had already driven ten thousand miles more than the average salesman, and his fear of an accident was becoming an obsession. He was losing business day after day and week after week because of this fear. He came to me and I explained to him the law of believing. The man changed his believing and has not had an accident to this day.

The world around us builds fear in people. The psychology prevalent in our society today is fear. If

44

you do not use this brand of toothpaste, you are going to have an increased number of cavities; you are afraid of increasing your cavities so you buy this kind of toothpaste. If you do not do this, you are going to get that. It is all based on fear.

Have you ever picked up a newspaper and noticed how positive the stories are? Ninety per cent of what one reads in the newspaper is negative. Automobile accidents, murders, suicides — all negative. Why? Because this is what people have been living. We have been living on negatives so long that when somebody else comes along with a positive diet, we think he must be crazy.

Proverbs 29:25 says "The fear of man bringeth a snare ...." Every time a man has fear he is ensnared, he is bound.

Isaiah 8:12:
Say ye not, A confederacy, to all *them to* whom this people shall say, A confederacy; neither fear ye their fear, nor be afraid.

These people were being enslaved as a nation because they were afraid of other people. Yet The Word said, "Neither fear ye their fear, nor be afraid."

There are many examples like this in The Word. I

45

am just selecting a few.

> Jeremiah 49:24:
> Damascus is waxed feeble, *and* turneth herself to
> flee, and fear hath seized on *her* ....

The reason she had waxed feeble and turned to flee
was that she was afraid.

> Job 3:25:
> For the thing which I greatly feared is come
> upon me, and that which I was afraid of is come
> unto me.

Job received that of which he was afraid.

> Psalms 34:4:
> I sought the Lord, and he heard me, and deliv-
> ered me from all my fears.

As long as he was in fear he was encased.

> II Timothy 1:7:
> For God hath not given us the spirit of fear; but
> of power, and of love, and of a sound mind.

God did not give us fear so fear must come from
some other source. If fear came from a source other
than God, then it has to be negative. Fear is always

wrong.

Remember in John 20 the disciples, also known as the twelve apostles, on the day of the resurrection were behind closed doors for fear of the Jews. But observe these same men fifty days later.

Keep in mind that, under ordinary circumstances, no adult changes drastically in forty or fifty days. But Acts 2 tells of common human beings who within fifty days from being full of fear became men of great boldness and great conviction. I want to focus on (1) the law of believing both negative and positive and (2) the cause of their change.

Acts 2:4 tells that all these men were filled with the holy spirit and then we read verse 14.

Acts 2:14:
But Peter, standing up with the eleven, lifted up his voice, and said unto them, Ye men of Judea, and all *ye* that dwell at Jerusalem, be this known unto you, and hearken to my words.

Where was Peter fifty days before? According to the Gospel of John, he was behind closed doors for fear of the Jews. But now Peter stood up with the eleven and lifted up his unquivering voice unto them, "Ye men of Judea, and all *ye* that dwell at Jerusalem,

be this known unto you, and hearken to my words."
Where did he get that boldness? What changed him
from being a man full of fear to being a great man of
confidence?

Acts 2:22,23:
Ye men of Israel, hear these words; Jesus of
Nazareth, a man approved of God among you by
miracles and wonders and signs, which God did
by him in the midst of you, as ye yourselves also
know:

Him, being delivered by the determinate counsel
and foreknowledge of God, ye have taken, and
by wicked hands have crucified and slain.

Fifty days previously Peter certainly would not
have said this. Why is he not afraid to say it now?

When I was attending seminaries and being instructed in homiletics and other arts of the ministry, I was told that when a person preaches a
sermon he should never say *you,* but to always say
we. Peter must have gone to the wrong seminary because when he was preaching here he said, "*You* have
crucified Him and *you* have slain Him."

Acts 3 contains a record of events after the day of
Pentecost.

48

Acts 3:12 and 14:
And when Peter saw *it*, he answered unto the people, Ye men of Israel, why marvel ye at this? or why look ye so earnestly on us, as though by our own power or holiness we had made this man to walk?

But ye denied the Holy One and the Just, and desired a murderer to be granted unto you.

That is boldness. Peter was no longer full of fear. Something must have changed this man.

Peter and John were then taken into custody because they were too bold.

Acts 4:23–29:
And being let go, they went [returned] to their own company, and reported all that the chief priests and elders had said unto them.

And when they heard that, they lifted up their voice to God with one accord, and said, Lord, thou *art* God, which hast made heaven, and earth, and the sea, and all that in them is:

Who, by the mouth of thy servant David hast said, Why did the heathen rage, and the people imagine vain things?

The kings of the earth stood up, and the rulers were gathered together against the Lord, and against his Christ.

For of a truth against thy holy child Jesus, whom thou hast anointed, both Herod, and Pontius Pilate, with the Gentiles, and the people of Israel, were gathered together,

For to do whatsoever thy hand and thy counsel determined before to be done .

And now, Lord, behold their threatenings: and grant unto thy servants ....

"Grant unto thy servants" a holiday, a vacation? No. We think it should say this because, after all, if we have been out there working for the Lord, carrying out the ministry, being imprisoned, whipped, and persecuted, certainly we ought to have a vacation with pay. When Peter and John came back and got in this prayer group, they said,

... Lord, behold their threatenings: and grant unto thy servants, that with all boldness [not with hesitancy, not with reluctance, not with fear.] they may speak [what the people want us to speak? No.] thy word.

They prayed for more boldness. As long as they were full of fear and behind closed doors, they had nothing to fear but fear itself, but once they got boldness and preached the Word of God, they accomplished work for the Lord. Men were healed, set free, and saved. Peter and John, however, were thrown into prison; but when they got out, they went back to the little prayer group and believed for more boldness. "Give us more of the boldness, Lord, that we may speak thy word."

Acts 4:30,31:
By stretching forth thine hand to heal; and that signs and wonders may be done by the name of thy holy child Jesus.

And when they had prayed, the place was shaken where they were assembled together; and they were all filled with the Holy Ghost, and they spake the word of God with [hesitancy? No. They spake the Word of God with] boldness.

What made them speak the Word of God with boldness? Verse 31 says that "they were all filled with the Holy Ghost." In Acts 2 on the day of Pentecost the twelve apostles received the fullness of the Holy Spirit. Verse 31 of Acts 4 says that they were all filled with the Holy Ghost "and they spake the word

51

of God with boldness." What changed those men? Between the resurrection record and Acts 2 there is nothing that could have changed the men except the new birth which is the power of the holy spirit which came on Pentecost. I have never seen one person get rid of his fear until he became born again of God's Spirit, filled with the power of the holy spirit. If you want to get rid of your fear, your frustrations, your anxieties, you have to be born again by God's Spirit, filled with His power. That is what changed Peter and the rest of the apostles and that is the power which will change your life.

Peter and John prayed. And when they prayed, the place was shaken where they were assembled. They were all filled with the holy spirit, and they spake the Word of God with boldness. I always become amused when I read that, thinking that if the power of God moved like that today in most of our churches, we would have many funerals. People would be shocked to death if the place was shaken where they prayed. In Acts 4 what they prayed for was boldness that they might speak The Word. Nothing but the power of the holy spirit in the Living Word in an individual takes the fear out of him.

That is what took the fear out of my life. I used to be afraid of my own shadow; I was afraid of meeting people, especially people in academic circles, in high

political circles, in elite religious circles. Today I have
no fear within me. Why? I believe that the power
from the Holy Spirit is within giving me the boldness,
the enthusiasm, the dynamics to stand up for the
integrity and the greatness of God's Word.

Fear builds unbelief. This is why fear always defeats the promises of God. Jesus Christ did many
signs, miracles and wonders in places like Galilee and
Capernaum in Galilee; but in Nazareth, his own home
town, He could not do much.

Matthew 13:58:
And he [Jesus] did not many mighty works
there because of their unbelief.

Could He not do many mighty works there because
He had changed? No. Jesus had not changed; the people had changed.

Unbelief is believing; it is negative believing. On the
negative side is doubt and on the positive side is confidence. Confidence versus doubt; trust versus worry;
faith versus fear. Doubt, worry and fear are negative
believing. Confidence, trust, and faith are positive believing. These laws work with precision not only in
the Word of God but in our own lives.

Carefully note that there are two specific types of

negative believing regarding spiritual power spoken of in the Bible: *apistia* and *apeitheia*. *Apistia* refers to those people who have never heard or who have never heard enough to believe; *apeitheia* refers to those who have heard but refuse to believe what they have heard.

Apistia is the unbelief of those who have never heard or who have not heard in enough detail to believe. For instance, if I have not heard enough of the Word of God to be saved, I have *apistia* unbelief. Look at Romans 10.

> Romans 10:13—15:
> For whosoever shall call upon the name of the Lord shall be saved.
>
> How then shall they call on him in whom they have not believed? and how shall they believe in him of whom they have not heard? and how shall they hear without a preacher?
>
> And how shall they preach, except they be sent? as it is written, How beautiful are the feet of them that preach the gospel of peace, and bring glad tidings of good things!

"How then shall they call on him in whom they have not believed? ... how shall they believe in him of

54

whom they have not heard?" These people were unbelievers in that they had never heard the Word of God so that they could believe.

Matthew 13:53—58:
And it came to pass, *that* when Jesus had finished these parables, he departed thence.

And when he was come into his own country, he taught them in their synagogue, insomuch that they were astonished, and said, Whence hath this *man* this wisdom, and *these* mighty works?

Is not this the carpenter's son? is not his mother called Mary? and his brethren, James, and Joses, and Simon, and Judas?

And his sisters, are they not all with us? Whence then hath this *man* all these things?

And they were offended in him. But Jesus said unto them, A prophet is not without honour, save in his own country, and in his own house.

And he did not many mighty works there because of their unbelief.

He could not do much in Nazareth because of the people's unbelief, *apistia*. Although Jesus tried to

55

teach, the community would not hear enough to believe because they did not think He could know anything since He was illegitimate, and thus they could not believe. Do you know what the people of Jesus' community said to Him? "Is this the carpenter's son? He is illegitimate because everyone knows that Mary was pregnant before she and Joseph came together in marriage." Contrary to what they thought, however, Jesus was not the carpenter's son; He was the Son of God by divine conception, born of Mary but conceived by the Holy Ghost, as the Word of God says.

"Is not this the carpenter's son? Is not his mother called Mary and his brethren, James, and Joses, and Simon, and Judas? And his sisters, are they not all with us? Whence then hath this *man* all these things?" The original text gives emphasis as follows: "Is not this the carpenter's son and his mother called Mary (You remember her.), and his brethren, James, and Joses, and Simon, and that Judas (Was he wild!), and his sisters, (Weren't they something.), Are they not all with us? Whence then hath this *man* all these things?" The community said that Jesus could not have such power because they looked at the family and said, "Nothing good can come out of this man. We know that family." Therefore, they would not hear enough to believe. They had unbelief (*apistia*).

"But Jesus said unto them, A prophet is not without honour, save in his own country, and in his own house. And he did not many mighty works there because of their unbelief [*apistia*]."

Luke 2 contains one verse of Scripture that for many years I was not able to understand.

Luke 2:42:
And when he [Jesus] was twelve years old, they went up to Jerusalem after the custom of the feast.

I knew that according to Jewish law, a boy became a man, going through *Bar Mitzvah,* when he was thirteen. But Jesus was taken to the temple when He was twelve. I could not understand it so I considered that there might be a mistake in the text. I looked in every critical Greek text that I could find and checked every other source I could think of; but I never found Jesus to be thirteen when He went to the synagogue. Every text concurred on the age of twelve. Finally I came across an old piece of literature which explained that according to ancient Jewish law when a boy was conceived illegitimately, this child was brought to the temple at the age of twelve instead of thirteen.

This explains why Jesus could not communicate with the people in His own hometown. They thought that a child conceived illegitimately certainly could not have great knowledge or do wonderful works. They were offended by Him, would not listen to hear enough to believe when He spoke, and thus suffered from *apistia,* unbelief.

In the critical Greek texts the word used for the second of the two types of unbelief is *apeitheia. Apeitheia* refers to those who have heard but still refuse to believe what they have heard. To illustrate, if I have heard enough of the Word of God that I could be saved but refuse to believe that Word of God, I have *apeitheia.*

Noting Romans 11:30, we find this type of unbelief, not for an individual, but in reference to Israel and the Gentiles as nations.

Romans 11:30:

For as ye in times past have not believed [*apeitheia*] God, yet have now obtained mercy through their unbelief [*apeitheia*].

The Gentiles had heard but refused to believe, as it states in Romans 1:21, "Because that, when they [the Gentiles] knew God, they glorified *him* not as God ...."

Again Hebrews 4 clarifies this *apeitheia* type of

unbelief.

Hebrews 4:6:
Seeing therefore it remaineth that some must
enter therein, and they to whom it was first
preached entered not in because of unbelief
[*apeitheia*].

It was first preached to them. They heard enough
to believe but they refused to believe.

Fear which culminates in unbelief is due either to
wrong teaching or ignorance. Wrong teaching may be
corrected or overcome by right teaching; while ignorance may be corrected or overcome by instruction.

If a person is full of fear because he is ignorant
regarding a particular subject he may overcome this
ignorance which causes fear by right teaching or right
instruction. For instance, a child who is afraid to
sleep in the dark is full of fear and wakes up scream-
ing in the middle of the night. Why is that child fear-
ful? Maybe because he has been wrongly taught. Perhaps the child was frightened by someone's saying
that if the child was not a good boy, he would be put
in the closet and the boogie man would get him. That
child is full of fear because of wrong teaching.

On the other hand, suppose an adult is afraid of

59

the boogie man in the closet. That is ignorance. He ignores the facts. For a child it is wrong teaching; but for an adult, it is ignorance. Fears, whether from ignorance or wrong teaching, are always encasing and always enslaving and they always defeat us because when we have fear in our lives, we cannot act positively on the promises of God's wonderful, matchless Word.

Matthew 10:16 is a positive record showing that God never meant for His believers to be ignorant; He meant for them to be bold and full of believing, full of power, full of positives.

> Matthew 10:16:
> Behold, I send you forth as sheep in the midst of wolves: be ye therefore wise as serpents, and harmless as doves.

God wants us to be "wise as serpents, and harmless as doves."

Romans tells us that we are to be wise concerning that which is good. The Epistle of James declares that God gives us wisdom: "If any of you lack wisdom, let him ask of God," who gives wisdom. God never meant for His Church nor His children to be ignorant; He meant for His Church to be wise; He wanted us to know the score.

Do you know from where this wisdom comes? It comes from the Word of God. Psalms 119:105 says that the Word of God is a lamp to our feet and a light to our path, and thereby imparts wisdom. Isaiah tells us that the Word of God imparts wisdom regarding salvation, that even a fool need not err therein. The way is so simple and so plain. I John 3:2 says, "Beloved, now are we the sons of God ...." It is the Word of God that imparts wisdom regarding our sonship relationship with Him. II Corinthians 2 tells about the devices of Satan of which we are not ignorant. We are not stupid and should not act unwisely.

The Gospel of John says that the Word of God imparts wisdom regarding the future life, the return of Christ, and heaven. The Word of God gives us wisdom regarding every subject necessary for man's complete knowledge of his redemption and of his salvation. This gives us confidence to manifest positive results. We need never fear for we are not ignorant; we have knowledge of God's Word.

Part II

The Bible
is the
Word of God

Chapter Five
The God-breathed Word

II Timothy 3:16 has great significance in our study of power for abundant living. It tells that The Word is God-breathed.

All scripture *is* given by inspiration of God, and *is* profitable for doctrine, for reproof, for correction, for instruction in righteousness.

The first word in II Timothy 3:16 is "all." Every time "all" appears, one must ask himself what the word "all" means, because in the Bible the word "all" is used in one of two ways: it is either *all without exception* or *all without distinction. All without distinction* means everyone in a certain designated class or group. If one wrongly considers the word "all," he will never rightly understand the Word of God or get its full impact.

> John 12:32:
> And I [Jesus], if I be lifted up from the earth,
> will draw all *men* unto me.

Is that *all without exception* or is it *all without distinction*? The answer is obvious. We know that not everybody in our community is a Christian; therefore, not all without exception have been drawn to Him. All who have believed, all without distinction, are the ones who have been drawn.

> Hebrews 2:9:
> But we see Jesus, who was made a little lower than the angels for the suffering of death, crowned with glory and honour; that he by the grace of God should taste death for every man [for all men].

Is the word "every" (or the word "all") *without exception* or *without distinction*? Did Christ taste death for all men without exception or for all men without distinction? He died for all without exception that whosoever wants to be saved can be saved. Christ died for every man without any exception and because of this anyone can be born again by God's Spirit.

In II Timothy 3, where it reads, "All scripture *is* given by inspiration of God," "all scripture" means

66

without any exception from Genesis 1:1 to Revelation 22:21.

The words "all scripture" are followed by the word "is." "All scripture *is* ...." The word "is" must be italicized. Where it is not italicized in a King James Bible, it was either a proofreader's oversight or a deliberate act for the printer's convenience. All italicized words in the King James Version are words which have been added to the text by the translators. One of the major reasons I have my students use the King James Version is that this version points out what has been added to the Stephen's Greek text from which it was translated.

Before going further, let us understand one thing. If a person deletes a word that is italicized, the Word of God has not been touched. The italicized word was added anyway so that by dropping it The Word itself is not touched. This becomes very important as we go further into the accuracy of The Word.

To go another step, there was no verb "to be" in the original Hebrew or Aramaic languages. There was a verb "to become." In other words, the words "is," "are," "was" and "were" literally were not in the original Hebrew and Aramaic.

This becomes very interesting in the first chapter of Genesis. Genesis 1:2 says "And the earth was ...."

67

Here the word "was" is not in italics; it is in regular print. Genesis 1:2 continues: "And the earth was without form, and void; and darkness *was* upon the face of the deep ...." The second usage of the word "was" is italicized. This tells us that the first word which is translated "was" is not the word "was"; it is the word "became." But the second "was" is added. Therefore verse 2 literally reads, "And the earth became without form, and void; and darkness upon the face of the deep." It *became* without form and void. God did not create it this way. If the word "was" is left in the text, "And the earth was without form," it appears to say that God created the earth this way. To the contrary, the earth *became* this way as Isaiah 45:18 substantiates.

> For thus saith the Lord that created the heavens; God himself that formed the earth and made it; he hath established it, he created it not in vain ....

"Without form" (*tohu*) in Genesis 1:2 is the same word used in Isaiah's "in vain" (*tohu*). God did not create it without form and void (*tohu bohu*). The earth became that way.

Let us go back to II Timothy 3:16. Observe carefully, "All scripture *is* given by inspiration of God ...." These five words, "given by inspiration of

68

God" are one word in the critical Greek texts. The word is *theopneustos*. This word is composed of two root words: *theo* and *pneustos*. Taken in parts, *theo* is "God" and *pneustos* is "breathed." *Theopneustos* literally means "God-breathed." "All scripture *is* given by inspiration of God" equals "all scripture *is theopneustos*" or "all scripture is God-breathed."

Now we ask, does God breathe? You and I breathe, but does God? John 4:24 records that "God *is* a Spirit ...." The Greek texts delete the article *a* and simply say, "God *is* Spirit." Furthermore, the Word of God says that a spirit has no flesh or bones. We cannot view a spirit with our eyes. Yet II Timothy 3:16 says that God breathed. We must search out exactly what is meant when God is attributed human characteristics. What does "God-breathed" mean?

Have you ever asked yourself what should be emphasized in the Word of God? If the Bible is God-breathed, *theopneustos*, and if the Bible is the Word of God, can you imagine for one minute that God would allow any mortal the privilege of deciding what should be emphasized in the Word of God? In this word, "God-breathed," *theopneustos*, is a great truth that has taken years to ferret out and study.

God is Spirit so God does not breathe, but we do.

The Bible is the Word of God

Whenever the Bible attributes human characteristics to God, as does this particular Scripture in II Timothy, it is called a *figure of speech*. The figures of speech in the Bible from Genesis 1:1 to Revelation 22:21 are God's markings in The Word as to that which He wants emphasized.

A figure of speech is not something to be guessed about. Figures of speech are legitimate grammatical usages which depart from literal language to call attention to themselves. For instance, if we have not had any rain for a long time, I could say, "The ground is dry." This would be a plain statement of fact. The dust is blowing around and the cracks are gaping. But if I say, "The ground is thirsty," that is a figure of speech. The figure of speech is always more vivid than the literal statement itself. When I say "The ground is dry," I place an indistinct idea in your mind; but the moment I say "The ground is thirsty," then you have a clear picture. A figure of speech always augments, always vitalizes, the statement.

The Word of God is to be accepted literally whenever and wherever possible. But when a word or words fail to be true to fact, they are figures of speech. Figures of speech have a God-designed emphasis which must be grasped and understood in order to fully obtain the impact of The Word. Men are prone to use figures of speech haphazardly, but in

The God-breathed Word

the Word of God figures of speech are used with divine design. Each and every one of them may be accurately catalogued and analyzed with precision. There is absolutely no guesswork. Except for the figures of speech and the Oriental customs and mannerisms, The Word is literal.

There are 212 different figures of speech used in the Bible. As far as I can calculate, throughout history there must have been approximately 220 different figures of speech. Two hundred twelve of these are used in the Bible; sometimes there are as many as 40 variations of one figure. It is easy to see what a monumental opportunity for research the field of figures of speech is.

This figure of speech, "God-breathed," is so tremendous that I am taking this time to develop its greatness. Once you understand this, hundreds of Scriptures will become very plain to you.

God is Spirit, yet II Timothy says that "all scripture is God-breathed." This figure of speech is called in the Hebrew *derech benai adam* which translated means "ways of the sons of man," bringing God down to the level of man. Now the Greeks took *derech benai adam* and translated it *anthropopatheia* meaning "pathos of man." The Romans used this figure and called it *condescensio* in Latin from which is

71

derived our English word "condescension." Whenever the Word of God attributes human characteristics to God, the figure of speech is called in Greek *anthropopatheia* and in Latin, *condescensio*. This is the Holy Spirit's emphatic marking in II Timothy 3:16. The emphasis is not on the word "all" or on the word "scripture." The emphasis is on the source, *God-breathed*. God put the emphasis where He wanted it; He marked it by this figure of speech.

Another example of *condescensio* is Exodus 4:14 which says, "And the anger of the Lord was kindled." God is Spirit; He has no anger. When the Bible says the anger of the Lord, what figure is it? *Condescensio*. Isaiah 52:10 says, "The Lord hath made bare his holy arm ...." Does the Lord have an arm? No, He does not, but I do and you do. "To make bare the arm" is the figure *condescensio*.

What exactly was the process by which the God-breathed Word came about? The key to answering this question is in the Word of God.

II Peter 1:21:
For the prophecy came not in old time by the will of man: but holy men of God spake *as they were* moved by the Holy Ghost.

"Prophecy" is uniquely used in this verse of Scripture. When the average person thinks of prophecy, he thinks of foretelling the future. This definition is one of the usages of the word "prophecy," but is not the only one. The word "prophecy" can also mean "forthtelling."

Isaiah's prophecy of the coming of the Lord Jesus Christ and John's prophecy of the return of Christ (which is still in the future) are examples of foretelling. Some of the Word of God is foretelling. The verb "prophesy" also means "to forthtell, to state, to set forth, to speak forth." "Prophecy" literally means "that which is foretold and that which is forthtold." The whole Bible from Genesis to Revelation is either foretelling or forthtelling. "For the prophecy [all that which is foretold or forthtold, everything from Genesis to Revelation] came not in old time by the will of man ...." The Word of God, which foretells and forthtells, did not come by the will of man. Many theologians and religious leaders have taught that whenever a Biblical writer wanted to write he sat down and penned a part of the Word of God. The Word of God does not say that. Moses never sat down in the desert and said, "Well, now I think I am going to write the Word of God," and then got out his shorthand pad. He did not scratch his head and write, "In the beginning God created the heaven and the earth." "I like that." No. The prophecy came not by the will of man; in other words, man never willed the Word of

God. He never sat down and said, "Now I will to compose Genesis" or "I will to compose Matthew." "For the prophecy came not in old time by the will of man ...." This is basic to our understanding of a fundamental background of how The Word came about.

The Word of God never came by the will of man, "... but holy men of God spake ...." Holy men of God spoke. Who are holy men? Men who believe God are holy. The Bible was not written by God-rejectors, unbelievers or skeptics. The Bible was written by holy men of God who spoke as they were moved by the Holy Spirit.

I have asked many people about this verse, "Who did the speaking?" And do you know what they say? The Holy Spirit. That is not what the verse says. It says, "... holy men of God spake *as they were* moved by the Holy Ghost." It does not say God spoke; it says holy men of God did the speaking. That is what The Word says and that is what it means.

Do you know why there is such a difference between the books of Amos and Isaiah, between the Gospel of Mark and the Gospel of John? Can you speak with any vocabulary other than the one you have? For instance, if you have never heard of the word "idiosyncrasy," you can not use it. One can only use the vocabulary that he possesses. That is

74

exactly what The Word declares in II Peter 1:21, that holy men of God spoke. They used their own vocabularies and their own modes of expression. The Gospel of Mark is short and choppy: "and immediately," "and straightway," "and forthwith." These words are used because the writer of the Gospel of Mark was not a highly-educated man with a flowery vocabulary. But the Gospel of John is different. John wrote, "In the beginning was the Word, and the Word was with God, and the Word was God. The same was in the beginning with God. All things were made by him; and without him was not anything made that was made." How beautiful! Why? Because of John's style of writing. Amos' writing was terse; he was a herdsman. Isaiah used beautiful expressions. This accounts for the differences in writing styles that are found in the Bible. Holy men of God did the speaking and writing; they used their natural vocabularies. But they spoke *"as they were moved* by the Holy Ghost [Spirit]."

What does it mean to be "... moved by the Holy Spirit"? II Timothy 3:16 tells that all Scripture is God-breathed. Here in II Peter 1:21, The Word declares that these men were moved by the Holy Spirit. Whatever is "God-breathed" or to be "inspired of God" is to be "moved by the Holy Spirit."

Some people teach that God took the arm of

Moses and shoved it around and, in this way, made Moses write what God wanted written. No. It does not say "pushed around by the Holy Spirit"; it says, "... moved by the Holy Ghost." People are always guessing and offering opinions rather than reading the declared accuracy of God's Word. What is it to be God-breathed and moved by the Holy Spirit? Galatians 1:11 contains this record.

> But I certify [guarantee] you, brethren, that the gospel which was preached of me is not after man.

If the gospel had come after man, he, Paul, would have received it by the will of man and that would have been a contradiction with the rest of The Word. II Peter 1:21 emphatically states that The Word did not come by the desires of man. It did not come by the will of man. Galatians says, "... the gospel which was preached of me is not after man. For I neither received it of man, neither was I taught *it* ...." Then there must be another way to get information. All learning in our sense-knowledge world of mathematics, science, history and such — all our information — comes by the will of man. But in contrast, Paul said of his writing in Galatians 1:12,

> For I neither received it of man, neither was I taught *it,* but by the revelation of Jesus Christ.

The Word came "by the revelation of Jesus Christ." Now let us put these verses together.

II Timothy 3:16:
All scripture *is* given by inspiration of God [God-breathed], and *is* profitable for doctrine, for reproof, for correction, for instruction in righteousness.

II Peter 1:21:
For the prophecy came not in old time by the will of man: but holy men of God spake *as they were* moved by the Holy Ghost.

Galatians 1:11,12:
But I certify you, brethren, that the gospel which was preached of me is not after man.

For I neither received it of man, neither was I taught *it*, but by the revelation of Jesus Christ.

In II Timothy 3:16 is the "God-breathed word" which in II Peter 1:21 is to be "moved by the Holy Spirit" which in Galatians 1:11 and 12 is "revelation."

There is a mathematical axiom involved at this point: "Things equal to the same thing are equal to each other." Therefore, God-breathed word = moved by the Holy Spirit = revelation; or God-breathed means to be moved by the Holy Spirit which is revelation.

Before we go deeper into this particular verse in II Peter, let's look into the Old Testament and see how those holy men of God spoke who received this revelation. We have seen from John 4:24 that God is Spirit. God being Spirit can only speak to what He is. God cannot speak to the natural human mind. This is why The Word could not come by the will of man because the will of man is in the natural realm. God being Spirit can only speak to what He is — spirit. Things in the natural realm may be known by the five senses — seeing, hearing, smelling, tasting and touching. But God is Spirit and, therefore, cannot speak to brain cells; God cannot speak to a person's mind. It is a law and God never oversteps His own laws. The spirit from God had to be upon these men, otherwise they could never have received revelation as Paul declared in Galatians. Numbers 11:17 helps explain revelation.

> And I [God] will come down and talk with thee [Moses] there: and I will take of the spirit which *is* upon thee, and will put *it* upon them ....

God is Spirit and He could reveal Himself through

78

the spirit from God which was upon Moses. Then Moses, having a mind, used his vocabulary and wrote the revealed Word of God. That is the exact means by which the Word of God came into being.

A man of God, in Biblical usage, was a man upon whom was the spirit from God, also called the "spirit of wisdom" because God as Spirit is wise. Joshua was one of these men as told in Deuteronomy 34:9.

> And Joshua the son of Nun was full of the spirit of wisdom; for Moses had laid his hands upon him: and the children of Israel hearkened unto him, and did as the Lord commanded Moses.

Every man in the Bible who wrote the Word of God had the spirit from God on him. There is only one author of the Bible and that is God. There are many writers but only one author. God is the author while Moses wrote, Joshua wrote, Paul wrote, David wrote and many others wrote. God being Spirit spoke to the spirit upon the holy men and told them what He wanted said. Then the men of God used their vocabularies in speaking what God had revealed. "For the prophecy [all that is foretold or forthtold] came not ... by the will of man: but holy men of God spake *as they were* moved by the Holy Ghost [Spirit]." The original, God-given Word literally contained no errors or contradictions. Why? Because God was its author.

79

The Bible is the Word of God

Holy men simply wrote down what God revealed to them. This is how we got the God-breathed Word. It truly is tremendous.

Chapter Six
That Man May Be Perfect

After establishing how the Word of God came into existence, the next step in our building process is to find out what is the function of His Word. Let us look again at II Timothy 3:16.

> All scripture *is* given by inspiration of God-[God-breathed], and *is* profitable for doctrine, for reproof, for correction, for [which is] instruction in righteousness.

All Scripture from Genesis to Revelation is profitable. The Scripture does not put you in the red; it keeps you in the black. What is it profitable for? It "... *is* profitable for doctrine, for reproof, for correction, for instruction in righteousness." All Scripture is profitable in three areas: (1) doctrine, which is how to believe rightly; (2) reproof, which is to rebuke at the places where we are not believing rightly; and (3) correction, which is to put us back to right believing. The entire Word of God will do just that. It will

81

teach us how to believe rightly, it will reprove us at the places where we are believing wrongly, and it will correct us so that we can again believe rightly. All three of these are "instruction in righteousness."

Many times a critic of the Bible comes along and says, "Well, the Bible is not true. I feel that there are too many contradictions; the Bible really is just another book among the rest of them." This is not the testimony of the Word of God. The testimony of the Word of God is that all Scripture is God-breathed and is profitable for doctrine, which is to teach us how to believe rightly, how to believe positively. If we are going to tap the resources for the more abundant life we must know how to believe rightly. To the people who say that the Bible has lots of error in it, I would like to state that the true Word of God is accurate from Genesis to Revelation. The errors have come in by man propounding those errors. Men have brought their opinions and desires into The Word. When men come and say that they do not believe the Bible, we must remember that the Bible was never written for the unbeliever, the agnostic, or the infidel; the Bible was not written for the God-rejectors and the God-deniers. The Bible was written for men and women who want to find answers. The Word of God is given to men and women who want to tap resources for the more abundant life. This is why the critic who comes from the outside to the Word of

God has no footing to stand on to judge The Word
because The Word has already judged him.

The Bible was written so that you as a believer
need not be blown about by every wind of doctrine
or theory or ideology. This Word of God does not
change. Men change, ideologies change, opinions
change; but this Word of God lives and abides forever.
It endures, it stands. Let's see this from John 5:39.
"Search the scriptures ...." It does not say search
Shakespeare or Kant or Plato or Aristotle or V.P.
Wierwille's writings or the writings of a denomination. No, it says, "Search the scriptures ..." because
all Scripture is God-breathed. Not all that Wierwille
writes will necessarily be God-breathed; not what
Calvin said, nor Luther, nor Wesley, nor Graham, nor
Roberts; but the Scriptures — they are God-breathed.

John 5:39:
Search the scriptures; for in them ... ye have
eternal life: and they [the Scriptures] are they
which testify of me.

The Scriptures tell us the truth about the Lord
Jesus Christ, and about God; this is doctrine — it is
right believing.

John 17:8:
For I have given unto them the words which

> thou gavest me; and they have received *them*,
> and have known surely that I came out from
> thee, and they have believed that thou didst
> send me.

Jesus gave them the words which God gave to Him,
the Scriptures, the Word of God. John 17:14 says, "I
have given them thy word ...." Without the Word of
God, which is right believing, you and I could never
walk in the greatness of the power of God.

> John 17:17:
> Sanctify them through thy truth: thy word is
> truth.

The Word is truth. This is the testimony that The
Word gives of itself. Eventually we have to come to
the testimony of The Word itself and let it speak. We
never bring God's Word down to our level; we always
bring ourselves up to the level of God's Word. Never
come to the Word of God with your skepticism, your
doubt, your opinion. You come to the Word of God
and let it speak for itself and then you reevaluate and
readapt your living to the integrity and the accuracy
of God's Word.

What else does the Scripture do besides give doctrine? It is also profitable for reproof. The Scripture
reproves us when we are not believing rightly. The

Word tells us where we are off; it admonishes us for our wrong believing. No man has a right to reprove any other man. The Word of God has to do the reproving because what I might allow in my life, somebody else might not allow in his life.

> Romans 14:22:
> Hast thou faith? have *it* to thyself before God. Happy *is* he that condemneth not himself in that thing which he alloweth.

I have experienced people's reproof when they did not like the ties that I wore, to cite one example. I was then moving among circles that taught if you offend somebody by what you do, you should quit doing it. So I got rid of the old tie and found out that the next tie offended someone else. I tried every which way to please people because people were reproving me for wearing this or wearing that. I have come to the place in my life that I am concerned about what God thinks and not what people think. I take my reproof not from what people say, but from what The Word says. These Scriptures are God-breathed and these Scriptures are profitable for right believing. Where we are believing and acting wrongly, The Word reproves us.

After doctrine and reproof, what is the third thing the Scripture does? Not only does it teach us right believing and reprove us when we are not believing rightly, but it corrects us. The Word of God is profitable to correct us, to bring us back to believing rightly once more. Parents should utilize this technique in training their children. Most of us as parents say, "Don't do that." Seldom do we add the correction and tell them what they ought to do. But that is exactly what The Word does. It tells us where we are believing wrongly; but then it gives the correction and tells us how we can get back to right believing.

There are many examples of correction in the Bible. Take David, for instance. David was off the ball. He found beautiful Bathsheba and then had her husband shot while in the front lines of battle so that he, David, could have Bathsheba as his wife. A few people knew about the sequence of events leading to David's marriage, but nobody had a right to say anything because David was king and every woman in the kingdom was technically the property of the king or belonged to the king. However, there happened to be a little prophet whose name was Nathan with whom God had a conversation. One time God said to Nathan, "Nathan, you go over and tell David that he has sinned." And Nathan said, "Oh, Lord, not me. I don't want to go to David because old David is handy at chopping off heads." But the Lord insisted, "You go over and tell him about a man who had many sheep and his neighbor had just one little lamb and that little lamb was so precious to him that he took it to the table with him and he took it to bed with him; he mothered it in his bosom. You tell him that story. Tell him how the rich man once had a visitor. And instead of taking one of his own sheep to feed his visitor, the rich man went over to the neighbor and picked up his one lamb and butchered it."

So Nathan went to see David and he said, "King David, something terrible happened in this kingdom. A rich man had company coming, and do you know what this man did? He went over to his neighbor and got that one little lamb that was so precious, the only thing the poor neighbor had, and he brought it to his home and slaughtered it." Nathan told David the whole story. David became very angry and he said to Nathan, "You tell me who the man is. Give me his name and I'll have his head chopped off." Nathan looked David right in the eye and he said to him, "You are the man."

How would you like to have been Nathan? If Nathan had gone down there with any other story, do you know what would have happened to him? David would have had Nathan beheaded. But God told Nathan what to say so that David would trap himself. The moment David said, "Let me know who it is," Nathan said, "You are the man." At that moment David recognized the truth of what Nathan was bringing from God and David said, "Well, I am sorry." He turned to God and asked God to forgive him. Then it says in the Word of God that David was a man after God's own heart. He was not after God's heart when he was out fooling around with Bathsheba and having Uriah killed; no, but when he was back in line, David was a man after God's own heart. When we rightly divide The Word and we walk in the power of it — then we are men and women after God's own heart.

So all Scripture is God-breathed, profitable for doctrine — right believing, for reproof — reprimanding when we are believing wrongly, and for correcting us — for putting us back in line for God. This is instruction in righteousness. Isn't that a tremendous verse of Scripture when we examine it closely to see the greatness of God's Word.

After having the function of God-breathed Scripture — doctrine, reproof, and correction which are instruction in righteousness — disclosed in one concise verse, God follows with the next line in II Timothy 3 by giving the purpose of the God-breathed Word.

II Timothy 3:17:
That the man of God may be perfect, throughly furnished unto all good works.

The purpose, as it says, is "that the man of God ...." Let us see who is a man of God. The word "man" in this usage means "one who is a spokesman for God, one who speaks for God."

> Deuteronomy 33:1:
> And this *is* the blessing, wherewith Moses the man of God blessed the children of Israel before his death.

Moses was a man of God because he spoke for God. Deuteronomy 18:15 reads,

> The Lord thy God will raise up unto thee a Prophet from the midst of thee, of thy brethren, like unto me; unto him ye shall hearken.

Moses was this man of God. He was a prophet, one who speaks for God. The greatness of this is that every time that a believer speaks the accuracy of God's Word, he is like a man of God. When you speak the accuracy of God's Word, you are as a man of God. When we speak His Word, we are speaking as though God Himself were speaking.

God's purpose is "that the man of God [the one who speaks for God], may be perfect ...." Somebody may come along and say, "Well, you cannot be perfect." The Word of God says we are to be.

The Greek word for "perfect" is used only this one time in the Bible which makes it especially interesting in Biblical research and accuracy. The word "perfect" is the Greek word *artios* used as an adjective. *Artios* is defined in two ways. One way is describing a ship when it is equipped for its voyage, having on it everything needed to make a successful trip. Whenever that ship is so perfectly outfitted that it lacks nothing, then the word that is used in Greek is *artios*. The other usage of *artios* regards the ball-and-socket joint. As the ball of the hip fits into the socket, for example, is called *artios*. If one should have even the tiniest foreign particle in the ball-and-socket joint of the hip, the pain would be excruciating.

God's Word declares the purpose of the Word of God is that the man of God may be perfect, without one foreign body there to cause a blemish. The purpose is for the man of God to be so perfect that he has everything that is ever needed in every situation, not lacking one thing. He is completely prepared for a successful voyage.

Then in II Timothy 3:17 comes the next word: "That the man of God may be perfect, throughly ...." The word is "throughly," not "thoroughly." I have asked hundreds of people in classes to read this verse of Scripture, and 99 out of 100 will read that word "thoroughly." When we do not read what is written, how can we expect to understand the Word of God? People are constantly reading into it. Our minds project rather than read. It is basic that we read what is written. II Timothy 3:17 does not say "thoroughly;" it says "throughly." You may ask, "What is the difference?" You see, I can wash hands thoroughly, but I cannot wash my hands throughly. "Throughly" implies an inside job whereas "thoroughly" is for the external. The purpose of the Word of God is that the man of God may be perfect, not on the outside, but on the inside.

If the word "thoroughly" is in your Bible, it is a proofreader's oversight. If it were typed accurately, the word would always be printed "throughly." One cannot have perfection on the outside unless he first has perfection on the inside. The purpose of the Word of God is that the man of God may be perfect on the inside as a starting point.

"That the man of God may be perfect, throughly furnished ...." At this point, the translation has failed to communicate the impact of this verse. The word "furnished" is from the same root word in Greek as the word "perfect." The Greek word for "perfect" is *artios*; the Greek word for "furnished" in II Timothy 3:17 is *exartizō*. *Exartizō* is a verb whereas *artios* is an adjective. Literally it says, "That the man of God may be perfect, throughly perfected ...." Not only is the man to be perfect, but he is to be through and through and throughly perfected.

In two short verses of Scripture, The Word tells us both its own function and its purpose.

> II Timothy 3:16,17:
> All scripture *is* given by inspiration of God, and *is* profitable for doctrine, for reproof, for correction, for instruction in righteousness:
>
> That the man of God may be perfect, throughly furnished unto all good works.

What a foundational revelation to our study and understanding of the Word of God!

Chapter Seven
Man Shall Not Live By Bread Alone

Man's basic spiritual problem is not believing the integrity of the Word of God. Very few people believe that the Word of God is accurate, that it means what it says and that it says what it means. Thus man is in a constant dilemma in his quest for truth; he has no touchstone for truth because he will not go to The Word and study its integrity and accuracy.

In Matthew 4:4 the Word of God declares,

> ... It is written, Man shall not live by bread alone, but by every word that proceedeth out of the mouth of God.

Notice the words "out of the mouth of God." God has been attributed a human characteristic, but God does not have a mouth. Again the figure of speech is *condescensio,* the Holy Spirit's marking for emphasis.

Man cannot sustain himself solely on a diet of

physical food; he needs his food supplemented by every word that comes from God. Man cannot live by words that come from men, from different writers, from different theologians or from different church groups, but by words that come from God.

Man does need physical food for the maintenance of his physical body. But a man has more than just his physical body to care for. A man's soul needs nourishment also. Man's soul cannot be sustained by mashed potatoes, gravy and steak. Matthew 4:4 declares that man shall live not only by bread "but by every word ...." He needs not just a word here and a word there; not one verse here and another verse there; "but by every word that proceedeth out of the mouth of God." The Word of God is that food required by man so that he may renew his mind and thereby manifest the more abundant life.

Spiritual weakness and spiritual inability can be due only to an improper diet, that is, the neglect of the Word of God. For the most part, spiritual anemia caused by the neglect of the Word of God may today be attributed to the fact that the Bible is not understood when read. The Bible is not understood because we have never been taught how to understand it. Who has taught us figures of speech? Who has taught us what revelation is? Who has shown us the accuracy of The Word? That is why we have stories about the dust-covered Bible. One cannot really blame people for this. The blame should lay with those of us who have been preachers and teachers because we have not communicated The Word to today's man.

But what about the people whose Bibles are not dust covered and neglected, and yet they are still spiritually weak? Their spiritual malady must be caused by wrong usage of God's Word. The improper usage means that the Word of God is not being rightly divided. Some of us have been instructed to read the Bible at least once a day; but when we are through reading our daily Scripture, what do we know? We have not learned anything because we have not understood it. What happens when people fail to understand The Word? They succumb to all the doctrines and theories of man. These spiritually-hungry people are blown around from pillar to post with each new philosopher or new idea. The fleeting shadows of a few great names rather than the Word of God hold people spellbound. Far too many people believe what they have received from man and then endeavor to have their beliefs corroborated by going to the Bible and selecting Scriptures to substantiate their ideas.

A woman once wrote to me regarding one of our broadcasts. She had appreciated my preaching because it agreed with what she thought. Suppose the teaching had been The Word and that it had disagreed with what she thought. Would her beliefs have changed the Word of God? Whether or not we believe, it is still God's Word.

Several years ago I was teaching a class in a Southern state. After the second session a man came to me and said, "I think that this is the most logical Biblical teaching I have ever heard, but," he said, "it is upsetting me because I have always held other opinions and I do not want to change my mind. You are confusing me." This gentleman did not finish the class because he already had his mind closed. That was his privilege, but God's Word is still Truth whether or not we believe it.

When two parts of hydrogen and one part of oxygen are sparked together, water is going to result. I do not care whether you pray or do not pray, whether you are Christian or non-Christian, whether you believe or you do not believe; it does not make any difference because the law is that two parts of hydrogen and one part of oxygen is water. God's Word is as infallible as that. This is why we should honestly come to the point that we allow the Word of God to take pre-eminence in our lives no matter what ideas, no matter what theories, no matter what opinions we may have held. We must come to The Word, let The Word speak, and then adjust our thinking according to the integrity and the accuracy of The

96

Word. After we have let The Word speak, we must accordingly harmonize our beliefs, our actions and our living.

II Peter 1:3 says about The Word,
According as his [God's] divine power hath given unto us all things that *pertain* unto life and godliness, through the knowledge of him that hath called us to glory and virtue.

God by His divine power has given unto us all things that pertain unto life and godliness. If we want the things that pertain to life and godliness, we have to go to God's Word. If one plays football, he must go by the rules of the game of football. So logically, if we want to know God's will, where do we go? To the commentary, to the theologians, to the encyclopedia, or to last Sunday's sermon? No. We go to the Word of God.

I Thessalonians 2:13:
For this cause also thank we God without ceasing, because, when ye received the word of God which ye heard of us, ye received *it* not *as* the word of men, but as it is in truth, the word of God, which effectually worketh also in you that believe.

They received the Word of God which they heard of

Paul. People could have said, "That is just Paul talking," but they did not. Paul says that the Thessalonians "received the Word of God which ye have heard of us ... not *as* the word of men, but as it is in truth, the word of God, which effectually worketh also in you that believe."

The Word declares of itself in Psalms 12:6,

> The words of the Lord *are* pure words: *as* silver tried in a furnace of earth, purified seven times.

If the Bible has the words of the Lord then these words must be undefiled and absolutely pure. They are "... *as* silver tried in a furnace of earth, purified seven times."

> Psalms 119:162:
> I rejoice at thy word, as one that findeth great spoil.

Do you rejoice at The Word as one who finds great spoil? Would you rejoice at The Word as much as you would if you found a thousand dollars?

I Corinthians contains another testimony from the Word of God regarding the integrity of God's Word.

> I Corinthians 2:13:
> Which things also we speak, not in the words

which man's wisdom teacheth, but [words] which the Holy Ghost teacheth; comparing spiritual things with spiritual.

If these are words which the Holy Spirit teaches, then we ought to wash out our ears, get the cobwebs out of our minds, and begin to study The Word for its inherent accuracy.

> Jeremiah 15:16:
> Thy words were found, and I did eat them; and thy word [The Word, not what people said about it, not what some theologian wrote about it] was unto me the joy and rejoicing of mine heart ....

This does not mean that they found the Bible or The Word and chewed it or physically ate it. When The Word was found, they digested it; they lived on it; it was their life, their heartbeat.

The Word is almost unbelievable because it is so true. Too many ministers like to talk around The Word by taking one verse of Scripture, reading that verse as the text for the day, giving illustrations from Shakespeare and *Newsweek,* coming back and quoting the verse of Scripture, pronouncing the benediction and going home. How much of The Word then has the congregation learned? None! When the people

ate The Word as recorded in Jeremiah, they ate the
pure Word. We must preach the *pure* Word.

All God's creation is marvelous; but of all God's
works, the greatest of His works is His Word.

> Psalms 138:2:
> ... for thou has magnified thy word above all thy
> name.

God has magnified His Word above His Name. It
does not say that about the stars or the planets. He
set His Word above His name for He underwrote it;
He put His name underneath it, He guaranteed it. It is
just like a check. When I write a check for a thousand
dollars, I put my name underneath it. The check is
only as good as the signature. How good is The Word?
The Word of God declares that it is as good as God
for God signed His Name to it. The Word is as much
God as God is God. What God said was, was; what
God has said is, is; what God says will be, will be. Do
you see why we must come back to the integrity and
accuracy of God's wonderful Word? We cannot trust
man's word because man blows about being here today and gone tomorrow; but the Word of God "liveth
and abideth for ever." That Word endures.

Chapter Eight
In the Beginning Was The Word

The beginning of the Gospel of John states,

In the beginning was the Word, and the Word was with God, and the Word was God.

Notice there are three usages of the word "word" in verse 1.

John 1:2:
The same was in the beginning with God.

Logos means "word" or "communication." God is spoken of as the *logos* because He *is* The Word. Christ is the *logos*, God's Word in person; while the Bible is the *logos*, God's Word in writing.

Which *logos* is John 1:1 speaking of? "In the beginning was the *logos*, and the *logos* was with God, and the *logos* was God." The word used in this verse is both the written Word, which we speak of today as

The Bible is the Word of God

the Bible, and Christ, The Word in person.

The key to understanding John 1:1 and 2 is the word "with." If any other Greek word were used for the word "with" except *pros*, the whole Bible would crumble. The word *pros* means "together with, yet distinctly independent of." That is exquisite semantic accuracy. Jesus Christ in the beginning was together with God, yet He was distinctively independent of Him. The written Word was originally with God, yet distinctively independent of God. This is its remarkable usage because it refutes the erroneous teaching that in the beginning Jesus Christ was with God to start everything. This is not what The Word says. It says that He was with Him, but the written Word was also with Him. How? In what you and I would express as "in the mind of God." God in His foreknowledge knew of the coming of the Lord Jesus Christ. He knew of the prophets to whom He could give The Word, and of their faithfulness in writing and speaking The Word. This was all with God because of His foreknowledge. Do you know that you were with God from the beginning if you are a born-again believer?

Ephesians 1:4:
According as he [God] hath chosen us in him before the foundation of the world ....

If you were chosen before the foundation of the

102

world, where were you? Do not tell me that you already have lived in eternity with Him. No, but in the foreknowledge of God, God knew that some day you would believe, you would be born again of God's Spirit. That is why The Word says that He chose you and that you were in Him before the foundation of the world.

Observe another corroborating Scripture.

II Thessalonians 2:13:
... God hath from the beginning chosen you to salvation through sanctification of the Spirit and belief of the truth.

We were with Him from the beginning as Jesus Christ was with Him, as the written Word was with Him, and yet distinctively independent of Him. This explains the importance of the use of *pros*.

By deductive logic, if God is perfect, then the *logos*, Jesus Christ, has to be perfect. If God is perfect and Christ is perfect and The Word is given as holy men of God spake as they were moved by the Holy Spirit, then God's Word must be perfect also.

God is perfect, so Jesus Christ is perfect, so the revealed Word of God is perfect. Consequently the words which make up The Word must also be perfect.

103

This is why if any other word had been used than the preposition *pros* in John 1:1 and 2 the whole Bible would fall to pieces because of imperfect usage of words. To have a perfect Word, the words must be perfect and the order of the words must be perfect.

Have you ever asked yourself why John 3:16 is placed exactly where it is? Why is Galatians 5:4 exactly where it is? Why is I Corinthians 12 where it is? Why is I Corinthians 14 where it is? If they were at any other place the order of the words would be imperfect. A chain is no stronger than its weakest link. This is true of The Word too. If The Word can be broken at any one place, The Word crumbles from Genesis to Revelation. Either the whole Bible is God's Word from Genesis 1:1 to Revelation 22:21 or none of it is God's Word. Someone may say, "I believe John 3:16, but I do not believe I Corinthians 14, where Paul says, 'I would that ye all spake with tongues ....' " If one can believe John 3:16 and throw out I Corinthians 14, then I can believe I Corinthians 14, and throw out John 3:16. What have we got? Nothing. Men's opinion. All must be God's Word or none of it is.

God is perfect, The Word is perfect, and, therefore, The Word means what it says, and says what it means. God has a purpose for *everything* He says, *where* He says it, *why* He says it, *how* He says it, *to whom* He says it, and *when* He says it.

At one point I believed that the Word of God was full of myths. At one point I could have quoted you numerous theologians, but I could not have quoted the accuracy of God's Word. There was a time in my life when I did not even believe the words "Holy Bible." I did not believe in the miracles, I did not believe in the second coming. I was just a rank unbeliever. I learned my unbelief in the schools I attended which taught that the Bible is full of errors, that the Word of God is full of myths, that it has a lot of forgeries in it. If a minister does not believe that the Bible is God's Word and if he thinks that it is full of myths and forgeries, what would be the man's actions if he followed what he believes? He would get out of the pulpit if he were honest with himself.

I have very little respect for those who stand in the pulpits or stand behind podiums and declare, "This verse is all right, but that one is an interpolation, and that other one is a myth." Men want to teach us that the book of Genesis had four or five different writers in the first few chapters. That is a presumptuous teaching when the Word of God declares that holy men of God spake as they were moved by the Holy Spirit. Which are you going to believe – God's Word or men's opinions? We should be concerned about the integrity of God's Word.

105

The Bible is the Word of God

We have failed to walk in deliverance in this our day and time because The Word is not real, it is not alive, it is not dynamic to or in us. Consequently most people are spiritual cripples, spiritual hitch-hikers. They ride along on somebody else's beliefs. Many people today would much rather read and study the literature of the hour than the literature of eternity. Why? Because the word of man has had pre-eminence over the wonderful Word of God. If what man says contradicts what The Word says, they stick to man's word rather than The Word. If we want deliverance, if we want to tap the resources for the more abundant life, then God's Word demands that we study and live by this matchless Word.

Chapter Nine
Mightily Grew the Word of God and Prevailed

When the Word of God prevails, the power of God manifests itself in a tremendous way. This is documented in Acts 19 where the prevailing Word revolutionized not only a community but also a complete section of the world in a short period of time.

Acts 19 records that Paul went to Ephesus and found certain disciples there. He ministered the power of the holy spirit into manifestation, "and all the men were about twelve." Verse 8 begins the record that demonstrates the dynamics of the prevailing Word of God.

> Acts 19:8:
> And he [Paul] went into the synagogue, and spake boldly for the space of three months, disputing and persuading the things concerning the kingdom of God.

For three months Paul went into the synagogue

107

and showed them the Word of God. But three months was all he stayed because unbelievers spoke evil of that way.

Verse 9,

> But when divers [many] were hardened, and believed not, but spake evil of that way before the multitude, he [Paul] departed from them, and separated the disciples, disputing daily in the school of one Tyrannus.

Paul went into the synagogue for three months preaching and teaching the Word of God; but when they refused to believe the Word of God, Paul separated the believers. He said, "You people who want to believe come with me; we are going over to the school of Tyrannus. The rest of you who do not want to believe the accuracy of God's Word just stay here at the synagogue." Actually it was not Paul who broke up this synagogue. The hardened and evil-speakers with their unbelief were the ones responsible for the break-up of the Ephesian synagogue. What a break it was, for verse 10 says,

> And this continued by the space of two years; so that all they which dwelt in Asia [Biblically, "Asia" refers to a province.] heard the word of the Lord Jesus, both Jews and Greeks.

In two years and three months all Asia Minor heard the Word of God. In our day and time, with our multi-million dollars spent for foreign missions, publications, newspapers, radios, televisions and all other media, this event has never been repeated. We have never reached all Asia Minor with the Word of God in one generation. But the Apostle Paul and a handful of believers accomplished the feat in two years and three months. Either God has changed or Paul and these men who studied at the school of Tyrannus had tapped into something which they utilized to its capacity.

As a matter of record, each of these men acted boldly after being filled with the power of the holy spirit and knowing God's Word. As these men learned, they taught The Word to someone else, who in turn, taught other individuals so that all of Asia Minor heard the Word of God in two years and three months. This evangelistic campaign began under the ministry of one man.

Verse 11 tells us what happened.

> And God wrought special miracles by the hands of Paul.

When Paul believed The Word, preached The Word, and taught The Word, special miracles came to pass.

109

This stir which began in Ephesus with the Word of God prevailing had a reverberating effect. People whom Paul had not taught tried to get into the act too, but their actions boomeranged on them.

Verse 13,

> Then certain of the vagabond Jews, exorcists, took upon them [themselves] to call over them which had evil spirits the name of the Lord Jesus, saying ....

In Acts 19:13 people with evil spirits tried to cast out evil spirits. This verse will give one trouble until he understands that a more powerful devil spirit has command over the less potent devil spirits. Just as in the army when a captain tells the private to jump, the private does not ask how high; he simply jumps. That is what these various devil spirits were doing. These exorcists were endeavoring to cast out devil spirits by other devil spirits in the name of Jesus saying, "We adjure you by Jesus whom Paul preaches. Come on out."

Verse 15,

> And the evil spirit answered and said, Jesus I know, and Paul I know; but who are ye?

These sons of Sceva, chief of the priests, were casting out devil spirits by other devil spirits. But one of these devil spirits came out and talked back to the sons and said, "Wait a minute. Jesus we know and Paul we know, but who in the world are you?"

Verse 16,

> And the man in whom the evil spirit was leaped on them, and overcame them, and prevailed against them, so that they fled out of that house naked and wounded.

Can't you just see those frenzied fellows running away? Once the devil spirits were aroused, the man, in whom the devil spirit was, attacked these fellows, jerking off their clothes and beating them around so that they ran out of the house naked and wounded.

Verse 17,

> And this was known to all the Jews and Greeks also dwelling at Ephesus; and fear fell on them all, and the name of the Lord Jesus was magnified.

Verse 18,

> And many that believed came, and confessed, and shewed their deeds.

Verse 19,

Many of them also which used curious arts ....

Do you know what curious arts are? Curious arts are a part of the entire E.S.P. field; for example, ouija boards which we are selling every place today for kids to play with because we want children to get started right in the spirit world. We tell them it is just a nice little game to play with. In truth it is a little game to open their minds to devil-possession which will later control and use the children at the spirit's own will.

Today very few people know the difference between an evil spirit and a good spirit so we go along and say that God gives all. We make just one basic mistake — which god? The Bible says that there are two gods — one is the God and Father of our Lord Jesus Christ and the other god is the god of this world called Satan. Later on I am going to show this to you from the Word of God, line by line and word by word.

Acts 19:19:
Many of them also which used curious arts brought their books together, and burned them before all *men*: and they counted the price of them, and found *it* fifty thousand *pieces* of silver.

Mightily Grew the Word of God and Prevailed

Think how much 50,000 pieces of silver would be in present-day currency. Verse 20 gives the fulfilling joy and greatness of the ministry in Ephesus.

Acts 19:20:
So mightily grew the word of God and prevailed.

What grew? Not man's opinion. The Word of God grew and the Word of God prevailed. When that Word of God prevails, things begin to happen in our lives, in our community, and in our society. But as long as the growth of the Word of God is stunted, as long as people do not understand the fullness of God's Word, it can never prevail. God meant for His Word to prevail. God gave us His Word that we might lead people out of darkness into the glorious light of the gospel of redemption and salvation to make known His will.

All Asia Minor was revived by the ministry of one man. When The Word again becomes real, revival will break out again. People will be saved without newspapers, without radio, without television, without the cooperation of all the churches of a community. When we start living The Word, The Word begins to permeate our everyday lives. It is the Word of God that sparks faith for rebirth.

Romans 10:17:
So then faith *cometh* by hearing, and hearing by the word of God.

The Bible is the Word of God

Faith does not come by hearing what *Look, Life, Time,* or the *Reader's Digest* has to say. Faith comes by hearing one thing — the Word of God. The Word of God builds believing so that a man can be born again by God's Spirit and filled with the power of the holy spirit. The Word of God is faithful. What He has promised He is able to perform. His Word is the same yesterday, today and forever. Believe that Word, speak that Word, and it produces the same results today that it produced at any time in the history of civilization since that Word was given. The Bible says that we are to abide in The Word and that we are to let this Word abide in us. To the extent that we abide in The Word, this Word takes the Master's place in our lives.

I have never seen a man, woman, boy or girl whose soul was not thrilled when this Word of God started to unfold to them. Why? Because the Word of God reveals mysteries, as it says in Romans 16:25 and 26. The Word makes us wise unto salvation as II Timothy 3:15 tells us. According to Acts 17:11 we are to search the Word of God for truth. We do not search any secular sources for truth. We must search the Word of God because the Word of God is the Will of God. Once we know His Will and let it prevail in our lives, then we will see the power of God in manifestation.

114

Chapter Ten
The Rightly-divided Word

Time and again I have heard the statement that God's Word causes trouble in a community or in a church or in our society. After frequently hearing that and after searching The Word as to why there is division and lack of accord among Christians, I wrote a study entitled "Why Division?" Division comes not from the Word of God; it comes from the unbelief of those who refuse to believe the integrity and the accuracy of God's Word.

The subject of this chapter is the accuracy of God's Word and a workman's responsibility to that Word. II Timothy 2:15 is our point of departure in studying this topic.

Study to shew thyself approved unto God, a workman that needeth not to be ashamed, rightly dividing the word of truth.

The one great requirement of every Biblical stu-

115

dent is to rightly divide the Word of Truth. The Bible, the Word of God in its originally-revealed form, is the Word of Truth. But when it is wrongly divided, the true Word does not exist. We have the Word of Truth only to the extent that the Word of God is rightly divided. Everybody at one time or another divides The Word. The question is not whether we divide The Word; the question is whether we rightly divide it.

Acts 17:2 is a verse of Scripture which a minister once handed to me. He said, "Dr. Wierwille, you are always talking about preaching nothing but The Word and not going to outside sources, but do you know that the Apostle Paul did not always use the Word of God, that he reasoned with people logically from outside The Word?" Then he quoted Acts 17:2 to prove to me that the Apostle Paul went outside of the Bible to reason with people about spiritual matters.

> Acts 17:2:
> And Paul, as his manner was, went in unto them, and three sabbath days reasoned with them out of the scriptures.

Did Paul reason with them from outside of the Scriptures? That is what the minister said, but that is not what The Word says. It says that he "reasoned with them out [out] of the scriptures," not *outside* the scriptures. That man divided The Word. Again, the question is whether he rightly divided it. We must study to show ourselves approved unto God as a workman who does not need to be ashamed by *rightly* dividing The Word.

Let me give another illustration of how people wrongly divide The Word. A man had been in a prayer meeting after which he came to the home of two students of the class on Power for Abundant Living. He said to them, "You know, we have just had the most tremendous meeting. We prayed until we had prayed the Holy Spirit into the meeting."

The Power for Abundant Living student said, "Do you mean you prayed so fervently that you prayed the Holy Spirit into your prayer group? I thought that God is the Holy Spirit and that He is everywhere present. How could you pray Him in?"

"Oh," the man said, "we did."

So the students asked the man to give them the chapter and verse. He turned to the book of Jude and gave this verse to prove that they had prayed the Holy Spirit into that meeting.

> Jude 20:
> But ye, beloved, building up yourselves on the most holy faith, praying in [in] the Holy Ghost.

117

Did he divide The Word? Yes. But did he rightly divide it? Is that what "praying in the Holy Ghost" means? Look again. "Building up yourselves on your most holy faith, praying in the Holy Ghost."

Anyone can take the Word of God and make it mean exactly what he wants by taking it out of its context or by adding to it or by deleting certain words. The story goes that a man once said that he could prove from the Bible that there is no God. He quoted from Psalm 14:1, "*There is* no God."

> Psalms 14:1:
> The fool hath said in his heart, *There is* no God ....

Does that verse say that there is no God? Yes, it does. It says, "There is no God." So one can go to the Bible and prove just what the man said. He just forgot to include the first part of the verse, "The fool hath said in his heart ...."

A person can prove anything from the Bible by isolating a text or by changing it around. Anyone can substantiate a theological viewpoint by manipulating Scripture.

II Timothy does not tell us to divide The Word; it tells us to rightly divide it. II Timothy 2:15 is the only place in the Bible where the words "rightly dividing" are found. Again a singular usage in the Word of God shows that the expression is uniquely and dynamically significant. The English words "rightly dividing" are the Greek word *orthotomounta*. *Orthos* means "perfectly right" or "perfectly straight." *Temno* means "to cut." Putting these two words together in the word *orthotomounta,* translated "rightly dividing" in the King James Version, literally means "a perfectly right cutting." Its intricate nuance of meaning is that there is only one way to rightly cut The Word; all other ways are wrong cuttings. The teaching that many people give – that as long as you are sincere everything is wonderful – is not the teaching of The Word. II Timothy 2:15 says that we are to "study to show ourselves approved unto God by rightly dividing." There is only one way to rightly cut The Word; all other ways are wrong cuttings. Now do you understand why we have splits, denominations and sects in so-called Christianity? They stem from the wrong dividing of The Word.

The first word in II Timothy 2:15 is "Study." The very first thing a person must do to rightly divide The Word is study. He is not told to study commentaries or secular writers; he must study The Word. If we are ever going to rightly divide The Word, we have to study The Word and not what people say about it.

For years I did nothing but read around the Word

of God. I used to read two or three theological works weekly for month after month and year after year. I knew what Professor so-and-so said, what Dr. so-and-so and the Right Reverend so-and-so said, but I could not quote you The Word. I had not read it. One day I finally became so disgusted and tired of reading around The Word that I hauled over 3,000 volumes of theological works to the city dump. I decided to quit reading around The Word. Consequently, I have spent years studying The Word — its integrity, its meaning, its words.

Why do we study? Because God expects us as workmen to know what His Word says.

> I Corinthians 12:1:
> Now concerning spiritual *gifts* [matters], brethren, I would not have you ignorant.

Since God would not have us ignorant, there is only one way He would have us to be — smart.

We are to study to show ourselves approved unto God, not to man. You do not study to show yourself approved unto the leading financier in your community, or to the heads of your denominations. Whether men approve you or not isn't of primary importance; the primary thing is to stand approved before God. And the only way you are going to stand approved

120

before God is to study and rightly divide The Word.

Romans 16:10:
Salute Apelles [who is] approved in Christ ....

It does not say that he was approved in the community or by the society or in the denomination, but he was approved in or of Christ.

Acts 2:22:
Ye men of Israel, hear these words; Jesus of Nazareth, a man approved of God ....

We study to show ourselves approved of God because we are workmen who do not need to be ashamed of our workmanship. If I were a carpenter and built a house with joints and mortises that were gaping, I would stand in disapproval for my workmanship when the owner came to look. A workman is approved or not approved by the people who employ him. So we study The Word that we may be approved before God because we are held accountable to Him for our workmanship.

Matthew 12:36,37:
But I say unto you, That every idle word that men shall speak, they shall give [an] account thereof in the day of judgment.

For by thy words thou shalt be justified, and by

121

thy words thou shalt be condemned.

Romans 14:12:
So then every one of us shall give account of himself to God.

The Word says and means that everyone shall give an account of himself. To have God's approval we must study The Word and study it in the right way. The right way is the right cutting of the Word of Truth to have the true Word.

Jesus Christ, God's only-begotten Son, rightly divided The Word. According to Luke 24:44 Jesus divided the Old Testament into the Law, the Prophets and the Psalms. "Psalms" means "writings" in Biblical usage. I had been taught to divide the Old Testament into the books of the Law, the books of History, the books of Poetry, the Major Prophets and the Minor Prophets. I put them into five categories whereas Jesus Christ put them into three. Who do you think was right? Jesus Christ rightly divided The Word.

Psalms 116:15 is another verse which is frequently wrongly divided. This is a verse of Scripture which we often hear at a funeral when a good man of God has died.

Psalm 116:15:
Precious in the sight of the Lord *is* the death of
his saints.

We say, "It is precious, it is good, in the sight of
the Lord that he is dead." Talk about wrongly dividing The Word! It is not good in the sight of the Lord
that Herman died or that John died or that Mary died
because they cannot help God any after they are
dead. The only time they could help God is when
they were alive. The word "precious" in the text is
"costly."

We speak of a diamond as a precious stone because
it is costly and rare. The more costly it is, the more
precious it is. This is what is meant by "precious in
the sight of the Lord *is* the death of his saints." It
does not cost God anything when an unbeliever or a
God-rejector dies. They have not done anything for
God anyway. But if a believer died, it would be costly
to God. That is why the Psalmist said, "Costly in the
sight of the Lord *is* the death of his saints."

The Word of God is the true Word only when it is
rightly divided. When it is wrongly divided we have
error at the particular place where it is wrongly
divided. To illustrate, if I rightly divide the Word of
Truth on salvation, I will have the true Word on salvation. But if I wrongly divide the Word of Truth on
the subject of the Holy Spirit, then at that place I do

123

not have the true Word. Naturally I will be sincere on both salvation and the Holy Spirit; but sincerity is absolutely no guarantee for truth. Sincerity is wonderful, but it is not synonymous with truth. I like sincere people, but I have also been hoodwinked by them. The insincere people have never deceived me, but the sincere people have.

Sincerity or insincerity is not the determining factor for truth. The Word of God is Truth. When we rightly divide it, we have the true Word; when we wrongly divide it, we have error.

In the matter of standing approved before God, people are again in disagreement. People say that we stand approved before God if we pray a certain way or if the flowers are on the altar at the right place. It does not make a bit of difference to God where the flowers are on the altar. It may make a difference to us, but it does not make any difference at all to God. The Word of God says we study to show ourselves approved unto God by rightly dividing The Word. To the end we rightly divide The Word, we stand approved; to the end we wrongly divide it, we do not stand approved. We must come to the position of using The Word as our authority. Christian believers can never be brought together on other extraneous, superficial, ritualistic matters. They can only be brought together when they stand approved before God by rightly dividing The Word.

An example of people trying to stand approved of God is a sadly ridiculous commentary on so-called Christians. Many years ago when I was doing research in the archives of the University of Chicago Divinity School, I came across a clipping from a newspaper on a denomination which had two factions. The cause of the rift was the question whether or not God originally had created Adam and Eve with or without navels. Incredible! One group said that Adam and Eve did not have navels while the other faction believed that God had given both Adam and Eve navels. The one group built a new church just across the street from the old one and called their new denomination the First Church of the Navelites. Christians bring disapproval to themselves when they become sidetracked on such irrelevant matters.

It does not make any difference to God whether one wears a long dress or a short one; it does not make any difference to Him whether I wear a tie or whether I do not. I could teach The Word just as effectively with a tie as without one. The greatness is not in what we wear or how we adorn ourselves, but whether we rightly divide The Word. This Word of God is the greatest thing in the whole world and rightly divided it gives us the true Word; it gives efficacy, power, exuberance and the more abundant life which Jesus Christ made available.

Chapter Eleven
The Translations of the Word of God

In proceeding as a workman, there is basic information which must be kept in mind, the first of which is that no translation or version of the Bible may properly be called the Word of God.

The Bible from which I have been quoting is called the King James Version. It is not the King James translation. If I had the King James translation in my hands, I would have a Bible that is worth a great deal of money as a collector's item. Once a translation has been made from an original text, like the Stephens Text from which the King James was translated, the first copy is called a translation. When scholars begin to rework the translation in any way, it becomes a version.

Now I said that no translation, let alone a version, may properly be called the Word of God. As far as anybody knows, there are no original texts in existence today. The oldest dated Biblical manuscript is

127

from 464 A.D. and written in Aramaic in Estrangelo script. There are older Aramaic manuscripts written in the Estrangelo script which predate 464 A.D., but these are not Biblical texts. What students or scholars refer to as "originals" really date from 464 A.D. and later. These manuscripts are not originals — the originals are those which holy men of God wrote as they were moved by the Holy Spirit. At best we have copies of the originals. When I refer to the Word of God, I do not mean a copy or a translation or a version; I mean that Word of God which was originally given by revelation to holy men.

Since we have no originals and the oldest manuscripts that we have date back to the fifth century A.D., how can we get back to the authentic prophecy which was given when holy men of God spoke? To get the Word of God out of any translation or out of any version, we have to compare one word with another word and one verse with another verse. We have to study the context of all the verses. If it is the Word of God, then it cannot have a contradiction for God cannot contradict Himself. Error has to be either in the translation or in one's own understanding. When we get back to that original, God-breathed Word — which I am confident we can — then once again we will be able to say with all the authority of the prophets of old, "Thus saith the Lord."

Note carefully the following about The Word:

128

(1) there are no original texts in existence today; (2) there were no chapter divisions in the original manuscripts; (3) there were no verse divisions in the original manuscripts. Chapters were first put into the Bible in 1250 A.D. Verses first appeared in the Geneva Bible in 1560 and then in the 1611 translation known as the King James.

God cannot be blamed for the error in the division of verses or chapters. Chapters and verses are good only for quick reference. But we must keep in mind that chapters and verses are all man-made and, therefore, devoid of authority in rightly dividing the Word of Truth.

Let us look at some examples of poor divisions in chapters and verses.

Genesis 1:31:
And God saw every thing that he had made, and, behold, *it was* very good. And the evening and the morning were the sixth day.

Then comes chapter 2 which begins with "thus." That first word immediately tells me that something is wrong because "thus" shows the result of what has already been said. Chapter 1 closed with "And the evening and the morning were the sixth day." And chapter 2 begins,

Thus the heavens and the earth were finished, and all the host of them.

Verse 2,

And on the seventh day God ended his work which he had made; and he rested on the seventh day from all his work which he had made.

Verse 3,

And God blessed the seventh day, and sanctified it: because that in it he had rested from all his work which God created and made.

Verse 4,

These *are* the generations of the heavens and of the earth when they were created ....

Verse 4 is an entirely new thought. The first three verses of chapter 2 finish the thought of the first chapter. The second chapter should begin with verse four, "These *are* the generations ...."

John 2 is another example of bad chaptering. One of the reasons the story of Nicodemus has not been understood is that we have never read the verses preceding it as part of the context. John 2:23 should

130

logically be John 3:1.

> Now when he [Jesus] was in Jerusalem at the passover, in the feast *day,* many believed in his name, when they saw the miracles which he did.

Verse 24,

> But Jesus did not commit himself unto them, because he knew all *men,*

Verse 25,

> And needed not that any should testify of man: for he knew what was in man.

Chapter 3, verse 1,

> There was a man of the Pharisees, named Nicodemus, a ruler of the Jews.

Reading those three verses before beginning the present third chapter explains the context for the coming of Nicodemus. Jesus knew what was in Nicodemus. With this introduction or background to the setting of the story, Nicodemus is easily understood.

John 7:53 is an example of a chapter that is divided in the middle of a verse.

131

And every man went unto his own house.

Chapter 8, verse 1 begins,

Jesus went unto the mount of Olives.

It should read, "And every man went unto his own house. Jesus went unto the mount of Olives." Then there should be a chapter division to begin, "And early in the next morning he came again into the temple ...."

If chaptering was not in the originals, what about chapter headings? Chapter headings are also not part of the original God-breathed Word. Chapter headings are found below the chapter markings and are usually in italics. These are what man has added. An example of an erroneous chapter heading in some King James editions is Isaiah 29. Chapter 29 heading says, "The heavy judgment of God upon *Jerusalem.*" The heading on chapter 30 says, "God's mercy toward His *Church.*" The text says in Isaiah 1:1, "The vision of Isaiah the son of Amoz, which he saw concerning Judah and Jerusalem." Either the man who put "To the church" at the top of chapter 30 is wrong or The Word in Isaiah 1:1 is wrong.

Paragraphs and center references are all man-made. Paragraphs are interpretations of what the translators think. They indicate when one subject is complete and

132

when a new paragraph should begin. Sometimes translators fail to recognize proper subject division. Center references, which run down a long column in the center of each page, tell what the editors think has some connection with that verse. Sometimes they are right, sometimes they are wrong. All these markings have been added and they can confuse the average new student in the Bible because he may think they have been given by God Himself.

God gave the original Word. He is not at all responsible for the errors that men have introduced by their chapter headings or by their center references or by their paragraph markings. Man made all those mistakes.

Punctuation is another man-made trickery. If you want the Bible to say something to substantiate your theology, all you have to do is to manipulate the punctuation. The Word of God can be made to say something that it does not really say by just putting in a comma. Each translator followed his own plan or his own pattern which makes all punctuation devoid of divine authority.

Let us observe the punctuation in the book of Luke.

Luke 23:43:
And Jesus said unto him [the malefactor],

133

> Verily I say unto thee, To day shalt thou be with me in paradise.

Some translations have the comma after the word "today" so that is read, "Jesus said unto him, Verily I say unto thee To day, thou shalt ...." The King James puts the comma before "today" while other translations put the comma after "today." Why? Because one group teaches that the moment one dies, he goes to heaven, while other groups teach that the moment one dies, he does not necessarily go to heaven for there is a period before going to heaven. If there is a waiting period between death and heaven then He could not say to that malefactor, "Today you are going to be with me in heaven," for the malefactor would have had to wait a duration. On the other hand others say man goes to heaven immediately after death so that comma before the word "today" fits in with their theology.

If a man is going to heaven today, heaven must be available. Some teach that heaven is available. If they had studied The Word, they would know that heaven is not available. However, this verse talks about paradise — and paradise is not heaven. Heaven is heaven and paradise is paradise. When the Word of God says "paradise," it means "paradise." Paradise is present in Genesis chapters 1 and 2, at the end of which paradise is no longer accessible. It is not again available until the book of Revelation which speaks of a new heaven and a new earth wherein dwells righteousness.

Paradise is always a place upon earth. If we are going to paradise, it has to be available. Was Jesus saying to the malefactor that day, "... Verily I say unto thee To day," or was it "... Verily I say unto thee, To day ..."? Since paradise was nonexistent on the day of the crucifixion, Jesus had to say to the malefactor that sometime in the future he would be with Him, not in heaven, but in paradise.

Let us read the sentence with the literal accuracy of the word "paradise" in mind.

> ... Verily, I say to you To day, thou shalt [the day is coming in the future when you are going to] be with me in paradise.

This fits with the rest of the Word of God. One little comma has caused so much error in dividing The Word.

Another example of a grave punctuation error is in Acts 21 which, when I first saw it, I found difficult to believe. I had been taught that the men of God in the Bible — like Abraham, and Paul, and John — never made mistakes. These men were on a pedestal while we other lowly Christians stared in awe with mouth

135

agape at such men to whom we thought we could never aspire. The record of the Apostle Paul in Acts 21 gave me quite a jolt when the error in using a comma was discovered.

> Acts 21:14:
> And when he [Paul] would not be persuaded, we ceased, saying, The will of the Lord be done.

This verse, the way it is punctuated, obviously says that they endeavored to persuade the Apostle Paul to change his mind and not go to Jerusalem; but when Paul would not change his mind, they finally said to him "All right, Paul, go out and do the will of the Lord. Go to Jerusalem." But this is not what it says.

To understand the background of this situation, let's go back to Acts 20:22.

> And now, behold, I go bound in the spirit unto Jerusalem, not knowing the things that shall befall me there.

Paul was bound in the spirit. To be "bound in the spirit" means that one is not spiritually free. Paul wanted to go, but something nagged his mind saying, "Don't go." Paul said, "I am going to go to Jerusalem"; but when he made this statement, he was bound in the spirit, he felt restrained. He knew he

136

should not go.

Verse 23,

> Save that the Holy Ghost witnesseth in every
> city, saying that bonds and afflictions abide me
> [if I go to Jerusalem].

Verse 24,

> But none of these things move me, neither count
> I my life dear unto myself, so that I might finish
> my course with joy, and the ministry, which I
> have received of the Lord Jesus, to testify the
> gospel of the grace of God.

Doesn't that sound wonderful, sincere, devout?
But what good was Paul's sincerity in going to Jerusalem when the spirit had already told him not to go
there?

> Acts 21:3,
> Now when we had discovered Cyprus, we left it
> on the left hand, and sailed into Syria; and
> landed at Tyre: for there the ship was to unlade
> her burden.

Verse 4,

> And finding disciples [there], we tarried there

137

> seven days: who said to Paul through the Spirit, that he should not go up to Jerusalem.

What then was the will of God? For Paul *not* to go to Jerusalem. But who was determined to go?

Verse 8,

> And the next *day* we that were of Paul's company departed, and came unto Caesarea: and we entered into the house of Philip the evangelist, which was *one* of the seven; and abode with him.

Verse 9,

> And the same man had four daughters, virgins, which did prophesy.

Verse nine does not say what the virgins prophesied. I would bet you, however, that they did not prophesy about the price of coffee or about who would win the next ball game. What is the context talking about? It is about a man who wanted to go to Jerusalem while the will of the Lord was for him not to go. Paul persisted, however. In context we know what the topic of the virgins' prophecy was.

After a period of time there came another message

to Paul.

Verse 10,

> And as we tarried *there* many days, there came
> down from Judea a certain prophet, named
> Agabus.

Look at the pains God was taking to keep the
Apostle Paul out of a mess. First of all, He told Paul
personally not to go to Jerusalem; Paul was bound in
the spirit. Then Paul was warned by a group in Tyre
who told him by the spirit not to go. Paul continued
on his trip to Caesarea where four Christian believers
prophesied. Finally God sent a prophet all the way
from Jerusalem to Caesarea to intercept Paul on his
journey and say, "Paul, don't go to Jerusalem."

> Acts 21:11:
> And when he [Agabus] was come unto us, he
> took Paul's girdle [a strip of cloth four or five
> inches wide which they tie around their loosely
> flowing garments], and bound his own hands
> and feet, and said, Thus saith the Holy Ghost,
> So shall the Jews at Jerusalem bind the man that
> owneth this girdle, and shall deliver *him* into the
> hands of the Gentiles.

Agabus foretold that when Paul got to Jerusalem
he, Paul, would be delivered into the hands of the
Gentiles.

Verse 12,

> And when we heard these things, both we, and they of that place, besought him not to go up to Jerusalem.

God had done everything to keep His man out of a big dilemma, but Paul was determined to get in it. God can try to tell you; but if you will not listen, He cannot force you.

Verse 13,

> Then Paul answered, What mean ye to weep and to break mine heart ...

Paul moaned, so-to-speak, "Don't you people know that I am ready not to be bound only, but also to die at Jerusalem for the name of the Lord Jesus?" Doesn't that sound magnanimous and sincere! But Paul was totally wrong. The will of the Lord was for him not to go to Jerusalem.

After translators accurately gave The Word thus far, they reached verse 14. The translators tried to help Paul save face in the modern translations by simply putting in commas.

140

Verse 14:
And when he would not be persuaded, we
ceased, saying, The will of the Lord be done.

If the commas are left in, there is error upon error
for the truth of the record is clearly obvious. Four
times the word of the Lord to Paul was not to go to
Jerusalem. If that was the Word of God, then it has to
fit with verse 14 too. What did the translators do?
They put in commas to substantiate their theology
because they could not believe that the Apostle Paul
ever made a mistake. Let me ask, did Paul go to Jerusalem? Surely, he went to Jerusalem. Did he get into
trouble? He surely did; he almost lost his life there.
This mightly man of God, under whose ministry all
Asia Minor heard the Word of God in two years and
three months, in the following two years won not one
soul for the Lord Jesus Christ. The only record is in
Acts 26:28 when he witnessed to Agrippa, the king
who said to Paul, "... Almost thou persuadest me to
be a Christian." If the evangelists who use this text
realized what it really implies, they would never use
it again. In the context the quote is about the ministry of a man who was outside the will of God. The
nearest Paul came to winning anybody for the Lord
in all those years was "almost."

Take the commas out of Acts 21:14.

And when he [Paul] would not be persuaded, we

141

ceased [stopped] saying the will of the Lord be done.

At one time his Christian friends were saying to Paul, "Do the will of the Lord. Don't go to Jerusalem." They tried their best to persuade him, but when he would not be persuaded they "... stopped saying 'do the will of the Lord' " because Paul was determined to do his own will. Now your Bible fits like a hand in a glove; now we have the Word of God.

Commas have all been added by man. In the original Word of God there were no periods, no commas, no semi-colons, no chapters, no verses, no chapter headings and no center references.

All of these things have gone through periods of change. In this study on *Power for Abundant Living* in which we are interested in the accuracy and integrity of God's Word, we must get back to that original Word which was given when holy men of God spoke as they were moved by the Holy Spirit. We must strip off the translators' theologies which have come about with man-made devices and once more discover the perfect God-breathed Word.

Part III

How the Bible
Interprets Itself

Chapter Twelve
In Its Verse

II Peter 1:20 is a Scripture that I ordinarily begin with in my classes. In this book I have gone into more background to point out the accuracy of The Word so that now we are ready to study this verse.

> II Peter 1:20:
> Knowing this first, that no prophecy of the scripture is of any private interpretation.

This is the first thing one must know if he is going to understand the greatness of God's revelation in His Word. No prophecy, not one verse of Scripture, is of any private interpretation.

If I say, "This is what I think it means," I am giving my private interpretation. If you say, "This is what I think it means," or if any denomination writes, "This is what our denomination says it means," we have private interpretation. Give two men the same Scripture verse and, by privately inter-

preting it, they will come to two completely diver-
gent conclusions. All our splits in Christianity come
because we do not study The Word from its inherent
accuracy. It matters nothing what we think, what our
opinions are. The crucial element is what The Word
says. You and I have to do our thinking according to
the accuracy of The Word.

II Peter 1:20 is the only place that *idios* is translated "private." At the other places in the Bible it is
translated either "one's own" or "his own." The
word "interpretation" is the Greek word *epilusis*
which occurs at no other place in the Bible. The
Greek verb form of *epilusis* is *epiluō* meaning "to let
loose upon," as a hunting dog is let loose upon game.
Idios plus *epilusis* equals "of no personal letting
loose." One does not just let his mind run vagrantly
as when turning a dog loose upon the game; one does
not let his mind wander and give all kinds of interpretations to the Scripture. "Knowing this first, that
no prophecy of the Scripture is of any personal
letting loose."

After eliminating private interpretation, two alternatives remain in interpreting God's Word: (1) either
there is no interpretation possible or (2) The Word
must interpret itself. If there is no interpretation possible, then we might as well forget the whole project
of understanding The Word. But this is not the case.

There is another answer — The Word interprets itself.

The Word interprets itself in one of three ways: (1) it interprets itself in the verse where it is written; or (2) it interprets itself in its context; or (3) the interpretation can be found by its previous usage in The Word.

It was a remarkable revelation to us who do Biblical research to discover that the vast majority of the Word of God does interpret itself right where it is written. I would estimate that from Genesis to Revelation 85 to 90 per cent of the Word of God interprets itself in the verse.

If the interpretation is so obvious, why have we not understood it? First of all, we have not read it; and secondly, we have not remembered what we read. We get sloppy and read "thoroughly" instead of "throughly."

Let us look at some examples where Scripture interprets itself in the verse.

Genesis 1:1:
In the beginning God created the heaven and the earth.

Where does this verse interpret itself? One needs no commentary to understand this verse.

147

John 3:16:
For God so loved the world, that he gave his only begotten Son, that whosoever believeth in him should not perish, but have everlasting life.

Where does this verse interpret itself? Right where it is written. Verse after verse is just like that.

Matthew 11:28:
Come unto me, all *ye* that labour and are heavy laden, and I will give you rest.

Hebrews 13:5:
... I will never leave thee, nor forsake thee.

A person doesn't need commentaries, seldom even a dictionary, to understand these verses.

1

One note which we must heed is that the words must be understood according to the definitions at the time the translation was made. The meanings of words change. We would have a problem three weeks from now if a new translation were published today because of changed definitions and usage of words.

To illustrate a change in expression, check Isaiah 1:13.

148

Bring no more vain oblations; incense is an abomination unto me; the new moons and sabbaths, the calling of assemblies, I cannot away with ....

"I cannot away with" Biblically means "I cannot tolerate them." The Lord could not tolerate all the ritual of the incense, the new moon and the sabbaths that everybody was going through in the holy days.

Mark 7:9:
And he said unto them, Full well ye reject the commandment of God, that ye may keep your own tradition.

"Full well" means "with full knowledge" in King James usage. "With full knowledge you reject the commandment of God."

James 5:1:
Go to now, *ye* rich men, weep and howl for your miseries that shall come upon *you*.

When the Bible tells somebody to "go to" it means "come now." A current translation would read, "Come on now, you rich men, weep for your miseries ...."

149

> Luke 17:9:
> Doth he thank that servant because he did the things that were commanded him? I trow not.

"I trow not" means "I imagine not" according to King James usage.

> Luke 21:9:
> But when ye shall hear of wars and commotions, be not terrified: for these things must first come to pass; but the end *is* not by and by.

The words "by and by" in the King James mean "immediately." "But the end is not immediately." When you and I think of "by and by," we think of "eventually" or "in due time," or of the old song "In the Sweet By and By." That is an example of how drastically expressions can change.

> I Thessalonians 4:15:
> For this we say unto you by the word of the Lord, that we which are alive *and* remain unto the coming of the Lord shall not prevent them which are asleep.

The word "prevent" in its seventeenth century usage meant "precede." Today when we prevent someone, we hinder him. In the times of King James if you prevented someone, you went before him.

150

Matthew 25:35:
For I was an hungered, and ye gave me meat: I was thirsty, and ye gave me drink: I was a stranger, and ye took me in.

To "take someone in" means "to give hospitality."

II Timothy 3:6:
For of this sort are they which creep into houses, and lead captive silly women laden with sins, led away with divers lusts.

Today when we talk about silly people, we think of people who show little sense. When the King James uses the word "silly," it means "harmless."

These examples illustrate that we must understand that Scripture interprets itself in the verse where it is written, but that sometimes the word or words must be understood according to their usage when the translation was made.

2

There is another point. Verses that are self-interpreting must be in harmony with all other Biblical references on the same topic. In Matthew 27 is a verse that sticks out in the Word of God like a sore thumb. Every Easter when the "seven last words" are sermon topics, this one verse is mangled.

151

Matthew 27:46:
And about the ninth hour Jesus cried with a loud voice, saying, Eli, Eli, lama sabachthani? that is to say, My God, my God, why hast thou forsaken me?

This verse of Scripture should have arrested our attention from the beginning. Why did the translators leave in the foreign words? This should have caused us to make an inquiry as to the translators' deviation from the usual.

We understand this verse word by word except for the foreign words. Yet this verse contradicts other verses in the Word of God. It would appear that God forsook Jesus because Jesus became sin and God could not stand sin; consequently, God left Jesus to die by Himself.

Let us go to The Word and see exactly what The Word says. Look at John 16:32.

Behold, the hour cometh, yea, is now come, that ye shall be scattered [Jesus is talking to His apostles.], every man to his own, and shall leave me alone: and yet I am not alone, because the Father is with me.

Jesus was talking about the time of His crucifixion

and of His death; He said, "the Father is with me."
Yet in Matthew 27:46 it says, "My God, my God,
why hast thou forsaken me?"

John 10:30:
I and *my* Father are one.

II Corinthians 5:19:
To wit, that God was in Christ, reconciling the
world unto himself ....

How can one be separated? Check Colossians 2:9.

For in him [in Christ] dwelleth all the fulness of
the Godhead bodily.

How are we going to separate the fullness of the
Godhead which dwelt in Christ's presence on earth?
How could Jesus say, "My God, my God, why hast
thou forsaken me?"

There are many examples in The Word which are
blatantly contradicted by Matthew 27:46. Matthew
cannot do this if it is the Word of God.

What Christ said at the time He was taken captive
is recorded in Matthew 26:53.

Thinkest thou that I cannot now pray to my

Father, and he shall presently give me more than twelve legions of angels?

One has to be on "talking terms" with God to get that kind of assistance. The Father would have given Jesus 72,000 angels. Jesus could have walked right out from among this group of men if He had wanted to. Why? Because "I and my Father are one," "the Father is with me," "I always do the Father's will." Jesus must have been doing God's will when He was dying upon the cross. Yet Matthew 27:46 says, "Jesus cried with a loud voice, saying, Eli, Eli, lama sabachthani? that is to say, My God, my God, why hast thou forsaken me?" This verse contradicts the rest of The Word.

What is the problem? First of all, the foreign words inserted in that verse are Aramaic words. Jesus spoke Aramaic. (Aramaic is called Hebrew in the King James Version. It might more accurately have been called Syro-Chaldee.) These Aramaic words are left in this particular Scripture because the translators really did not know what to do with them. They let the verse set and added the English interpretation. There are a few other examples in the New Testament to this day where the translators have allowed the Aramaic words to remain in the text.

The word *eli* means "my God," but there is no

154

Aramaic word like the word *lama*. There is a word *lmna*. *Lmna* is always a cry of victory, a declaration of "for this purpose," or "for this reason." The root of *sabachthani* is *shbk*. *Shbk* means "to reserve," "to leave," "to spare" or "to keep."

It was about the ninth hour, three o'clock in the afternoon, when Jesus spoke from the cross. Hanging on the cross at that crucial hour, Jesus came forth with this utterance from the depth of His soul. "My God, my God, for this purpose was I reserved, for this purpose was I spared." The last words that He uttered were "It is finished." What was finished? Your redemption and mine. Jesus Christ had given His own life. He who knew no sin had become sin so that you and I might become the righteousness of God in Him. Your redemption and mine was then finished. The next chronological verse of Scripture is John 19:30, "... and he ... gave up the ghost." They did not take His life. It was not the nails driven through His hands that held Him to the cross, nor the rope tied around His midriff nor the nails driven through His feet. Why did He keep hanging on that cross? Because Jesus Christ loved us. He could have walked off that cross: He could have had twelve legions of angels at His command. But He kept hanging on the cross because He so loved us that He gave His own life for us. When He was dying upon the cross He did not cry, "My God, my God, why hast thou forsaken me," but "My

155

God, my God, for this purpose was I reserved, for this purpose was I spared."

Translations from the Far East read of Matthew 27:46, "... My God, my God, for this purpose was I spared." The Occidental or the Western translations wrongly read, "... My God, my God, why hast thou forsaken me?"

Suppose you had an only son and right now your son was dying, would you be sitting reading this book on the accuracy of God's Word or would you be with your son? And yet your son has not always done your will. Your son has done things contrary to what you would like for him to do. Still you would want to be with him. Do you think that God Almighty is not as good as you are? Jesus Christ was God's only-begotten Son and always did the Father's will. When He was dying upon the cross, where do you think the Father was? With Him.

God stayed with His Son. This was not only their triumphal hour, but ours also for it was at this point that Jesus Christ, the second Adam, fulfilled all the legal requirements for our redemption and salvation. This was Christ's purpose. Now we have an accurate translation of Matthew 27:46, one of the most difficult verses of Scripture in the King James. Now this verse fits with the other passages in the Word of God.

To reiterate points: (1) Scripture usually interprets itself in the verse in which it is written; (2) the vocabulary must be understood in the terms of the day in which the translation was made; (3) all Scripture must be in harmony with itself; that is, Scriptures relating to a given subject cannot contradict each other.

3

Now let us proceed to the issue of *narrative development*. Narrative development means that several passages of Scripture on an identical incident or subject may augment the information given in each other. Each passage of Scripture relating to the same incident may not give the same details but the Scriptures must complement and agree with each other or we do not have the true Word of God.

One pitfall which we must now avoid is that we do not call situations *identical* that are only *similar*. For instance, if in one Gospel there are two men coming out of a certain city talking to Jesus and in another Gospel there is one man coming out of the city talking to Jesus, these are not identical situations. Did you have supper today and yesterday? Let us suppose you had a bologna sandwich and tea yesterday and today you had a bologna sandwich and tea again. Was the supper identical or similar? It could not be identical because you did not eat the same sandwich to-

157

day or drink the very same tea today that you drank yesterday. The timing was different — twenty-four hours apart — so the situations were similar but not identical.

In studying the development of identical situations in various passages of Scripture, it becomes vitally important to observe The Word with a keen eye and perceptive mind to see the depth of it. For example, Matthew may say something regarding a situation; Mark, on the other hand, talking about the identical situation, might not say that which Matthew said, but he could mention other details which Matthew did not give. However, what Mark would add to Matthew would not dare to contradict that which Matthew had said or the situation would not be identical. If the situations are identical, that which is set forth in one Scripture cannot contradict that which is set forth in the other.

Let us observe a highly developed narrative pertaining to the crucifixion of Christ. Matthew, Mark, Luke and John speak of the very same incident, but each record gives different details about the crucifixion. Once all four narratives are put together, we get a total, expansive picture with no flaws in it.

Matthew 27:35–37:
And they crucified him [Jesus], and parted his

garments, casting lots: that it might be fulfilled
which was spoken by the prophet, They parted
my garments among them, and upon my vesture
did they cast lots.

And sitting down they watched him there;
And set up over his head his accusation written,
THIS IS JESUS THE KING OF THE JEWS.

Here is the sequence of events according to time:
(1) they crucified Jesus, (2) they parted His garments,
(3) they set up over His head an accusation. After
the soldiers parted the garments, they sat down. In
the East when a person sits down, he stays awhile.
After sitting for a while, the soldiers put up over His
head His accusation. To get this accusation, they may
have had to go back to Jerusalem to get permission
and then they had to make the sign. All of this takes
time. That is exactly what Matthew is pointing out.

Matthew 27:38:
Then [after all that] were there two thieves crucified with him, one on the right hand, and
another on the left.

The King James says "two thieves"; the Greek
words are *duo lēstai* of which *duo* is "two," *lēstai* is
"robbers." The Greeks used an entirely different
word for a thief, *kleptēs*. A thief is one who acts

stealthily while a robber is one who deliberately plans and openly does his dirty work. In legal terms robbery is a worse crime than thievery. Thieves would be punished but not by such an extreme sentence as crucifixion. Robbers could receive a crucifixion sentence because of more extreme actions. *Duo lēstai,* two robbers, were crucified with Jesus after an interim of time.

Matthew tells us that the soldiers took Jesus and crucified Him; they sat down and they watched Him; they placed over His head His accusation; and *then* they crucified two robbers, one on the right hand of Jesus and the other on the left.

There is another interesting observation which should be made about Matthew 27:44.

The thieves [the robbers, the *duo lēstai*] also, which were crucified with him, cast the same in his teeth.

The gallery of people at the crucifixion were saying, as the verses before indicate, "He trusted in God, let Him save Himself"; soon the two robbers became involved in the conversation and both of the robbers "cast the same into his [Jesus'] teeth." They said to Jesus, "If you are really the Son of God, why do you not come down off that cross?" Both of the robbers reviled Him. This is the record which Matthew sets forth.

The next Gospel record on the crucifixion is found in Mark 15:26,27,32. Mark wrote no further information which is not given in the other Gospels. So to conserve time, let us go to Luke 23:32.

And there were also two other, malefactors [*kakourgoi,* malefactors, not robbers] , led with him to be put to death.

When Jesus Christ was led out of Jerusalem toward Calvary, they led with Him, Luke tells us, two malefactors. A malefactor is an evil-doer. A robber, for instance, would be a malefactor; but not every malefactor would be a robber. A murderer, for instance, is an evil-doer; but not every evil-doer is a murderer. When Jesus was led out of Jerusalem, according to the Gospel of Luke, two malefactors were led with Him to be put to death.

Luke 23:33:
And when they were come to the place, which is called Calvary, there they crucified him, and the malefactors, one on the right hand, and the other on the left.

The word "malefactor" is the word *kakourgos*; the

161

word "robbers" is *lestai*. Luke uses an entirely different word because entirely different people are involved. They were not two robbers; they were two *kakourgoi*, malefactors, who were brought at the *same time* as Jesus to be crucified.

> Luke 23:39,40:
> And one of the malefactors which were hanged railed on him, saying, If thou be Christ, save thyself and us.
>
> But the other answering rebuked him [the first malefactor], saying, Dost not thou fear God, seeing thou art in the same condemnation?

Both of the robbers, according to Matthew, "cast the same in his teeth." But in the Gospel of Luke, only one of the malefactors spoke revilingly to Jesus; the other said to the malefactor, "You had better be quiet because you are in the same condemnation as He is." How can anybody logically say that the two robbers as recorded in Matthew are the same as the two malefactors in Luke. In Matthew the soldiers crucified Jesus, parted His garments, sat down, put up His accusation, then they brought the two robbers. While according to Luke, the soldiers led the two malefactors with Him to be put to death.

Putting together the two records of Matthew and

162

Luke is simple. When Jesus was led out to be crucified, they led two malefactors with Him. The soldiers crucified Jesus and the malefactors, one on the
right hand and the other on the left. Both of the robbers reviled Jesus, but only one of the malefactors reviled Him. To the conscientious malefactor who said
to Jesus"... Lord, remember me when thou comest
into thy kingdom," Jesus said, "Verily, I say unto
thee To day thou shalt [future tense] be with me in
paradise."

According to the accurate Word of God, how many
men were crucified with Jesus? Two malefactors plus
two thieves makes four people. All the teaching that
we have had saying Jesus was on the center cross with
one culprit to the right and the other to the left is
proven faulty. The reason we have believed this is
that rather than reading The Word, we believed the
paintings we have seen. When a person goes to the
Word of God and sees the narrative development of
Matthew and Luke on an identical situation, he sees
very plainly that there were four crucified with Jesus.

The crucifixion record from the three Gospels is an
example of how the Scripture interprets itself in
Scriptural or narrative development. Watch the time
and notice the place of action. One Scripture may tell
some details and another may tell others; but the one
Scripture dares not contradict what the other Scrip-

ture says. From Matthew, Mark and Luke one observes that there were four men finally crucified with Jesus.

We have one Gospel record, John, left to consider. Matthew, Mark and Luke were specifically concerned about time while John is concerned about the place of action.

> John 19:18:
> Where they crucified him, and two other with him, on either side one, and Jesus in the midst.

Matthew informed us that there were two robbers crucified; Luke informed us that there were two malefactors, which totals four men. But John says, "Where they crucified him, and two other with him, on either side one." If there was only one on either side, one plus one makes two. Now we have an apparent discrepancy.

Remember when there is an apparent discrepancy, the first place we look is in our minds. Do we understand what is written? If we understand what is written, as we do here, then the error can only be at one other place and that is in translation for the true Word of God cannot contradict itself.

John tells us, according to King James, "Where

they crucified him, and two other with him, on either side one, and Jesus in the midst." One small word from John 19:18 should immediately attract our attention, and that is the word "midst." It means "middle." The word "midst" is a key word because grammatically one individual would not be crucified in the "midst" of two. With the use of the word "midst," four, six or eight are indicated. When a person is situated with one on either side, he is not in the midst; he is between. A person is between two, but in the midst of four.

An interlinear translation of the Stephens Text, from which the King James was translated, reads in John 19:18, "and with him, others two on this side and on that side." Then there is the word "one" in English, but no corresponding Greek word is above it. To indicate that the translators added the word "one," it was put in brackets. The King James translators, therefore, also added the word "one." If the word "one" is not in the critical Greek texts, why is it in the King James? Because by 1611 the Western world had been so indoctrinated by a picture showing Jesus on a cross with one evil-doer on either side of Him that, when the translators were translating this particular verse of the nineteenth chapter of John, they inserted the word "one."

Take out the commas and the word "one," and

read the verse again. "Where they crucified him and two others with him on either side and Jesus in the midst." The same words, *enteuthen kai enteuthen,* are used in Revelation 22:2.

> In the midst of the street of it, and on either side of the river ....

Enteuthen kai enteuthen is translated "on either side." These are the same words as in the Gospels with the exception that John has the word *duo. Duo enteuthen kai enteuthen* equals "two on this side and two on that side and Jesus in the midst." What a great accuracy from God's Word.

> John 19:32:
> Then came the soldiers, and brake the legs of the first [one of the robbers], and of the other [one of the malefactors] which was crucified with [The prefix *sun* means "in close proximity with."] him [meaning the first robber].

To illustrate how we have been mistaught about how the soldiers went about breaking the legs of the miscalled two thieves: the soldiers broke the legs of the first; then they must have by-passed Jesus and gone around His cross which was really a tree to the second miscalled thief. Finally these soldiers came back to Jesus and said, "My goodness, he is dead already." This type of routine is not very reasonable. As a matter of fact, it is senseless. When you read the accuracy of The Word, the soldiers came and they broke the legs of the first (robber) and of the next (malefactor) progressing in the row; when the soldiers came to Jesus in the third place, they found him already dead.

"Then came the soldiers, and brake the legs of the first, and of the other which was crucified with him." Who was "the other who was crucified with [with] him"? Luke said that when they led Jesus out of Jerusalem, they led two malefactors with Him. "... The soldiers came and brake the legs of the first, and of the other which was crucified with him," who was the malefactor.

The word "other" in verse 32 — and of the other which was crucified with him" — is another key to add to the proof that four men were crucified with Jesus. There are two different words translated "other" in John 19 and Luke 23. One word is *heteros*, and the other Greek word is *allos*. Both *heteros* and *allos* are translated "other," but *heteros* means "other when only two may be involved," while *allos* means "other when more than two may be involved." The word "other" in John 19:32 is *allos*.

Allos is used when more than two may be involved. Two malefactors, two thieves and Jesus are involved, making five. So the soldiers broke the legs of the first

167

and of the other (*allos*) of the five involved.

In Luke 23:32, "other" was also used.

> And there were also two other, malefactors, led
> with him to be put to death.

Which Greek word had to be used to have the true
Word? The word is *heteros* because only two categories are involved, Jesus and malefactors. This is the
sharp accuracy of God's Word.

When Jesus was led forth, they led two malefactors
with Him. Later, after the soldiers had crucified
Jesus, they parted garments, they cast lots, they sat
down, they put up an accusation, then finally they
brought two robbers and they crucified them. When
the soldiers came, they broke the legs of the first and
of the other (the *allos*, more than two involved); but
having come to Jesus, they found that He was dead
already. Why? Because the prophets of old had
prophesied that no one would ever break the Messiah's legs. (Psalm 34:20, Exodus 12:46, Numbers
9:12). The Jews and soldiers did not take Jesus' life
upon Calvary's cross; He laid it down, He gave up His
life. He did not die because they crucified Him; He
died because He gave Himself for you and for me.
This is the accuracy with which the Word of God fits,

168

and this is the remarkable usage of The Word as it develops the Scriptures by interpreting itself right where it is written. In comparing Scriptures on an identical incident, the Scriptures can complement each other but never contradict each other if we have the true Word.

While studying how Scriptural passages concerning identical situations develop, we must study the great accuracy of the day Jesus Christ died and arose again from the dead.

A number of years ago when I was teaching in India, a reputable government leader, a Hindu educated in an American mission school, asked me, "Dr. Wierwille, on what day did Jesus Christ die?" The man continued, "I have asked missionary after missionary to explain to me how he gets three days and three nights from Good Friday to Easter Sunday morning." Although this intelligent man had been trained in a mission school, he was still a Hindu because the missionaries understood less of The Word than the Indian. The man pointed out Matthew 12:40. "For as Jonas was three days and three nights in the whale's belly; so shall the Son of man be three days and three nights in the heart of the earth."

"Furthermore," he said, "what about the record in I Corinthians 15:4, where your Bible declares that

169

Jesus Christ was '... buried, and that he rose again the third day according to the scriptures.' " How could Jesus be dead three days and three nights from Good Friday to Easter Sunday morning and still rise the third day?

The Indian official and I had a good discussion unfolding The Word with the principles that one Scripture doesn't necessarily tell the complete story, but that complementary Scriptures about an identical situation cannot contradict each other.

First, let us examine traditional teaching concerning the death and resurrection of Jesus. The record in Matthew said that Jesus would be three days and three nights in the heart of the earth. Matthew does not say that Jesus would be in the heart of the earth from the time He died, but from the time He was buried. We will give people the benefit of the doubt, though, and grant them from the time He died, which would be from 3:00 P.M., Good Friday. If time is marked from Friday 3:00 P.M. to Saturday, 3:00 P.M., we have a day and a night; now if Jesus arose early on Easter Sunday morning – squeezing time for all it is worth – the most we can come up with is three days and two nights. The traditionalists say that Matthew did not literally mean three days and three nights – it means "segments," any portion of a day may be counted as a day. This is fallacious

170

teaching for whenever the Word of God mentions a day and a night, it is not a portion of time; a day and a night or a night and a day is a literal period of twenty-four hours. The reason night comes before day in the Word of God is that Jewish reckoning of time started with Jewish sunset so the night preceded the daylight hours of a day. Matthew 12:40 said "three days and three nights" which would mean three periods of twenty-four hours each. How can three days and three nights be figured from Good Friday 3:00 P.M. until Easter Sunday morning? By early Easter Sunday morning (which would be the third day) Jesus Christ had already risen; so where is the third night? This teaching does not fit. What are we going to do? We are going to study it in the same way in which we researched the men crucified with Jesus. When the Word of God fits, there are no contradictions, no errors. We must go to the Word of God to find the day, the hour and the details involved in Jesus' crucifixion, burial and resurrection to have the Word of God rightly divided.

According to the Word of God, the first day of the Passover was always a holy convocation, a high day, a Sabbath. For instance, if the first day of the Passover came on a Tuesday, that Tuesday was a Sabbath day. If the first day of the Passover came on a weekly Sabbath, on a Saturday, then it still was a high day and it would have pre-eminence over the weekly Sabbath.

171

This is similar to our holidays. For example, if Christmas happens to come on a Tuesday, it is a holiday; but if Christmas comes on a Sunday, the special day of Christmas takes priority over the weekly Sunday. This point has bearing upon the death and resurrection of our Lord Jesus Christ.

The first day of the Passover was always on the fifteenth of Nisan.

Leviticus 23:5:
In the fourteenth *day* of the first month at even [evening] *is* the Lord's passover.

The fourteenth day at even is the fifteenth for the fifteenth of Nisan begins at sunset, the even. The fourteenth is the day before the Passover.

Leviticus 23:6,7:
And on the fifteenth day of the same month *is* the feast of unleavened bread [which is the Passover] unto the Lord: seven days ye must eat unleavened bread.

In the first day ye shall have an holy convocation ....

The first day of the Passover, the fifteenth, will

always be a holy convocation, a Sabbath day, a high day.

Leviticus 23:8:
But ye shall offer an offering made by fire unto the Lord seven days: in the seventh day *is* an holy convocation ....

In other words, the first day of the Passover and the seventh day of the Passover were Sabbath days, holy convocation days.

Let us gather more verses of Scripture to understand the Jewish reckoning of time.

Exodus 12:2:
This month [Abib or Nisan] *shall be* unto you the beginning of months: it *shall be* the first month of the year to you.

Exodus 13:4:
This day came ye out in the month Abib.

The name of the month of Abib was later, after the Babylonian captivity, changed to the month of Nisan. In Esther 3:7, which was written after the Babylonian captivity, it says, "In the first month, that *is,* the month of Nisan ...." The month of Abib, the first month, is the only month God named in the

Bible. God refers to all other months as the second, the third, the fourth, the fifth, the sixth, the seventh month and so on. When man changed the name of the first month from Abib to Nisan, he also gave names to the other months which God had only numbered. In the first month of the year and on the fifteenth day was the Passover. So the day before Passover was logically the fourteenth day of Nisan or Abib.

There is further documentation of the time of Jesus' death in the Gospel of John.

> John 19:31
> The Jews therefore, because it was the prepara-
> tion [the day before the fifteenth of Nisan],
> that the bodies should not remain upon the
> cross on the sabbath day, (for that sabbath day
> was an high day,) besought Pilate that their legs
> might be broken, and *that* they might be taken
> away.

The Word plainly states that it was the preparation day, which would be the day before the Passover, the fourteenth of Nisan; the bodies could not remain on the cross on that high day. The greatest point of confusion among scholars has been their not differentiating between the Sabbath day, the first day of the Feast of the Passover, and the weekly Sabbath. The day before the weekly Sabbath was Friday; therefore

174

the teaching has been that Jesus died on Friday. But the Passover was not the weekly Sabbath, as John says. This point is even in parentheses in the King James: "(for that sabbath day was an high day)." Jesus was crucified the day before a special holy convocation, before a special day, the high day, which was the first day of the Feast of Unleavened Bread, the Passover. On which day of the week Jesus was crucified is yet to be seen.

Concerning the time of the resurrection of Jesus Christ, all four Gospels clearly agree.

Matthew 28:1:
In the end of the sabbath [this is the weekly sabbath], as it began to dawn toward the first *day* of the week [which you and I know as Sunday], came Mary Magdalene and the other Mary to see the sepulchre.

This is early Sunday morning. In verse 6 the report was that "He is not here: for he is risen ...." It does not say in verse 6 that He arose on what we call Easter Sunday morning. It says that by the time the women got to the tomb, the report of the angel to the women was that Jesus was not there for he had already risen.

Mark 16:1 and 6:
And when the sabbath was past, Mary Magdalene, and Mary the *mother* of James, and Salome, had bought sweet spices, that they might come and anoint him.

And he [the angel] saith unto them, Be not affrighted: Ye seek Jesus of Nazareth, which was crucified: he is risen; he is not here: behold the place where they laid him.

It does not say that He just arose. The declaration of the angel again was, "He is already up."

In Luke 24:6 the angel declares to those at the sepulchre on Sunday morning, "He is not here, but is risen ...." Again, The Word simply declares that He was already up.

It does not tell in Matthew, Mark or Luke exactly when He got up but it does tell that by the time the women came, which was very early, Christ had already risen. Not one of the Gospels — Matthew, Mark, Luke or John — states that Christ arose on Easter Sunday morning. That is tradition, not The Word.

In order to put the pieces together, we are going to have to go other places in The Word to find out precisely when Jesus Christ died and when He arose.

> Matthew 12:40:
> For as Jonas [Jonah] was three days and three nights in the whale's belly; so shall the Son of man be three days and three nights in the heart of the earth.

The Bible occasionally uses the word "day" as an idiom meaning a portion of time; but when "day and night" are used together, the time is to be taken literally. Jesus was to be buried three days and three nights which equals seventy-two hours.

A legal standard is involved in "the three days and three nights in the heart of the earth." In Biblical times no one could be officially pronounced dead until he had been interred for seventy-two hours, three days and three nights. Why did God not resurrect Jesus immediately after He was buried since God obviously had the power? The reason God did not raise the Lord Jesus Christ immediately after His burial is that Jesus Christ had to fulfill the law; that is, He had to be in the grave three days and three nights and not just part of it.

Our failure to recognize that the first day of the Passover was a high Sabbath Day, a holy day, a special convocation, and our failure to understand that

177

the Jewish day began at 6:00 p.m. or sunset have caused most of the difficulty regarding the time of the death and resurrection of Jesus Christ. The Bible says in John 19:31 that Jesus was crucified and buried on the day of preparation, the fourteenth day of Nisan. The Word tells us that Jesus died about 3:00 P.M. our time, which is the ninth hour by Jewish reckoning. Jesus had to be buried before sunset because sunset began the next day, which was the Passover. It was against the Jewish law to be carrying on burial and other servile activities on Passover thus the soldiers had to break the legs of the others crucified with Jesus. The soldiers had to get their work completed before sunset which was the beginning of the fifteenth of Nisan, Passover.

Jesus died at 3:00 P.M. and was buried before sunset on the fourteenth of Nisan. Jesus had to be buried three complete nights and days to fulfill the law. To get three complete nights and days beginning with sunset on the fifteenth of Nisan, the seventy-two hour duration would end with the afternoon of the seventeenth of Nisan. Jesus had to have been buried between 3:00 P.M. and sunset on the fourteenth of Nisan. So that was the time He was resurrected on the seventeenth of Nisan — seventy-two hours later. Now we must count backward to see the days of the week. We know that when Mary Magdalene came to the tomb early on Sunday, the first day of the week, the tomb was already empty and Christ had already risen. So Christ had to have arisen sometime between 3:00 and sunset on Saturday, the seventeenth of Nisan. That means He would have had to have been buried between 3:00 and sunset on Wednesday, the fourteenth of Nisan, three days and three nights or seventy-two hours previously. Jesus Christ literally fulfilled the law; He carried out the Word of God by being buried on Wednesday afternoon and being raised seventy-two hours later on Saturday afternoon.

Now I am not going to advocate that we change to Good Wednesday instead of Good Friday for the book of Colossians says that we are not to be observers of days or times or special hours. But I am going to stick to the accuracy of God's Word and acknowledge its truth. The pieces of the puzzle fall into place when the days of the months are rightly divided, when the hours of the days are rightly divided, and when the special days are understood. These tie together the whole story of the death and resurrection of Jesus Christ. The Word of God always is so accurate.

Studies in Abundant Living, Volume III contains the minute study of this topic in the chapter entitled "The Day Jesus Christ Died."

In Luke 24:21 we read of two disciples on the way

to Emmaus the first day of the week.

> Luke 24:21:
> But we trusted that it had been he which should
> have redeemed Israel: and beside all this, to day
> is the third day since these things were done.

This is the Scripture which unbelievers will question after they have been taught the great accuracy of
The Word. In the language of King James' day the
usage of the expression "the third day since" meant
that it was the fourth day because on the fourth day
three days had gone by. Moffatt's translation has this
Scripture very clearly and accurately presented. He
translated it, "and it is three days ago." The Aramaic
has it as follows, "And lo, three days have passed
since all these things have come to pass." See how
accurate The Word really becomes.

Perhaps someone will now ask you as I have been
asked hundreds of times, "What difference does it
make if Jesus died on Wednesday and was resurrected
on Saturday; so what if there were four crucified with
Jesus?" Does it make any difference? It makes all the
difference between an unerring, accurate Word and a
crumbling jumble of writing. Yes, it matters. We
acknowledge the importance of accuracy in every
other field except in God's Word. When we go to the
bank, we demand accuracy. If we were astronauts in a

180

capsule ready for the count-down, we would want accuracy. How much more we need accuracy and precision in the greatness of God's Word to get a cash reserve in the outer space of heaven. If God thought it important enough to sacrifice His only-begotten Son for the integrity of His Word, then we ought to think it supremely important to rightly and accurately divide that Word.

Chapter Thirteen
In Its Context

II Peter 1:20 declares, "Knowing this first, that no prophecy [none of that which is foretold or forthtold in the Word of God] ... is of any private interpretation." Since I dare not interpret it, or you, or any other person in the world, all Scripture must interpret itself either in the verse or in the context or in previous usage. We have so far exclusively studied the first point that Scripture interprets itself in the verse where it is written. For these Scriptures we noted that the verses not only interpreted themselves, but that (1) the words in the verses must be interpreted according to the meaning of the words at the time of the translation, (2) that any one verse must always be in harmony with all Scripture relating to the identical subject and (3) that one Scripture may not tell all the details; other Scriptures may add to it without contradicting each other.

The second point of how Scripture interprets itself is in its context. If Scripture does not interpret itself in its own verse, then read the verse in its context. The context is that which makes up the whole story, the enveloping idea.

For an example read Psalms 2:8. Missionaries have often used this text when talking about winning the heathen for the Lord Jesus Christ.

> Psalms 2:8:
> Ask of me, and I shall give *thee* the heathen *for* thine inheritance, and the uttermost parts of the earth *for* thy possession.

Isn't this a tremendous missionary sermon? Not if it is read in its context. Read the next verse.

> Psalms 2:9:
> Thou shalt break them with a rod of iron; thou shalt dash them in pieces like a potter's vessel.

Psalms 2:8 does not make a good missionary sermon because in context the verse is, to say the least, inappropriate.

In Matthew 22 is a verse of Scripture that is frequently used at the memorial service for a saint of God who has worked diligently for the local church. This person was a fine influence in the community and, having passed away, the minister selects Matthew

22:32 as his text at the funeral.

> ... God is not the God of the dead, but of the living.

The saint's body is lying in the casket, he is dead; but somehow or other, we say he is not dead, he is living. Why not check the context? What is Matthew talking about when he says that "God is not the God of the dead, but of the living"?

The twenty-third verse says, "... which say that there is no resurrection, and asked him ..."; and verse 31, "But as touching the resurrection ...." What is the context? The context is talking about the resurrection, not about death. Death and resurrection are far removed subjects.

Let us read the whole story from Matthew 22.

> Matthew 22:23–29:
> The same day came to him the Sadducees, which say that there is no resurrection, and asked him,
>
> Saying, Master, Moses said, If a man die, having no children, his brother shall marry his wife, and raise up seed unto his brother.
>
> Now there were with us seven brethren: and the

185

> first, when he had married a wife, deceased, and, having no issue, left his wife unto his brother:
>
> Likewise the second also, and the third, unto the seventh.
>
> And last of all the woman died also.
>
> Therefore in the resurrection [This is the subject.] whose wife shall she be of the seven? for they all had her.
>
> Jesus answered and said unto them, Ye do err, not knowing the scriptures, nor the power of God.

Jesus said to those Sadducees, who did not believe in the resurrection, "Ye do err, not knowing the scriptures, nor the power of God." This is exactly why we are still so confused regarding the coming of the Lord, the resurrection and the gathering together. The teaching that when one dies he is really not dead because he is alive some place else is error. To believe this shows that we do not know the Scriptures nor the power of God.

> Matthew 22:30–32:
> For in the resurrection they neither marry, nor are given in marriage but are as the angels of

God in heaven.

But as touching the resurrection of the dead, have ye not read that which was spoken unto you by God, saying,

I am the God of Abraham, and the God of Isaac, and the God of Jacob? God is not the God of the dead, but of the living.

When is God not the God of the dead but of the living? Not now, but at the time of the resurrection. Where is Abraham now according to the Word of God? The Bible says he is dead. Where is Isaac? He is dead. Where is Jacob? He is dead. How long will they remain dead? Until the resurrection, and the resurrection has not yet come. At the time of the resurrection, Abraham, Isaac and Jacob will be made alive. This is the true Word when read in its context.

To talk of people dying and then their being alive and in heaven can lead one into many devious fields such as the so-called research and learning in extra-sensory perception, in parapsychology and in subjects dealing with survival after death. I have been through this field in which masses of people believe and which is becoming increasingly popular. The so-called gift of prophecy is being promoted. Some people knew ahead of time that President Kennedy was going to be killed. What good was it to know ahead of time since he was still killed? When God talked to a prophet and told him that the army from the north was going to come to Israel at a certain place, God did not reveal this knowledge and yet have all the people slaughtered. God told the prophet, the prophet told the king, the king activated his army, and Israel was protected against attack. There was profit gained from God's warning. There is always a profit in the revelation if it comes from the right source. The reason that Satan is having such a grand picnic is that few people believe in Satan or in devil spirits. They all say there is only one God. The Bible says there are two. One is the God and Father of our Lord Jesus Christ; the other is the god of this world who is Satan. Devil spirits possess minds, they control, they give information. Many times the information from the devil spirits is accurate because if it were always inaccurate nobody would believe them. This is like evil; evil is a parasite and could not exist without truth upon which to feed. Devil spirits, evil spirits, wrong sources of information which possess people, could not exist if it were not for the true God. Just because somebody takes a Bible and holds it up and says, "I read the Bible," does not mean that he is not a counterfeit. Even Satan knows the Word of God; he can even quote (misquote out of context) The Word.

The Bible says that when a man dies, he is dead

and he stays dead until the return of Christ and the resurrection. Nobody who has died is living with the exception of the Lord Jesus Christ, whom the Bible declares God raised from the dead. All the rest are waiting the return of Christ. If the Church would teach this accurate Word, the spiritualists would be out of business. If the dead are alive and in heaven now having such a glorious time, then the spiritualists are not producing counterfeits when they bring back the so-called dead into manifestation in ectoplasmic or other forms. Ectoplasmic forms are merely deceiving spirits; they are counterfeits.

The reason spiritualists keep propounding the counterfeit is that the accuracy of the Word of God has never prevailed in our time in the Protestant or the Roman Catholic Church. Most groups have taught that when one dies, he is not really dead; somehow or other he goes to heaven or paradise, as they call it. The Bible says that when one dies, he stays dead until he is raised. Why should there be a raising of the dead if a person is already alive? The reason we have to have people raised is that people are dead. Some people say to me that God has to bring one's spirit back and reunite it with his body. How silly. If a person got along for a hundred years without a body, why should he take time to come back and pick one up? You see, we have gotten into this mess because of the error in wrongly dividing The Word regarding the

189

dead.

Where are the dead? They are dead. How long are they going to stay dead? They are going to stay dead until Christ returns.

People try to confuse the accuracy of God's Word by giving the example of Moses and Elijah who appeared to Jesus and three of His disciples on the Mount of Transfiguration and with whom Jesus talked. The Word of God says that they saw Moses and Elijah *in a vision.* A vision is not producing the men themselves.

Unknowing people say Enoch was such a good man that he never saw death because God translated him. Let us read the record in context.

> Hebrews 11:5:
> By faith Enoch was translated that he should not see death; and was not found, because God had translated him: for before his translation he had this testimony, that he pleased God.

"By faith Enoch was translated," The word "translated" is the word "transported," meaning "taken from one place to another." He was not taken from one spot *up* to another place; he was taken from one place *over* to another "... that he should not see

190

death." The word "see" is *eidon*, which means to "look at with actual perception with one's eyes" or literally "to see someone die." In checking the Old Testament, we discover that Enoch had never seen anybody pass away. He pleased God all the time for which God so loved him that God took him from the place where Enoch's loved ones would die and put him at a place where he should not see death. Enoch did not see anyone else die, but he himself died. The Bible says so in Hebrews 11:5, "By faith Enoch"; verse 8 says, "By faith Abraham"; verse 11 says, "By faith Sara ...." Then in verse 13, after listing Enoch, Abraham, and Sara, Hebrews 13 says, "These all died ...." All without exception died. If they all died, then Enoch is dead. That is what The Word says and that is what it means.

Sensitives or mediums or spiritualists who want us to believe we are surrounded with a great cloud of living witnesses continue to misquote The Word by using Hebrews 12:1.

Hebrews 12:1:
Wherefore seeing we also are compassed about with so great a cloud of witnesses, let us lay aside every weight ....

These people who wrongly divide The Word say that the "cloud of witnesses" is composed of believers who died and are living in heaven. That is not what it says. The cloud of witnesses are the people listed in chapter 11 of Hebrews who believed God and of whom the Word of God says, "These all died ...." Still we are surrounded with their examples of believing. Their believing gives us incentive to trust and believe also.

Contortionists of The Word also come with the reference from Philippians 1:21 where Paul says, "For to me to live *is* Christ, and to die *is* gain." Philippians does not say that the gain is immediate. Paul says that the return of Christ is better than living or dying; for when Christ returns the mortal shall put on immortality.

Skeptics talk about the rich man and Lazarus in Abraham's bosom; they talk about Saul and the Witch of Endor. Not one person in the Bible is living except the Lord Jesus Christ, and God raised Him from the dead. All the rest are dead. In a small book entitled *Are The Dead Alive Now?* I have examined all Scripture in the Bible that deals with any segment of the Lord's return and the resurrection. The accuracy of God's Word shows that the dead are dead and will remain dead until Christ comes. Also, a book of interest on this topic is *The Challenging Counterfeit*. Its author, Raphael Gasson, at one time was in spiritualism. He relates in this book what God in His

192

Word has already told us. Spiritualism is counterfeit. Yet nations are run by it, governmental men are used by it as are people in any occupation or economic group who seek information from sensitives. Sensitives do give information that will be right at some places; but just when a person needs sound knowledge, the sensitives' information breaks down and the person seeking knowledge breaks too.

We must always go to The Scripture and its context and find out exactly what it says before we make any other statement or we shall be led into confusion by the wrong dividing of The Word.

Matthew 13 contains another example of how Scripture interprets itself in its context.

> Matthew 13:24:
> Another parable put he forth unto them, saying, The kingdom of heaven is likened unto a man which sowed good seed in his field.

I ask the members in my class, "What is the good seed?" Johnny jumps up and says, "I think the good seed is the Word of God." And I say, "Wonderful, wonderful!" Then Maggie says, "Well, I think Johnny's idea is wonderful, but I think the good seed is Christ." And I say, "Great." Then I say, "Henry, what do you think it is?" And he says, "Well, I think

193

that the good seed represents the good works of man." What is wrong with finding out what The Word means by questioning my friends? "Knowing this first, that no prophecy of the scripture is of any private interpretation." Johnny, Maggie and Henry all guessed. Each one offered private interpretation. Quit thinking and guessing; say what The Word says. Matthew 13:24 simply says, "... The kingdom of heaven is likened unto a man which sowed good seed in his field." What is the good seed? That verse does not tell us; and if a verse does not tell us, we do not know. It is no disgrace not to know; it is a disgrace to indicate we know when we do not know or when we are guessing. When we don't know, we had better continue reading.

Matthew 13:25:
But while men slept, his enemy came and sowed tares among the wheat, and went his way.

What are the tares? We don't know so we just keep on reading until some place, somewhere, sometime, the meaning is going to be explained. If it is not explained, we will never know.

Matthew 13:26–30:
But when the blade was sprung up, and brought forth fruit, then appeared the tares also. [Has that verse explained it? No.]

So the servants of the householder came and said unto him, Sir, didst not thou sow good seed in thy field? from whence then hath it tares?

He said unto them, An enemy hath done this. The servants said unto him, Wilt thou then that we go and gather them up?

But he said, Nay; lest while ye gather up the tares, ye root up also the wheat with them.

Let both grow together until the harvest: and in the time of harvest I will say to the reapers, Gather ye together first the tares, and bind them in bundles to burn them: but gather the wheat into my barn.

Has The Word explained what the good seed is, what the field is, what the tares are? No, so we do not know. The parable ends with verse 30 and another parable begins.

Matthew 13:31:
Another parable put he forth unto them, saying, The kingdom of heaven is like ....

The next four verses continue this parable about the kingdom of heaven.

> Matthew 13:36:
> Then Jesus sent the multitude away, and went into the house: and his disciples came unto him, saying, Declare unto us the parable of the tares of the field.

How wise they were. The disciples did not guess. They did not say, "I think it is this" or "I think it is that." They went to the Master and they said, "Declare unto us the parable of the tares of the field."

> Matthew 13:37—39:
> He answered and said unto them, He that soweth the good seed is the Son of man [So the sower is the Son of man, no guesswork.];
>
> The field is the world; the good seed are the children of the kingdom; but the tares are the children of the wicked *one;*
>
> The enemy that sowed them is the devil; the harvest is the end of the world; and the reapers are the angels.

Could this be made any simpler or more plain? This parable is interpreted in its context. We need guess no longer.

The book of Revelation is considered by many people to be a very difficult book. The reason it has been difficult is that we have never allowed it to interpret itself in the verse or in the context. Things in Revelation which are symbolic have been taken literally, and things that are literal have been taken symbolically.

> Revelation 1:12:
> And I turned to see the voice that spake with me. And being turned, I saw seven golden candlesticks.

Does that verse tell what the seven golden candlesticks are? No, it just says, "I saw seven golden candlesticks." Before looking for the interpretation of this verse, look at verse 16.

> Revelation 1:16:
> And he had in his right hand seven stars: and out of his mouth went a sharp twoedged sword: and his countenance *was* as the sun shineth in his strength.

The twelfth verse talked about the seven golden candlesticks and the sixteenth spoke of the seven stars. What are the seven golden candlesticks, and what are the seven stars? That verse does not tell so we continue reading.

Revelation 1:20:
The mystery of the seven stars which thou sawest in my right hand, and the seven golden candlesticks. The seven stars are the angels [messengers] of the seven churches: and the seven candlesticks which thou sawest are the seven churches.

There is the answer. This is how the Scripture interprets itself in its context.

Chapter Fourteen
In Its Previous Usage

If Scripture does not interpret itself in the verse or in the context, then the interpretation is found in its previous usage. In the first usage of a word, expression or idea, the explanation is usually complete enough to carry through in all other references in the Bible. If God ever changed the usage of a word or expression, He always explained it.

To see this great truth on how The Word interprets itself in its previous usage observe II Corinthians 12. II Corinthians 12 is the passage on Paul's thorn in the flesh which has been a problem to many people. I have a collection in my library of different things ministers and theologians have through the years written to explain Paul's thorn. These men have come up with fourteen different conclusions. The Word tells us what Paul's thorn in the flesh was and thus we do not rely on guesswork and cannot, therefore, have fourteen contradictory opinions.

II Corinthians 12:7:

And lest I should be exalted above measure through the abundance of the revelations, there was given to me a thorn in the flesh, the messenger of Satan to buffet me, lest I should be exalted above measure.

Does that verse tell what Paul's thorn in the flesh was? No. But it tells who sent the thorn. The people who teach that Paul's thorn in the flesh was sickness which was sent by the Father of our Lord Jesus Christ must have lied because this verse says that it was sent by Satan. Why did Satan send it? To hinder and obstruct Paul in his work.

II Corinthians 12:8–10:

For this thing [thorn in the flesh] I besought the Lord thrice, that it might depart from me.

And he [God] said unto me, My grace is sufficient for thee: for my strength is made perfect in weakness [or humility]. Most gladly therefore will I rather glory in my infirmities that the power of Christ may rest upon me.

Therefore I take pleasure in infirmities, [It does not say sicknesses.] in reproaches, in necessities, in persecutions, in distresses for Christ's sake; for when I am weak [humble], then am I strong.

The thorn in the flesh still has not been explained

though we know more about it. None of the remaining New Testament explains the thorn in the
flesh. So what do we do? We have to turn in our
Bibles to the place at which the words "thorn in the
flesh" were used for the first time.

> Numbers 33:55:
> But if ye will not drive out the inhabitants of
> the land [unbelievers] from before you; then it
> shall come to pass, that those which ye let re-
> main of them *shall be* pricks in your eyes, and
> thorns in your sides, and shall vex you in the
> land wherein ye dwell.

The inhabitants, the people, shall be pricks in their
eyes and thorns in their side. Do you mean that a
Canaanite was hanging in one's eye and another
Canaanite attached to one's rib? What are "pricks in
your eyes and thorns in your side"? They are figures
of speech and are not to be taken literally.

This one verse alone, since it is the first usage of
the expression in the Bible, says that "pricks in your
eyes" and "thorns in your sides" are people. Previous
usage then explains Paul's thorn in the flesh. We do
not need guesswork or private interpretation. Satan
sent Paul a thorn in the flesh to hinder him in his
work. What hindered Paul? People. This verse in the
book of Numbers interpreted the figure of speech so

201

that we can understand II Corinthians 12:7. For good measure let us check two more Scriptures to further clinch the meaning of the thorn in the flesh.

> Joshua 23:13:
> Know for a certainty that the Lord your God will no more drive out *any of* these nations from before you; but they [nations, which are made up of people] shall be snares and traps unto you, and scourges in your sides, and thorns in your eyes, until ye perish from off this good land which the Lord your God hath given you.

Joshua shows the same truth because people again were "snares and traps unto you, and scourges in your sides, and thorns in your eyes." Can you imagine a nation of people like the Amorites being in one fellow's eye? That is not what it means. The thorn in the flesh always represents people who are pricking and trying to buffet and discourage.

Judges 2:3 witnesses to the same truth.

> Wherefore I also said, I will not drive them [people] out from before you; but they shall be *as thorns* in your sides, and their gods shall be a snare unto you.

The people were to be as thorns in their sides. Now

reread II Corinthians 12:7.

> And lest I should be exalted above measure through [because of] the abundance of the revelations, there was given to me a thorn in the flesh, the messenger of Satan to buffet me ....

What was the thorn in the flesh? People. Everywhere Paul went people constantly tried to alter the gospel which Paul preached. These people who followed him were thorns in his sides, pricks in his eyes, thorns in the flesh. People were the messengers of Satan sent to buffet, to obstruct his ministry, to weaken his work.

Remember the record in Acts which tells that after Paul finished preaching, people took him outside the city, stoned him and left him as dead; but the next morning Paul was preaching again. Listen to another record of Paul.

> II Corinthians 11:24:
> Of the Jews five times received I forty *stripes* save one.

The Jews whipped Paul five times with an instrument similar to our black snake whip. Who beats people? People. If we had been Paul, I would imagine by that time we would have been praying too, "Lord, take this thorn out of my flesh, remove these thorns."

> II Corinthians 11:25:
> Thrice was I beaten with rods, once was I stoned, thrice I suffered shipwreck, a night and a day I have been in the deep.

Three times Paul was beaten with rods, rods being whips which had pieces of metal or bone at the end of the thongs. Three times they beat him with rods, thirty-nine lashes each time. I hear people say, "Oh, we sacrifice for the Lord; we put our dollar in the collection plate." Look at the Apostle Paul. Five times they whipped him; three times they beat him with metal on the end of the thongs; once they stoned him and left him for dead.

> II Corinthians 11:26–28:
> *In* journeyings often, *in* perils of waters, *in* perils of robbers, *in* perils by *mine own* countrymen, *in* perils by the heathen, *in* perils in the city, *in* perils by the wilderness, *in* perils in the sea, *in* perils among false brethren:
>
> In weariness and painfulness, in watchings often, in hunger and thirst, in fastings often, in cold and nakedness.
>
> Beside those things that are without, that which

cometh upon me daily, the care of all the churches.

Who was responsible for all these happenings to Paul? Satan, the Devil. He inspired and possessed people who obstructed Paul. Satan inspired religious as well as irreligious people to act as messengers for him in hindering Paul.

No wonder Paul said in II Corinthians 12:8, "For this thing I besought the Lord thrice, that it might depart from me." When Paul prayed, the Lord answered, as recorded in verse 9, "And he said unto me, My grace is sufficient for thee: for my strength is made perfect in weakness [your humility]." In other words the Lord said, "As long as you keep your eyes upon Me, Paul, I will take care of the rest, for My strength is made perfect in your being challenged to handle the situation."

"Paul's Thorn in the Flesh" is a chapter in my work entitled *Studies in Abundant Living,* Volume I. There it is studied in more detail than we have just examined. The key to be understood here is that of interpretation in previous usage. This takes all the guesswork out and all private interpretation.

"Knowing this first, that no prophecy [not one word of that which is foretold or forthtold in the

Word of God] ... is of any private interpretation." It must interpret itself in its own verse or in the context of the entire story or in its previous usage. Those are the three major ways in which the Word of God interprets itself.

Chapter Fifteen
To Whom The Word is Written

Most people believe that the entire Bible — from Genesis to Revelation — is written to them. This is not true. Believing that the entire Word of God is written to everyone throughout history has caused confusion and contradiction in rightly dividing The Word. There are some passages in the Word of God that just do not fit with other sections unless we understand to whom the passage is specifically addressed.

Suppose I received a letter today addressed to Victor Paul Wierwille. Is it addressed to Mrs. Wierwille? No. It has my name on it. But suppose she reads my letter; could she possibly learn something from the information in the letter?

So it is when it comes to the Word of God. That part which is addressed *to* us must be applied by us. All the rest of the Scripture which does not have our name on it, which is not addressed to us, is *for* our learning.

How many groups of people can different segments
of The Word be addressed to? In I Corinthians 10:32
God discloses His system of classification.

> I Corinthians 10:32:
> Give none offence, neither to the Jews, nor to
> the Gentiles, nor to the church of God.

God lists Jew, Gentile, the Church of God — three
categories. Galatians 3:28 says that a person is either
a Jew or a Gentile until he becomes born again of
God's Spirit at which time he joins the Church of
God. The entire Bible is addressed to one or the other
of these three groups. Unless one understands to
whom a passage or book or section is written, he will
never be able to rightly divide the Word of Truth.

Romans was written after Pentecost, the day on
which the Church of God was founded, the Church to
which you and I belong.

> Romans 15:4:
> For whatsoever things were written aforetime
> [before the day of Pentecost] were written for
> our learning, that we through patience and com-
> fort of the scriptures might have hope.

Those things written before the day of Pentecost
208

are not addressed *to* us but are *for* our learning.

In I Corinthians we are shown the same truth of understanding as to whom The Word is addressed.

> I Corinthians 10:11:
> Now all these things happened unto them [Israel] for ensamples [examples]: and they are written for our admonition, upon whom the ends of the world are come.

All Scripture before Pentecost is not addressed to us but is for our learning. No one could be born again and belong to the Church of God until the Church was established on Pentecost. This is why The Word says in I Corinthians 10:11 that all Scripture before Pentecost is an admonition to those of us who belong to the Church of God.

Then what about the laws of Exodus, Leviticus and Numbers — all those things in the Old Testament? Are they addressed to us? No. To whom are they addressed? They are addressed to the Jews or to the Gentiles because the Church of God had not yet come into being. The Old Testament, therefore, must be for our learning. It is not addressed to us, it does not have our name on it; but it can help us learn. For instance, the Ten Commandments are not written to us, but we can learn from them. Yet we in the Prot-

209

estant churches still teach as if the Ten Commandments were specifically to us rather than for our learning. All Scripture before the day of Pentecost is for our learning; so the Ten Commandments of the Old Testament, along with others, are for our learning.

To this point, people usually understand. But now take this key a step further in accurately dividing God's Word. To whom were the Gospels addressed? To a period before or after Pentecost? The Bible indicates that the four Gospels — Matthew, Mark, Luke and John — basically took up with the birth of Christ and terminated with His ascension ten days before the day of Pentecost. So are the Gospels addressed to us? Not if the Word of God is right for Romans says that all Scripture before the day of Pentecost is for our learning, and the Gospels obviously come before the founding day of the Church of God. The records in the Gospels are addressed at times to Israel and at other times to the Gentiles, but never to the Church of God. One of the greatest errors in the translation of the Bible was placing the four Gospels in the New Testament. The Gospels logically belong in the Old Testament. Jesus came to Israel, His own people. He was the prophet who fulfilled the law of the Old Testament; therefore, the Gospels complete the Old Testament.

Romans says that Jesus Christ was a minister to the

circumcision.

> Romans 15:8:
> Now I say that Jesus Christ was a minister of
> [to] the circumcision ....

I do not belong to the circumcision, and neither do
you if you are born again of God's Spirit; for if we
are born again of God's Spirit, we belong to the
Church of God in which there is neither Jew nor Gentile. Jesus Christ did not come to start the Church on
the day of Pentecost; Jesus Christ came as a minister
to the circumcision. He was the completion, the fulfillment of the Old Covenant, the Old Testament.

Had the Gospels been placed in the Old Testament
rather than at the start of the New Testament, much
confusion could have been avoided. The New Testament actually begins with the book of Romans,
with Acts being the book of transition between the
Old Covenant and the New. The book of Acts gives
the story of the rise and the expansion of the Christian Church telling that on the day of Pentecost men
were born again of God's Spirit and filled with the
power of the holy spirit and that the Church continued to grow. Then the book of Romans addresses
its informative contents to the Church with a few sections specifically directed to the Jews or Gentiles. All
Scripture before Acts and Pentecost is for our
learning.

We must be continually conscious of the part of the Word of God which is written for our learning and separate it from that part which is written to us. These two prepositions, *for* and *to*, make the critical difference between truth and error when it comes to rightly dividing the Word of God.

> I Corinthians 1:2:
> Unto the church of God ....

This letter is addressed to someone just as if I received a letter addressed to me. To whom is Corinthians addressed? The Church of God. That is what it says and that is what it means.

> Ephesians 1:1:
> Paul, an apostle of Jesus Christ by the will of God, to the saints which are at Ephesus, and to the faithful in Christ Jesus.

Who are the saints? The saints are the born-again believers. To whom is Ephesians addressed? It is addressed to the Church.

This is so simple. The entire Old Testament plus the four Gospels are addressed to either the Jew or to the Gentile. But the Epistles such as Romans, I and II Corinthians, Galatians, Ephesians, Philippians, Colossians, I and II Thessalonians are addressed specifically to the Church as are the personal Epistles like Timothy, Titus and Philemon. Hebrews is not addressed to the Church in the sense that we know the Church established on Pentecost. Hebrews is addressed to believers who are born again of God's Spirit but who have never walked in the freedom or the greatness of the new birth; Hebrews is written for those who are still zealous for the law. Likewise the book of James is addressed to the same Old Testament-minded believers.

James 1:1:
James, a servant of God and of the Lord Jesus Christ, to [to] the twelve tribes which are scattered abroad, greeting.

Could God write the address any more directly? It is addressed to the twelve tribes who are scattered, the dispersed Jews. The reason James is so applicable to many believers today is that believers who are born again of God's Spirit still do not want to believe the Scripture which is addressed to them; they seem to want to put themselves under the law again. This was the problem in the early Church too.

Acts 21:20:
And when they heard *it*, they glorified the Lord, and said unto him, Thou seest, brother, how many thousands of Jews there are which believe; and they are all zealous of the law.

These Jews were born again of God's Spirit, they were saved after Pentecost; but they were still zealous for the law. They never walked into the greatness of the revelation that came on the day of Pentecost which the Apostle Paul set forth and declared so boldly.

Galatians 5:1:
Stand fast therefore in the liberty wherewith Christ hath made us free, and be not entangled again with the yoke of bondage.

The word "liberty" means a state of being unrestricted, unfettered, free." "Stand fast therefore in the liberty [in your unrestricted condition] wherewith Christ hath made us free, and be not entangled again with the yoke of bondage." What is the yoke of bondage? The law.

Those Epistles that are addressed to us must be specifically applied by us. All other Scripture is for our learning. We do not have to keep the Ten Commandments; they are not addressed to me. There is a greater law to the Church than the Ten Commandments. We have the law of the love of God in Christ Jesus. If we live love with the power of God in us and the renewed mind, will we keep the Ten Commandments? Definitely. We will not go around breaking the Ten Commandments for we live on a higher plateau; we live by a greater law.

What about the Lord's Prayer? Is it addressed to those after the day of Pentecost or did Jesus teach it to His disciples before Pentecost? The Word of God declares in Matthew that He taught it to His disciples, to Israel. Yet almost every Sunday in all major denominations, the members stand and the minister says, "Now let us pray the prayer which the Lord taught us. 'Our Father which art in heaven, Hallowed be thy name. Thy kingdom come. Thy will be done in earth, as *it is* in heaven. Give us this day our daily bread.' " Why can I *not* pray that? Because the Epistles, which are addressed to the Church, say that He *has supplied* all our need according to His riches in glory. Certainly then God has supplied my daily bread. When we pray, "Give us this day our daily bread," we are asking Him to give us something which has already been given to us.

"And forgive us our debts, as we forgive our debtors." Why can I not accurately pray this? Because my forgiveness is not dependent upon forgiving others for God said to the church of the Gospels that "whosoever ... shall confess me before men, him will I confess also before my Father which is in heaven." The Lord's Prayer says, "Forgive us our debts [our trespasses or our sins] as we forgive our debtors [those who sin against us]." In other words, it is condi-

215

tional — if I do not forgive John Doe for his sins, God will not forgive me mine. In The Word addressed to me this is not indicated. It does not say anything about forgiving anybody else. It says to confess with your mouth the Lord Jesus; it does not say to confess your sin. Do you see the difference?

To see the importance of knowing to whom a passage of Scripture is addressed read the record in Romans 8.

Romans 8:37–39:
Nay, in all these things we are more than conquerors through him that loved us.

For I am persuaded, that neither death, nor life, nor angels, nor principalities, nor powers, nor things present, nor things to come,

Nor height, nor depth, nor any other creature, shall be able to separate us from the love of God, which is in Christ Jesus our Lord.

Nothing can separate me from the love of God which is in Christ Jesus my Lord. Later, as I continue reading, I come to Romans 11.

Romans 11:21,22:
For if God spared not the natural branches, *take*

heed lest he also spare not thee.

> Behold therefore the goodness and severity of
> God: on them which fell, severity; but toward
> thee, goodness, if thou continue in *his* goodness:
> otherwise thou also shalt be cut off.

Romans 8 says that nothing can separate me from
the love of God; and yet three chapters later, Romans
11 says that if I don't continue in His goodness, I am
going to be cut off. What's going on? Look to see to
whom each passage is written.

> Romans 9:3:
> For I could wish that myself were accursed from
> Christ for my brethren, my kinsmen according
> to the flesh.

Who were Paul's kinsmen according to the flesh?
Verse 4 says, "Who are Israelites ...." To whom is it
addressed? Verse 4 says to the Israelites, the Jews.
Paul continued talking to Israel. Paul wrote in chapter
10 verse 1, "Brethren, my heart's desire and prayer to
God for Israel is, that they might be saved." This is still
addressed to Israel. In chapter 11, verse 1, he says,
"I say then, Hath God cast away his people? God for-
bid. For I also am an Israelite, of the seed of Abraham, *of* the tribe of Benjamin." Paul was still writing
to Israel. But in verse 13 Paul changed to the Gentiles

in his speech.

> Romans 11:13:
> For I speak to you Gentiles, inasmuch as I am
> the apostle of the Gentiles ....

Verse 21 of chapter 11: "For if God spared not the natural branches ...." Who are the natural branches? the natural branches are Israel. "... *take heed* lest he also spare not thee." "Thee" who? Gentiles. Why should God spare the Gentiles if He did not spare the Jews? Gentile and Jew both now had to be born again of God's Spirit. We are neither Jew nor Gentile; we belong to the Church of God and nothing can separate us from the love of God which is in Christ Jesus. But if a person is a Gentile and not born again, "For if God spared not the natural branches [Israel], *take heed* lest he also spare not thee." Verse 22, "Behold therefore the goodness and severity of God: on them [Israel] which fell, severity: but toward thee [the Gentiles], goodness, if thou [Gentiles] continue in *his* goodness ...." What does it mean for a Gentile to continue in His goodness? The Gentile is to be saved, born again of God's Spirit. Unless the Gentile continues in His goodness by making the confession of Romans 10:9, "... thou [Gentiles] also shalt be cut off." All must now be born again.

As a part of understanding to whom the Word of

God is written a person must accurately recognize the administrations in the Bible.

I Corinthians 9:17:
For if I do this thing willingly, I have a reward: but if against my will, a dispensation [an administration] *of the gospel* is committed unto me.

Paul says that an administration of the Gospel was committed unto him. The word "dispensation" is completely misleading, for an administration is accurately the administering of an entire era as in one of our government administrations. The previous term of office was someone else's administration. In rightly dividing the Word of Truth, we must understand that these Biblical administrations have to remain within the confines in which God has placed them with His Word.

As far as I have been able to study the integrity of the Word of God, there are these major administrations in The Word: (1) the Original Paradise, (2) the Patriarchal, (3) the Law, (4) the Christ Administration, (5) the Church, (6) the Appearing, and (7) the Final Paradise or Glory Administration.

The First or Original Paradise Administration terminated very abruptly. It is documented from the beginning of Genesis through its third chapter. In the

219

twenty-fourth verse of Genesis 3, the Original Administration sharply ended.

> Genesis 3:24:
> So he drove out the man; and he placed at the east of the garden of Eden Cherubims, and a flaming sword which turned every way, to keep the way of the tree of life.

When God drove Adam and Eve out of Eden, the Original Administration where God dwelt with man came to a sudden end.

The second administration was the Patriarchal Administration of Abraham, Isaac and all the patriarchs until the laws of Moses. Things that were given to Moses before the law were unwritten laws. Things that were sins before the law was written became transgressions after the law was given.

> Romans 2:12:
> For as many as have sinned without law shall also perish without law: and as many as have sinned in the law shall be judged by the law.

There is another reference to the Patriarchal Administration in Acts 17:30.

And the times of this ignorance God winked at;

but now [He] commandeth all men every where to repent.

"The times of this ignorance" refers to the patriarchal period when the law was an unwritten law, so God winked at the time of this ignorance. That means that He just closed His eyes to it.

After the Patriarchal Administration comes the Law Administration. And the Law Administration which was initiated under Moses terminated when Jesus Christ came.

The difference between the Law and Christ Administrations is that Christ was personally on earth to keep and fulfill the law so that preparation might be made for the fifth administration, the Church.

Romans 10:4:
For Christ *is* the end of the law for righteousness to every one that believeth.

Matthew 27:51 tells us that when Jesus Christ died, "... behold, the veil of the temple was rent in twain from the top to the bottom ...." The veil that separated the Holy of Holies from the Holy Place was torn from top to the bottom. The veil of the temple, once it was ripped into two parts, no longer separated the priests from the people. The whole area was then

221

open to all both literally and figuratively. The priests no longer had to make intercession for the lay people once Christ had fulfilled the law; the people's intercessor became Christ Himself.

The fifth administration, The Church of Grace, began at Pentecost with the mystery of the Church first being made known several years after Pentecost to the Apostle Paul. This is the administration under which we now are living.

The sixth administration is the Appearing Administration. The Appearing Administration starts with the gathering together of those believers who were born again after Pentecost during the period before the return of Christ. The record of the gathering together of the believers is given in I Thessalonians 4:17 and II Thessalonians 2:1 and following. The Appearing Administration is also called the Revelation Administration from the book of Revelation. During this period Christ will appear, gather the Church, and come back to earth with His saints. The Appearing Administration ends when Satan is destroyed and the great white throne judgment takes place.

The final administration is the Paradise or Glory Administration. The Paradise Administration complements the Original Administration for that which was started in Genesis 1 and 2 and terminated with Gene-

sis 3:24 takes up again in Revelation 21. Paradise will
once more be on earth. There shall be a new heaven
and a new earth wherein dwells righteousness, where
there is no more sickness, no more sorrow, no more
death.

This has been a brief analysis of the administrations
which are encompassed in the Word of God. We must
understand that the rules of life change in the various
time periods so that we must see each administration
within its distinct context. When we look to see to
whom a particular Scripture is addressed, we must
also see which administration governs the rules.

As an example of understanding The Word in its
proper administration, turn to Deuteronomy 6:25.

> And it shall be our righteousness, if we observe
> to do all these commandments before the Lord
> our God, as he hath commanded us.

To whom is Deuteronomy addressed? To the Jews,
to Israel. If they kept the law, they would be made
righteous. Deuteronomy can be set under law, but it
cannot be set under the administration of the Church
of Grace. If we observed all the commandments, we
would not be righteous because our administration,
the Church, operates under changed rules.

For contrast in administrations look at Romans
3:20.

Therefore by the deeds of the law there shall no flesh be justified in his sight ....

On the surface, Deuteronomy 6:25 and Romans 3:20 appear contradictory. But they are not if we recognize to whom they are written. Deuteronomy was addressed to Israel under the Law Administration while Romans is addressed to the Church under the Church Administration.

Let me briefly point out one final key in understanding Biblical truth. What course of action does a person follow when he cannot make sense of a very difficult verse — when the verse, the context and previous usage are not satisfactory in giving him understanding?

The difficult verse must be understood in the light of clear verses. There may be one verse that stands out as difficult, while there are many verses on the same subject which are clear. Modern man has magnified the difficult one and forgotten the many clear ones. That is not honest. That is not rightly dividing The Word. We must see that the one fits with the many, not by squeezing it but by working it. Sometimes I have waited ten years to fit one thorny verse with the rest of the accuracy of The Word. Time is not important when studying a verse; the keys in The Word are. When we rightly divide The Word as to whom it is written, we understand that the one difficult verse must always fit in the light of the clear verses on the same subject.

We must always remember this first: that no prophecy — not one thing of that which is foretold or forthtold — is of any private interpretation. All Scripture interprets itself either in its verse, in its context, or by its previous usage. In the light of this basic foundation, we will be able to study the integrity and the accuracy of God's Word.

Part IV

The New Birth

Chapter Sixteen
Body, Soul, Spirit — Formed, Made, Created

The foundations have been set for understanding the accuracy of God's Word regarding how Scripture interprets itself, how the Word of God came into existence, and how this Word of God can be trusted when rightly divided. Now we are ready to proceed to working The Word to bring it into fruition in our understanding and our lives.

One of the great subjects in the Word of God is the new birth; it is the crux of Christianity. The new birth is the miracle of all miracles. I cannot explain it; but I believe that, by God's mercy and grace, we can approach The Word and it will explain itself so that we can understand.

Before we move into the depth of the new birth, we must realize some fundamental terms. When I speak of the "natural man," I speak of the man of body and soul, the man who is *not* born again of God's Spirit. This is the accurate Biblical usage of *natural man.* The five senses are the only avenues of learning that the natural man has to gain knowledge. Everything that ever comes to a natural man's mind must come by one or a combination of these five senses: seeing, hearing, smelling, tasting, touching.

We gather information through our five senses from a source or sources outside ourselves. We come to conclusions from our accumulated knowledge, and thus we believe what we believe. Being aware of the process of learning, I came to the conclusion many years ago that for me the Word of God (not the King James Version, but the Word of God which was given when "... holy men of God spake *as they were* moved by the Holy Ghost") would be my source for truth. This is my center of reference for learning.

For years I read around the Word of God with the writers of outside works being centers of reference for me. Soon I suffered from a common disease called mental confusion because equally great men regarding the same verse of Scripture would contradict each other. When I began to consider the process of learning, I finally came to the conclusion that instead of spending my life in confusion with men's opinions I would accept one center of reference for truth which was outside myself, and that was the Word of God.

If the Word of God is wrong, I am going to be

wrong; but if the Word of God is right, then I have everything to gain by taking it as my sole center of reference. I believe that The Word takes the place of the absent Christ, and that the holy spirit takes the place of Christ in us through God's Word. I believe that the Bible gives the truth regarding man's redemption, his dominion and authority and power over all God's creation. I believe that the Bible gives the truth regarding Jesus Christ, His coming, His death, His resurrection, His ascension, God's giving of the truth regarding the new heaven and the new earth which God is going to establish. I believe that the Bible gives truth, not facts. Anything man does, anything man makes, is a fact. I believe that the Word of God is Truth — Truth which is eternal, the same yesterday, today, and forever. I believe that the revelation of the Word of God is an absolute necessity for the natural man. If the senses man is going to be a complete man, he must have an accurate knowledge of God's Word.

A very condensed Scripture which we must thoroughly master to understand the origin of man is Isaiah 43:7.

> *Even* [for] every one that is called by my name: for I have created him for my glory, I have formed him; yea, I have made him.

"I have *created* him, I have *formed* him, I have

made him." Are the three words "created," "formed" and "made" synonymous? Most people in my classes say, yes. If The Word means what it says and says what it means, these words cannot be synonymous. When God said *formed*, He meant *formed*. When He said *made*, He meant *made*. When He said *created*, He meant *created*. Had He meant *formed* all the way through, it would have said *formed* at all three places. But it says, "I created man, I formed man, I made man." We must now find out what is meant when He created, made and formed man.

> I Thessalonians 5:23:
> And the very God of peace sanctify you wholly; and *I pray God* your whole spirit and soul and body be preserved blameless unto the coming of our Lord Jesus Christ.

Are those three words "spirit," "soul" and "body" synonymous? They are no more synonymous than are *created, formed* and *made. Body* means *body, soul* means *soul*, and *spirit* means *spirit*. Now we must go to The Word and let The Word speak as to what is formed, what is made, and what is created, and what is body, soul and spirit.

In the beginning — whenever that was — man was formed, made and created. To follow Scriptural development, let us begin with Genesis 2:7.

232

Body, Soul, Spirit — Formed, Made, Created

And the Lord God formed man *of* the dust of the ground ....

The Hebrew word for "formed" is *yatsar*, "fashioned out of something that was already in existence." Genesis 2:7 says that God formed man of the dust of the ground. The word "man" is *adam*, meaning "red earth." Man's body is composed of the same elements that are in the dust of the earth.

> Genesis 3:19:
> In the sweat of thy face shalt thou eat bread, till thou return unto the ground; for out of it wast thou taken: for dust thou *art*, and unto dust shalt thou return.

The body of man was formed (*yatsar*) of the dust of the ground. And, because of the law that everything must ultimately return to its original state, the body must return to dust. Ecclesiastes 3:20 says, "... all are of the dust, and all turn to dust again."

The next word to observe is the word "soul" which in Hebrew is *nephesh*. What is soul? The soul in man is that which gives the body its life, its vitality. Look again at Genesis 2:7.

> And the Lord God formed man [man's body] *of* the dust of the ground, and breathed into his

233

> nostrils the breath of life; and man became a living soul.

"Breathed into his nostrils" is the figure of speech *condescensio*. God put life into Adam; He made man a living soul. The word "made" in Hebrew is *asah*, "a substance required of which the thing made consisted." The soul is nothing more and nothing less than that which gives life to a person's body. Sometimes it is called "the spirit of man." Soul has nothing to do with whether you are a Christian or a non-Christian. As long as a person breathes, he has a soul.

The confusion between the soul and the spirit has caused no end of difficulty for people. They say the soul is immortal, for instance. They talk about transmigration of the soul, the immortality of the soul. These are all erroneous usages of words which are used with exactness and precision in the Word of God.

To observe the use of the word "soul" look at I Peter 3:20.

> Which sometime were disobedient, when once the longsuffering of God waited in the days of Noah, while the ark was a preparing, wherein few, that is, eight souls were saved by water.

234

Body, Soul, Spirit — Formed, Made, Created

This verse is talking about the eight souls that were saved during the great flood. Were they Christians? No, Christ had not yet come. Noah, his wife, their three sons and their three wives — all eight people, eight souls — were saved.

> Acts 27:37:
> And we were in all in the ship two hundred threescore and sixteen souls.

The record in Acts refers to Paul's and Luke's ship sailing to Rome. Except for Paul and Luke, the rest on board were unbelievers, non-Christians; and yet the record says, "and we were in all in the ship two hundred threescore and sixteen souls." "Soul" means alive people; it is that part which gives life to the body.

The modern church has been illogical on this particular issue because it usually teaches that the soul is eternal life spirit and goes back to God; but then the teachers deny that a cow having a soul, life, must go back to God. If the soul came from God, it must ultimately go back to God, just as the body of man must ultimately go back to dust. If what they teach is true, all animals must return to God. But it isn't true, because the soul is not eternal life spirit. The soul is that which gives one breath-life.

235

The New Birth

>Genesis 1:30:
>And to every beast of the earth, and to every
>fowl of the air, and to every thing that creepeth
>upon the earth, wherein *there is* life ....

The word "life" in Genesis 1:30 is "soul." This
verse says that every beast has a living soul.

>Genesis 1:20:
>And God said, Let the waters bring forth abun-
>dantly the moving creature that hath life ....

The word "life" is the word "soul." If there is a
soul, there is movement, there is breath-life.

>Genesis 1:21:
>And God created great whales, and every living
>creature that moveth ....

The word "creature" is the word "soul."

>Genesis 1:24:
>And God said, Let the earth bring forth the
>living creature ....

The word "creature" is again the word "soul."
These are some of the places in Genesis 1 where the
word "soul" is used regarding creatures as well as
man. The soul, then, is that which gives a being its
life. The word *nephesh* is "soul." *Chai* means
"moving life, *moving soul.*" *Nephesh chai* is always
236

used in the Word of God as living life, in contrast to a dead soul, a soul that perished.

God *made* every beast wherein there is a soul, a life. The question we must now ask is where is the soul life of man and beast.

> Leviticus 17:11:
> For the life of the flesh *is* in the blood ....

The soul life is in the blood and is passed on when the sperm impregnates the egg at the time of fertilization.

What ultimately happens to the soul? As the body goes back to dust, the soul is passed on from one person to his progeny. If a person has no offspring, his soul is gone when he dies; it is no more. If my soul is gone, I am a dead person and the Bible speaks of me as a dead soul. There is nothing immortal about the soul, no more so than there is anything immortal about dust. Man's body is made of dust and it goes back to dust. When man takes his last breath, his soul life terminates.

After studying "formed" and "made," we still must consider the Biblical usage of the word "created." What part of man was created?

To find the first use of "create," we look at the

The New Birth

first book in the Bible.

> Genesis 1:1:
> In the beginning God created the heaven and the earth.

To "create" (*bara*) literally means "to get something out of nothing" or "to bring into existence something which never existed in any form before."

Many Sunday School teachers (if they still use the Bible) say that "on the first day God *created* thus and so, and on the second day God *created* something else," and so on. But that is not what the Word of God says. In verse 3 God said, "... Let there be light ...." Why didn't He have to create it? Because whatever light is composed of had already been created in Genesis 1:1 in the beginning when God created the heaven and the earth. All he had to do was "speak" light into existence.

Verse 6 says, "And God said ...." Verse 9, "And God said ...." Verse 11, "And God said ...." Verse 14, "And God said ...."

In verse 21 God *created* "great whales, and every living creature that moveth ...." Their bodies were brought forth abundantly out of the waters. Water and earth already existed, so the substance which

238

made up their bodies did not have to be created. What had to be created at this point? Soul life, because it never existed before. In verses 24–26 God brought forth from the earth the cattle, the beasts, and man — all having the soul life that was created in verse 21.

As God progressed in His work of forming, making and creating the earth and its inhabitants, He finally came to bringing about His culminating work — man.

Genesis 1:27:
So God created man in his *own* image, in the image of God created he him; male and female created he them.

God had already formed and made man; man already had a body and soul. So what was God doing in creating man in his own image? What is the image of God? John 4:24: "God *is* a Spirit ...."

A spirit has no flesh or bones. God created within man His Spirit (*ruach*), His image. Thus man became body, soul and spirit. After God created man in His own image, God had a companion — not in the body and soul parts of man, but in the spirit. It is that part of man which made it possible for God to talk to man and for man to communicate with God. This gave them fellowship. This is the man we read about in

239

Isaiah and Thessalonians where the Scriptures say that man was formed, made and created, and that he was body, soul and spirit.

Scientists today talk about creating life. That is a misnomer. They may rediscover, revamp, reorganize, readapt, or recompose; but they cannot create because to create something is to bring something into existence which did not exist in any form. The scientists always start with some substance so they are not creating.

Genesis 1:1,2:

In the beginning God created the heaven and the earth.

And the earth was [became] without form and void; and darkness *was* upon the face of the deep.

There is a long period of time between Genesis 1:1 and Genesis 1:2. I do not know how long, but I do know that when verse 2 came into being, "the earth was [became] without form, and void ...." The earth was not created without form and void; it became that way.

Now, the question is: what caused this original creation in Genesis 1:1 (which was perfect) to become formless and void. To see the tremendous

240

accuracy of The Word, we have to study Scriptures like Isaiah 14:12; Ezekiel 28:15–19; Romans 8:22; I Timothy 3:6; Revelation 12:4. These Scriptures explain that in the beginning God created angels under three leaders: Gabriel, Michael and Lucifer. These three archangels were responsible for all the other angels. Lucifer, who was called an angel of light, wanted to usurp the throne of God. He caused a mutiny in heaven, so to speak. Therefore Lucifer was cast out of heaven along with one-third of the angels who, under Lucifer's leadership, had conspired against God. After being cast out of heaven, Lucifer became "Satan," "the serpent," "the Devil." He and one-third of the angels of heaven make up the evil-spirit or the devil-spirit world about which people know very little and believe less.

The mutiny in heaven of Lucifer and his angels was so cataclysmic that while the war was taking place, all that God had originally created in Genesis 1:1 fell into ruin. Thus, verse 2 of Genesis 1 says, "And the earth was [became] without form, and void ...."

How much time was there between Genesis 1:1 and 1:2? I don't know. There could have been eons of time. Verse 3 simply begins the record of God's actions in making the earth habitable for mankind — mankind of body, soul and spirit.

Were there "men" before the man of body, soul

and spirit? To the scientists, yes; but not man as Genesis 1:27 defines him. When a scientist looks at a fossil or a skeleton and the relic suggests a man-like form, he puts it in the species of *homo sapiens.* What scientists do not know and what they cannot see is the life that was in that being.

The reason I am concerned about this accuracy is that verse 24 of the first chapter tells us that God created man as we know him — body, soul and spirit. What kind of life there was in the so-called man before Adam and Eve, I do not know because the Bible does not tell me. Nor do the scientists know because they cannot re-enact that life. I do know, however, that whatever that life was then, it was not the life that God created when He created soul life for animal. The possibility of there being a different kind of life is indicated by the word "replenish" in Genesis 1:28.

> And God blessed them [man], and God said unto them, Be fruitful and multiply, and replenish the earth ....

How can the earth be *re*plenished if it had previously had no beings? Genesis 1:28 will corroborate and substantiate science because of "replenish."

There are many things one ought to know about

242

the great accuracy of God's Word in Genesis because in it is the foundation of the accuracy of His matchless Word.

Genesis 1:11 says,

> And God said, Let the earth bring forth grass, the herb yielding seed, *and* the fruit tree yielding fruit after his kind ....

"His kind" should be translated "its kind." To bring forth after its kind means, for example, when a tomato seed is planted tomatoes are reaped. When an onion seed is planted, onions are produced. Everything comes after its kind. The word "kind" is the Greek word *genos* which is transliterated into English as "genus." If cows are bred, a calf is born. If dogs are bred, puppies are born. A dog and a cat cannot be bred to get a kitten-pup. Crossing a cow and a horse doesn't bring a horsey-cow or a cowy-horse. Why? Because of the law of everything after its kind. That is why you can have variety within species but not in genus, not in kind. There is a great difference in characteristics between a Guernsey cow, a Jersey, and a Brown Swiss, for instance; but they belong to the same kind — the genus is bovine. There is no overlapping of genus. You cannot breed a cow to a horse because they are not of the same genus. There is evolution within species, but not between genus. All

theories of evolution die before they start unless kept
within the category of species and not genus.

The Word of God says, "... the fruit tree yielding
fruit ... whose seed *is* in itself ...." The seed is always
in itself and it is the seed that has life. Take a seed,
put it in the ground, add a little moisture and sun-
shine, and soon a leaf shoots up. Why? Because the
seed has life in itself.

When it comes to man, who has the seed? The life
which is in the flesh is contributed by the sperm of
the male. When the sperm impregnates the egg, the
sperm carries soul life and the soul life is in the seed.
This becomes singularly important to man when
studying the birth of the Lord Jesus Christ.

How many times did God create soul? The Bible
says that (except for the birth of Jesus) God created
it just once and that was when animals first came
into being.   God simply took the previously
created soul life and gave it to man when God formed
and made Adam. Adam then had progeny; and his
sons and daughters, in turn, had progeny. The soul
life which was in Adam was carried on in his children
and in his children's children. When Adam took his
last breath, his personal soul was gone; but his soul
life lived on in Cain, in Seth and in the rest of his
sons and daughters. To this day the same soul life

244

continues in mankind which God originally put in Adam when God made him.

Acts 17:26:
And [God] hath made of one blood all nations of men for to dwell on all the face of the earth ....

If all men come from the same blood, our soul life being derived from one common source (Adam), why are there so many physical variations among people? For instance, why are some people white, some yellow, some black and some red? How does one account for all this? To understand physical variations, we must have a knowledge of genes and chromosomes and dominant and recessive characteristics. Mendel's Law explains the process of dominant and recessive characteristics in plants and animals. Breeding controls or determines the variations within species.

In the beginning of man, the gene which determined the coloring of the skin carried both the dark and light characteristics. After generations of the darker-skinned marrying darker-skinned and fairer-skinned marrying fairer-skinned people, eventually strains end up with darker darks and lighter lights than originally existed, all due to natural selection and dominant characteristics. Thus came about the different colors and the different races of men that

245

dwell upon the face of the earth today. It does not contradict any of God's Word and it does not contradict the science of genetics.

Another question always arises as to whom the children of Adam and Eve married. Since there were no neighbors around, whom could the children take as their mates? Whom did Cain marry, for instance? He married his sister. Whom else could he marry? Finding a mate was no problem because, as Genesis 5:4 says,

> And the days of Adam after he had begotten Seth were eight hundred years: and he begat sons and daughters.

The sons of Adam married their own sisters. If we had a pure blood stream, we could marry our sisters. The reason we are not allowed now to marry sisters is that the impurities in our blood streams would cause complications in the next generation and in those following.

Because of purer blood people lived longer lives as the early Biblical records tell. Some people explain early man's longevity by saying that their years weren't as long as ours. But time then was the same as now. The reason for such longevity was that their blood had not become so contaminated, so impure.

246

Marriage and sin eventually began to produce weaker people who, therefore, died at an earlier age.

Previously "soul" has been defined as "breath-life." Plants do not have breath-life and yet they obviously have life in that they grow and bear fruit. Plants have growth-life, but they do not have breath-life. Animals have both growth-life and soul or breath-life. Man, as he originally was created, surpassed the animal realm in that he not only had body and soul but also spirit. It was the spirit which set man apart from the rest of creation. Because man had spirit, God could communicate with his final masterpiece.

Chapter Seventeen
"... Thou Shalt Surely Die"

In God's communication with Adam, God oriented the first human to the rules of life. The only reservation which God made to Adam is recorded in Genesis 2.

Genesis 2:16,17:
And the Lord God commanded the man, saying, Of every tree of the garden thou mayest freely eat:

But of the tree of the knowledge of good and evil, thou shalt not eat of it: for in the day [not *a* day, but in *that very day*] that thou eatest thereof thou shalt surely die.

In the beginnning there was only one who was above Adam, and that was God. Except for God, Adam was the supreme being. As earth's ruler, Adam had only one "hands-off" stipulation with the consequence being "... for in the day that thou eatest thereof thou shalt surely die."

In the beginning, the spirit in man made it possible for God to talk to him and for man, in turn, to talk to God. The natural man of body and soul only has his five senses whereby to acquire knowledge. In contrast, the first man not only could acquire knowledge through his five senses, but he could also attain knowledge through his communication with God, made possible by the spirit from God within him. Adam had two ways whereby he could know things, and he had the freedom of will to choose whether he was going to gather knowledge by his five senses or by spirit — God's speaking to him.

When God created spirit within man, man had perfect fellowship, perfect communion, with the Creator at all times. Adam also had supreme power on earth over that which God gave him dominion.

> Genesis 1:26:
> ... Let them [man] have dominion over the fish of the sea, and over the fowl of the air, and over the cattle, and over all the earth ....

Adam had dominion over all God's creation because God had given him this dominion; and as long as Adam walked by the spirit, he had perfect fellowship with God. But the moment Adam let his senses

250

rule over his mind and body instead of walking by the spirit, calamity resulted. Why? Because then he was no longer God-ruled. Adam had the option of walking by his senses or walking by the spirit. He determined by his free will whether to be led by what he could see, hear, smell, taste and touch or to be led by God.

In Genesis the story of Adam develops. Remember that Lucifer, who had fallen, is also called the serpent.

> Genesis 3:1:
> Now the serpent was more subtil than any beast of the field which the Lord God had made. And he said unto the woman, Yea, hath God said, Ye shall not eat of every tree of the garden?

Did the serpent know what God had said? He knew what God had said. With this knowledge, the serpent went to Eve and said, "Has God really said this? Did God say ye shall not eat of every tree of the garden?"

In observing the downfall of man, we can carefully observe how the Devil consistently operates. The first things that the Devil had Eve do — and the first thing he will get us to do — is to question the integrity and accuracy of God's Word. He said to her, "Did God really say ye shall not eat of every tree of the garden?" The Devil knew what God had said. The Devil

251

also knew that he wanted to instill a doubt in Eve's mind. This is the beginning of trouble. The Devil slyly gets people to doubt the accuracy and integrity of God's Word as he disguises himself as an angel of light. The Devil is not so stupid as to barge into one's affairs in a straight-forward, obnoxious way. He slyly questions, "Did God really say that you couldn't eat of every tree of the garden?"

With this doubt placed in Eve's mind, she reacts to the serpent as recorded in verse 2. "And the woman said unto the serpent ...." This is the next pitfall. A person cannot stop satanic influences from approaching, but one can stop them from lodging or staying in his mind. We cannot always help it if a bad thought comes, for instance; but we can keep from harboring and incubating it. The complication of the situation with Eve was not that the Devil had said to her, "Hath God not said, Ye shall not eat of every tree of the garden?" The trouble rooted itself when Eve started to participate by conversing and "reasoning" with the Devil.

> Genesis 3:2:
> And the woman said unto the serpent, We may eat of the fruit of the trees of the garden.

Is that what God had said? God had said, "Of every tree of the garden thou mayest freely eat." Do

you know what Eve did? She omitted the word
"freely." If one word is omitted from the Word of
God, is it still the Word of God? No, it has become
private interpretation. By omitting one word, Eve
no longer had The Word. Eve continued her
conversation.

> Genesis 3:3:
> But of the fruit of the tree which *is* in the midst
> of the garden, God hath said, Ye shall not eat of
> it, neither shall ye touch it, lest ye die.

God never said anything about touching the fruit.
Now what had Eve done? She had added to the Word
of God. When one adds to the Word of God, is it still
the Word of God? Again, it becomes private interpretation. The moment a word is deleted or added,
one no longer has The Word. God never said what Eve
quoted Him as saying. But was she sincere? She was
sincere, but she was totally wrong.

What else did Eve do to God's Word? "Ye shall
not eat of it, neither shall ye touch it, lest ye die."
God had said, "For in the day that thou eatest thereof
thou shalt surely die." There was no equivocating
about it. Eve changed the truth of God's Word from
"the day that thou eatest thereof thou shalt surely
die," to "lest [maybe, perhaps] ye die." She ques-
tioned the integrity of God's Word.

In following the pattern, the first thing the Devil induced Eve to do was question God's Word. Eve made the second mistake by considering the question that the Devil had propounded. Thirdly, Eve omitted from God's Word; fourthly, she added to God's Word; and fifthly, she changed the Word of God from an absolute to a perhaps. Here is the spiraling road downward. To this day, whenever Satan wants to attack men and women of God, he always leads them to question the integrity of The Word and then to change it so The Word no longer exists.

The third chapter of Genesis is as timely today and tomorrow as it was the day it happened many thousands of years ago when Adam and Eve went through the experience. When men and women throughout history have listened to Satan they began by questioning the integrity of God's Word. People say, "Oh, it isn't God's Word anyway," or "It has a lot of myths in it, a lot of interpolations, a lot of error. After all, you can't believe all that because it was just written by human beings." Thus people begin to question the integrity of The Word; they begin to doubt it. The next thing that happens is that these people speak to us. We start considering their doubts. "Well, now, maybe you are right. Maybe man did come from a one-celled animal." Before we know it, we think it is a good idea that man came from an amoeba so we begin changing the Bible. We omit a

254

word or we add a word or we change a few words. We arrange The Word to suit ourselves and, therefore, we do not have the true Word.

After the woman, Eve, responded to the Devil, he carried on the conversation.

Genesis 3:4:
And the serpent said unto the woman, Ye shall not surely die.

The Devil eased Eve into questioning The Word by omitting a word, by adding a word, by changing a word. When he finally got Eve in a pliable state of mind, he came out and showed his true colors. The Devil boldly and bluntly said, "Ye shall not surely die." That statement is not an omission, an addition or a change. It is a straight-forward contradiction of what God had said in Genesis 2:17. The true Word of God said, "Thou shalt surely die," and the Devil said, "Ye shall not surely die."

The same devilish things happen today. When a man is dead, we go to the funeral home and look at his corpse. He's dead. But some sweet person comes and says, "Oh, he's not dead, he is flying up there in the sky because I heard from him last night in a seance." The same kind of lie the Devil propounded back in Genesis 3 is still propounded by churches

255

today. The Devil said, "Ye shall not surely die." The mourners of the dead say, "He is not really dead; he just moved out from this world into something better." These are out-and-out contradictions of God's Word.

The Devil's primary target is The Word because if he can get rid of The Word, there is nothing left. There is little of The Word left in today's churches. Satan is always causing factions on extraneous matters so that people won't care or have time to study The Word. The great tragedy is that he has pretty well succeeded. Today people just talk about The Word; they do not believe it. Furthermore, they cannot put The Word together so that it fits with exactness and precision. A person can attend most Bible colleges in the world and still not know the Word of God. One may gain an impressive knowledge around The Word, but he will not know The Word. Otherwise, we would not be falling into the same pitfalls as Adam and Eve if our teachers and preachers knew The Word.

When God said, "Thou shalt surely die" and the Devil said, "Ye shall not surely die," one of them had to be lying. Follow the Devil's speech in Genesis 3.

> Genesis 3:4,5:
> And the serpent said unto the woman, Ye shall not surely die:

For God doth know that in the day ye eat thereof, then your eyes shall be opened, and ye shall be as gods, knowing good and evil.

The Devil cajoles, "You are going to be as smart as God. You are going to know everything."

What ensues is recorded in Genesis 3:6. "And when the woman saw ...." Is "saw" in the world of the spirit or the senses? It is in the category of the senses. As long as Adam and Eve lived by God's revelation, life was perfect; but the moment the senses were allowed to dominate over the spirit, calamity resulted.

Genesis 3:6:
And when the woman saw that the tree *was* good for food, and that it *was* pleasant to the eyes [the senses], and a tree to be desired to make *one* wise, she took of the fruit thereof, and did eat, and gave also unto her husband with her; and he did eat.

Thus man fell because man was disobedient to God's Word. God's Word said, "You can do this, but not this." The Devil said, "You just go ahead and do it because you will be just as smart as God." Eve, as the record said, walked definitely by her senses; then Adam willingly followed her into the catastrophe. It says in the Bible that Eve was deceived by the Devil.

257

Adam was never deceived; he just followed along.

Adam's mistake was cataclysmic for God had said, "For in the day that thou eatest thereof thou shalt surely die." What died on the day Adam and Eve ate of the tree of knowledge of good and evil? Did Adam and Eve still have bodies and souls? Certainly. What they no longer had was their connection with God, spirit. This is why God said, "The day that thou eatest thereof thou shalt surely die." Many times clergy, theologians or commentaries have said, "Well, they didn't really die. It was just the seeds of spiritual death that were planted in them because the Word of God says that Adam lived some 800 years after that." The Word does not agree with this explanation. The Word says, "the day [the very day] that thou eatest thereof thou shalt surely [absolutely] die." One must understand the man of body, soul and spirit to be aware of exactly what happened on the day that Adam defied God's one rule.

The spirit disappeared. The reason the spirit was called dead is that it was no longer there. Their entire spiritual connection with God was lost. From that very day Adam and Eve were just body and soul — as any other animal.

Man, being body and soul, had to rely solely on his five senses. From the day Adam ate of the tree of

258

knowledge of good and evil until the day of Pentecost thousands of years later, God came into concretion whenever He wanted to talk to man. He had to come into some form for the man's senses to perceive and thereby understand. Moses, traveling along in the wilderness, saw a burning bush; and from the midst of the burning bush, he heard a voice. Moses' senses perceived God. The children of Israel could see the Ten Commandments. This was the means by which God came into concrete form to tell them what to do. Annually, on the Day of Atonement, the high priest entered into the Holy of Holies to make sacrifices. He laid his hands on the goat and then sent it into the wilderness to die. God had said that as surely as the Israelites saw the goat go into the wilderness, their sins went with it. They could see the goat, they could see the stone tablet, they could see the burning bush.

God had to come into concrete form because men had no means by which to understand spiritual things. But since man still did have the five senses, he could believe. This explains why Jesus Christ was born. Jesus Christ was born so that people could see Him; He had to be manifested in physical form. Jesus said, "... He that hath seen me hath seen the Father ...." God was in Christ reconciling the world unto Himself. Jesus was the concretion.

When a man of body and soul can say to me, "I

don't believe in your God." I say, "I know." He may look around stunned because he expected to fight for his position, but he gets no fight because I know the accuracy of The Word — he can't know God for he is a natural man who understands only the world of the five senses.

> I Corinthians 2:14:
> But the natural man receiveth not the things of the Spirit of God: for they are foolishness unto him: neither can he know *them*, because they are spiritually discerned.

Natural man cannot know spiritual matters because they are spiritually discerned. Having summed up the situation in one verse of Scripture, God couldn't have stated Himself more clearly. Because the things of God are spiritual, they must be known by the spirit. That is why The Word says that spiritual things are foolishness to the natural, scientific man. The natural man goes by his reason — by what he can see, hear, smell, taste and touch — and not by the revealed Word of God.

> I Corithians 1:21:
> For after that in the wisdom of God [spiritual wisdom] the world by wisdom [sense-knowledge wisdom] knew not God ....

After once understanding body, soul and spirit,

this entire section of the Word of God unfolds itself. Romans 8 becomes readily understandable.

Romans 8:1—8:

There is therefore now no condemnation to them which are in Christ Jesus, who walk not after the flesh [by the five senses], but who walk after the Spirit [by revelation from God's Word or by direct revelation from God].

For the law of the Spirit of life in Christ Jesus hath made me free from the law of sin and death.

For what the law could not do, in that it was weak through the flesh [by way of the senses], God sending his own Son in the likeness of sinful flesh, and for sin, condemned sin in the flesh:

That the righteousness of the law might be fulfilled in us, who walk not after the flesh [according to the five senses], but [who walk] after the Spirit.

For they that are after the flesh do mind [are obedient to] the things of the flesh; but they that are after the Spirit the things of the Spirit.

For to be carnally minded [sense-knowledge

261

minded] *is* death; but to be spiritually minded *is* life and peace.

Because the carnal mind *is* enmity against God: [The brain of many is in conflict with God — senses versus revelation.] for it is not subject to the law of God, neither indeed can be.

So then they that are in the flesh [who live by their five senses] cannot please God.

The flesh cannot please God because God is Spirit.

Previously we looked at the origin of the Word of God. Man did not write The Word by using his five senses. Galatians 1 bears further witness to this.

Galatians 1:11,12:
But I certify [guarantee] you, brethren, that the gospel which was preached of me is not after man.

For I neither received it of man, neither was I taught it ....

If man didn't receive the Gospel from man, he didn't receive it by way of the five senses. Paul continues,

... but by the revelation of [from] Jesus Christ.

262

Paul received the Gospel by revelation.

Jeremiah 17 also points out the natural man's inability to know God and matters associated with Him.

Jeremiah 17:5—8:
Thus saith the Lord; Cursed *be* the man that trusteth in man, and [who] maketh flesh [the five senses] his arm, and whose heart departeth from the Lord.

For he shall be like the heath in the desert, and shall not see when good cometh; but shall inhabit the parched places in the wilderness, *in* a salt land and not inhabited.

Blessed *is* the man that trusteth in the Lord, and whose hope the Lord is.

For he shall be as a tree planted by the waters, and *that* spreadeth out her roots by the river, and shall not see when heat cometh, but her leaf shall be green; and shall not be careful in the year of drought; neither shall cease from yielding fruit.

The one man trusts in the arm of the flesh and the other trusts in God. The contrast is obvious.

Look at the instruction in Proverbs 3.

> Proverbs 3:5,6:
> Trust in the Lord with all thine heart; and lean not unto thine own understanding.
>
> In all thy ways acknowledge him, and he shall direct thy paths.

Do you see the two divisions? Leaning to one's own understanding is going by the five senses while acknowledging God is to go by the revealed Word of God or by revelation.

Because Adam chose to walk by his senses rather than by God's Word, the position of Adam and the productivity of the earth drastically changed.

> Genesis 3:17:
> And unto Adam he said, Because thou hast hearkened unto the voice of thy wife, and hast eaten of the tree, of which I commanded thee, saying, Thou shalt not eat of it: cursed *is* the ground for thy sake; in sorrow [labor] shalt thou eat *of* it all the days of thy life.

In chapters one and two of Genesis there was no curse. Before sin came, before Adam and Eve acted contrary to the will of God, there was no cursing of

264

the ground. Adam was in absolute control of all earthly matters; but immediately after the fall, the record in The Word says that the ground was cursed. God said, "In sorrow [labor] shalt thou eat *of* it all the days of thy life; Thorns also and thistles shall it bring forth." There were no thorns and thistles in paradise. Where there was no sin, there could be no disruption like this. There was no sickness, there was no disease, there was no death. Why? Because there was no sin. Sin, whose originator is the Devil, produces sickness, disease, death; it produces every negative that is recorded after the third chapter of Genesis.

> Genesis 3:19:
> In the sweat of thy face shalt thou eat bread, till thou return unto the ground; for out of it wast thou taken: for dust thou *art,* and unto dust shalt thou return.

When Adam disobeyed the condition set by God, something occurred to establish physical death within man. Whenever we break the spiritual laws of God, we bring to ourselves physical calamities.

> Genesis 3:22,23:
> And the Lord God said, Behold, the man is become as one of us, to know good and evil: and now, lest he put forth his hand, and take also of the tree of life, and eat, and live for ever:

265

> Therefore the Lord God sent him forth from the garden of Eden, to till the ground from whence he was taken.

The true God and His archenemy the Devil were involved in an all-out battle. If Adam and Eve had been allowed to stay in paradise after the fall, the Devil could have defeated God. The Devil could then have kept man in that unredeemable state of sin forever if man had eaten of the tree of life after once sinning. So that this would not happen, God drove Adam and Eve out of the garden or paradise.

The question arises as to the rulership of this world after Adam listened to the Devil and disobeyed God. Jesus spoke of the rulership of this world while He was here upon earth.

> John 14:30:
> Hereafter I will not talk much with you: for the prince of this world cometh, and hath nothing in me.

In Chapters one and two of Genesis the prince of this world was Adam. In John 14, however, Jesus Christ declares that the prince of this world has nothing in Him. Who then is the prince of this world? It is the Devil. Observe Luke 4.

266

Luke 4:5,6:
And the devil, taking him [Jesus] up into an high mountain, shewed unto him all the kingdoms of the world in a moment of time.

And the devil said unto him [Jesus], All this power will I give thee, and the glory of them: for that is delivered unto me; and to whomsoever I will I give it.

The Devil said to Jesus, "All this power will I give thee." Can a person give something away if he does not have it? Yet Luke 4:5 says that the Devil was offering all the kingdoms, all the glory, all the power to Jesus Christ.

If at one time Adam had all power, dominion and authority, how then did the Devil come to have it? The Devil said, "that is delivered unto me." Who delivered it to him? Adam did. Adam transferred that which God had conferred upon him to God's archenemy the Devil. This made the original sin, in legal terms, high treason against God. Adam gave the power which God had given to him to God's archenemy.

In the beginning God had conferred the right of rulership, dominion, authority and power over all God's creation to Adam. Having freedom of will, Adam could choose how he wished to utilize what God had given him. The original sin was Adam's

267

choosing to transfer his conferred power to God's archenemy, the Devil. The Devil then became the god of this world.

> II Corinthians 4:4:
> In whom the god of this world [Satan] hath blinded the minds of them which believe not, lest the light of the glorious gospel of Christ, who is the image of God, should shine unto them.

So there are two gods. One is the God and Father of our Lord Jesus Christ and the other is the god of this world, the Devil. If a man says, "I believe in God," I always ask him which one. The Word says there are two.

The Devil now has the rulership, the dominion, the authority, the power which Adam originally possessed over God's creation. Whenever the Devil wants to flood a territory, he floods it out. When he wants to kill people, he kills them. All evil and disease are the opposite of what the true God would do. To read a classic example of human suffering, follow the biography of Job. It was the Devil who killed Job's children; it was the Devil who turned Job's wife against him; it was the Devil who sent the storm. Why? Because he has the power, the rulership, the dominion, the authority over this earth.

Chapter Eighteen
Faith Comes by Hearing the Word of God

When the Devil was given dominion and man became a being of body and soul, what happened to man's relationship with God?

> Ephesians 2:11,12:
> Wherefore remember, that ye *being* in time past Gentiles in the flesh, who are called Uncircumcision by that which is called the Circumcision in the flesh made by hands;
>
> That at that time ye were without Christ, being aliens from the commonwealth of Israel, and strangers from the covenants of promise, having no hope, and without God in the world.

They were without God because when man sinned he lost his spirit, his innate relationship with God. Man, being without spirit, was without God and without hope in this world.

269

Ephesians 2:1:
And you *hath he quickened,* who were dead in
trespasses and sins.

What does *dead* mean? Man appeared to be lively.
He had body and soul, but was dead in trespasses and
sins because he had no spirit. Psalms says that all men
are conceived and born in sin. This does not mean
that the parents were sinful in the way in which they
had intercourse. Man is conceived and born in sin
because he has no spirit.

Having only a body and soul, how does a natural
man ever again have a connection with the spiritual
realm? Spiritual things can only be known by the
spirit, even as things in the natural realm can only be
known by the five senses. Since natural man cannot
know God, what is the bridge that spans the chasm
between the natural man and God? The bridge is
faith.

But natural man does not have faith because faith
is a spiritual element. How then does he get faith to
span that chasm?

Romans 10:17:
So then faith *cometh* by hearing, and hearing by
the word of God.

Faith comes to the natural man by hearing. The

man of body and soul can hear. The man has freedom of will and he has a mind so that he can believe if he wants to.

"So then faith *cometh* by hearing ...." By hearing what? What John or Henry says, or what *Reader's Digest, Life, Look* and *Time* say? Faith does not come that way. Faith comes by hearing one thing — the Word of God.

Before going further, let us clarify the difference between the two words "faith" and "believing." These two words are not synonymous though the King James and other translations have used them interchangeably. Faith is an inner spiritual development, while believing is an action of the human mind. The natural man of body and soul can believe; but the natural man cannot have faith.

Galatians 3:22:
But the scripture hath concluded all under sin, that the promise by faith of Jesus Christ might be given to them that believe.

The natural man of body and soul, the unsaved man, does not have faith. Faith is spiritual and the natural man cannot have it. But the man of body and soul can believe.

Galatians 3 continues, "But before faith came ...."

271

Then there must have been a time when faith did not exist.

> Galatians 3:23,24:
> But before faith came, we were kept under the law, shut up unto the faith which should afterwards be revealed.
>
> Wherefore the law was our schoolmaster *to bring us* unto [until] Christ, that we might be justified by faith.

The law was the schoolmaster until Christ, that we might be justified by faith. Whose faith? The faith of Jesus Christ. We, natural men of body and soul, are to be justified by faith.

> Galatians 3:25:
> But after that faith is come, we are no longer under a schoolmaster.

Since faith came, I am no longer under the law because Christ was the end of the law.

If faith came by Jesus Christ, was there faith in the Old Testament? Was there then faith in the Gospels? There must not have been because Jesus Christ came to make it available, and the law was not entirely fulfilled until Pentecost. Absolutely nobody could

272

have faith until Jesus Christ made faith available.

Jesus did not bring it when He was born in Bethlehem; He did not bring it when He died upon the cross; He brought it when all was fulfilled on the day of Pentecost. There is no faith in the Gospels or in the Old Testament. When we read the word "faith" before the book of Acts, we are simply reading an error in translation. How many times do you think the word "faith" appears in the Old Testament in the King James Version? It appears only twice, once in Habakkuk 2:4 and once in Deuteronomy 32:20. Reading "faith" in context, one will see that it means "faithfulness, steadfastness." There is a vast difference between being faithful and having faith. Most people think there is faith in the Old Testament because of Hebrews 11: "By faith Noah," "By faith Abraham," "By faith Isaac," "By faith Jacob," "By faith Sara." Yet in the Old Testament, it does not say that Abraham had faith. It says that Abraham believed God, Isaac believed God, Jacob believed God. These men had body and soul; they could believe for they had a mind; they could hear The Word; they could see the Ten Commandments and believe what they saw. Galatians 3:6 says of Abraham, "he believed God, and it was accounted to him for righteousness." Hebrews 11 should accurately read, "By believing Noah," "By believing Abraham," "By believing Isaac," and so forth.

273

In the Old Testament, God covered their sins. Members of the Church of Grace do not have their sins covered; they are completely washed away. He cleanses us. God can cleanse us because one thing has come into being and that is faith.

> Romans 10:4:
> For Christ *is* the end of the law for righteousness to every one that believeth.

When the man of body and soul hears the Word of God and believes what he hears, Romans 10:9, he receives the "faith of Jesus Christ" and righteousness.

> Romans 3:22:
> Even the righteousness of God *which is* by faith of Jesus Christ unto all and upon all them that believe ....

How much faith is the faith of Jesus Christ? All one is ever going to receive. How can a person get more faith when The Word says that the "faith of Jesus Christ [is] unto all and upon all them that believe "?

> Romans 12:3:
> For I say, through the grace given unto me, to every man that is among you, not to think *of himself* more highly than he ought to think; but to think soberly, according as God hath dealt to

274

every man the measure of faith.

What is that measure of faith which God deals to every man when he believes? The Word says that it is the faith of Jesus Christ .

Galatians 2:16:
Knowing that a man is not justified by the works of the law, but by the faith of Jesus Christ ....

We are not justified by the works of the law; we are justified by the faith of Jesus Christ.

Galatians 2:20:
I am crucified with Christ [The original text is: I *was* crucified with Christ.]: nevertheless I live; yet not I, but Christ liveth in me: and the life which I now live in the flesh I live by the faith of the Son of God, who loved me, and gave himself for me.

When Christ was crucified, I was crucified with Him; nevertheless, I am still living — body and soul. Not only do I have body and soul, but I have spirit when I am born again. And now I live not by my senses, but by the faith of Jesus Christ which is spiritually given to me. I simply utilize my senses to put that faith in operation.

Look at Ephesians 2:8. "For by grace [divine

275

favor] are ye saved through faith ...." Whose faith? Not my own, but the faith of Jesus Christ which is the bridge that spans the chasm between the natural man of body and soul and God who is Spirit.

> Ephesians 2:8—10:
> For by grace are ye saved through faith [The faith of Jesus Christ is God's gift to every man when he believes on the Lord Jesus Christ.] ; and that not of yourselves: *it is* the gift of [from] God:
>
> Not of works [If salvation is of grace, it cannot be of works.] , lest any man should boast.
>
> For we are his [God's] workmanship, created in Christ Jesus unto good works, which God hath before ordained that we should walk in them.

When this natural man of body and soul hears the Word of Truth and believes, he receives the faith of Jesus Christ. A person can never receive or attain more faith than that. When a person receives this faith, he joins a family. God is the Father and we are His sons.

> Galatians 6:10:
> As we have therefore opportunity, let us do good unto all *men*, especially unto them who

Faith Comes By Hearing the Word of God

are of the household of faith.

Who makes up the household of faith? Those who
have been given the faith of Jesus Christ because they
believed.

Let us say that I am unsaved — a natural man of
body and soul. I hear The Word; I believe what I hear.
And, when I believe, God implants in me the faith of
Jesus Christ, which is "unto all and upon all them that
believe." Since He has put this faith in me, I am now
of the household of faith. God is my Father; I am His
son.

How are we to treat the other members of the
household of faith? The Word of God says that we
are to be especially good to the household of faith.
Often in our earthly domain we are good to everyone
outside the household; within the household, we act
unkindly toward each other. Christians, too, cannot
seem to get along with each other. We are always
fighting over whether or not Adam had a navel, or
whether or not six angels could sit on the head of a
pin, or whether we ought to march on Washington or
away from Washington. Christians are not at all good
to each other. And yet The Word says that we are to
be especially good to the household of faith. Why?
Because it is God's household and we therefore share
so much in common.

277

Titus 1:4:
To Titus, *mine* own son after the common
faith ....

The "common faith" is that faith which is common to every born-again believer. It is the household faith.

Titus 1:13:
... Wherefore rebuke them sharply, that they may be sound in the faith.

Make sure that the sons of God are acting properly as a part of the household of faith.

There are other kinds of faith in the Bible besides household or family faith. Once we have become members of the household of faith, we then can operate the manifestation of faith (believing) so that we can live with the power of God. The manifestation of faith (believing) is special renewed mind believing according to the revelation manifestations. Renewing one's mind consists of putting God's Word in the mind and then living it.

The manifestation of faith (believing) is often called one of the "gifts" of the Spirit. They are not *gifts* of the Spirit; they are *manifestations* of the spirit, as recorded in I Corinthians 12. The manifesta-

278

tion of faith is the manifestation of believing.

Galatians discloses another type of faith and that is faith as a *fruit* of the spirit. Good fruit comes from good cultivation. To cultivate, one uses good fertilizer or natural plant food. Galatians 5 tells about our personal, spiritual gardens.

> Galatians 5:22,23:
> But the fruit of the Spirit is love, joy, peace, longsuffering, gentleness, goodness, faith,
>
> Meekness, temperance: against such there is no law.

This is the fruit of the spirit. Notice that the word "fruit" is in the singular. It is stated that way because they are all in a group or on one cluster like grapes. Galatians 5:22 does not say, as do many commentaries, that love is a fruit of good works. When it says, "fruit of the Spirit," it means fruit of the spirit. If it had meant fruit of good works, it would have said fruit of good works.

One produces the fruit of the spirit by operating the manifestations of the spirit. The person who has the faith of Jesus Christ has the ability to operate the nine manifestations. He can speak in tongues, he can interpret, he can prophesy, he can operate the word

279

of knowledge, the word of wisdom, discerning of spirits, faith (believing), miracles and healing.

The various types of faith are: (1) believing, (2) faith of Jesus Christ, (3) household faith, (4) manifestation of faith (believing), (5) fruit of the Spirit faith. We must be alert to the various usages of this word if we are going to rightly divide the Word of Truth.

It was a great revelation to me when I discovered that never in the Word of God is the Church told to have faith. Why? Because to be born again of God's spirit is to have the faith of Jesus Christ. We are born again of God's Spirit, we are His workmanship, we have the faith of Jesus Christ. We cannot get any more faith than that. Every born-again believer has equally-measured faith. If God had given you more faith when you were saved than I received, then God is a respecter of person, which, of course, is a contradiction to the Word of God. The youngest child in the family of God has the same amount of faith as the oldest saint. All have the faith of Jesus Christ. Since most people who are born again of God's Spirit do not know that they have the faith of Jesus Christ, they cannot use it.

This explains the apparent difference in Christian people: why one believer is, so to speak, an anemic

Christian while another believer becomes a very healthy or robust Christian. They both have the same faith but one reaches a higher plateau of Christian living than the other one because he knows more, he believes more, and therefore, he operates more. Christian anemia comes from being taught little, believing less, and operating even less. The person who believes more receives abundantly; the other who believes little receives in proportion. Nobody ever receives until he first believes.

The Old Testament and the Gospels are about men who existed solely by their five senses. They could only understand and believe what they could see for faith had not yet come.

John 6:30:
They said therefore unto him [Jesus], What sign shewest thou then, that we may see, and believe thee? what dost thou work?

In the Gospels, faith had not yet come so men had to see first and then they would believe. They could understand nothing except that which was in the senses realm. Another example of this is given in John 20:8 when two disciples saw Jesus' empty tomb.

Then went in also that other disciple, which came first to the sepulchre, and he saw, and

281

[he] believed.

He was a sense-knowledge man who saw the empty tomb. He saw and then he believed. Another familiar example is found in John 20.

John 20:24—29:
But Thomas, one of the twelve, called Didymus, was not with them when Jesus came.

The other disciples therefore said unto him [Thomas], We have seen the Lord. But he said unto them, Except I shall see in his hands the print of the nails, and put my finger into the print of the nails, and thrust my hand into his side, I will not believe.
And after eight days again his disciples were within, and Thomas with them: *then* came Jesus, the doors being shut, and stood in the midst, and said, Peace *be* unto you.

Then saith he to Thomas, Reach hither thy finger, and behold my hands; and reach hither thy hand, and thrust *it* into my side: and be not faithless, but believing.

And Thomas answered and said unto him, My Lord and my God.

Jesus saith unto him, Thomas, because thou hast

seen me, thou hast believed: blessed *are* they that have not seen, and *yet* have believed.

Until the day of Pentecost, people saw and then believed. Today we believe first and then we see.

To those living on and after Pentecost during the Church Administration Romans 10 gives the steps for salvation.

> Romans 10:9,10:
> That if thou shalt confess with thy mouth the Lord Jesus, and shalt believe in thine heart that God hath raised him from the dead, thou shalt be saved.
>
> For with the heart man believeth unto righteousness; and with the mouth confession is made unto salvation.

The man who confesses Jesus as Lord and believes that God raised Jesus from the dead receives salvation. He believes first and then he receives.

> II Corinthians 4:18:
> ... we look not at the things which are seen, but at the things which are not seen: for the things which are seen *are* temporal; but the things which are not seen *are* eternal.

283

Anything that can be seen is in the category of the senses; and the things of the senses are always temporal. But that which you cannot see — the spirit of God, the faith of Jesus Christ, the righteousness of God, justification, sanctification — all these are the things which are eternal.

How can a man of body and soul get the faith of Jesus Christ? How can he get the justification of God, redemption and sanctification? The answer is simple. To receive all this from God we must do one thing — believe. The next question is: what are we to believe?

To answer this, we must first see what God wrought in Christ, which in turn Christ works within us as we of body and soul believe.

Jesus Christ was God's plan from the beginning to manifest God who is Spirit on the level of the senses so that sense-knowledge man might be redeemed. God in His foreknowledge knew that Adam and Eve would sin and that He would have to send His Son to redeem mankind. God, being consistent and law-abiding, had to work within a legal framework to redeem man. Since by man came sin and death, by man also would have to come the redemption from sin and death. Jesus Christ was a human being who physically had all the fundamental life processes and endured all things. Hebrews 4:15 says that He "... was in all

284

points [things] tempted like as *we are, yet* without sin." Jesus Christ was God's plan for manifestation in the senses world. John 14:9 records, "... he that [who] hath seen me hath seen the Father." Jesus Christ manifested God in the world which understood only what it saw, heard, smelled, tasted or touched.

To understand God's manifesting Himself in the flesh through His Son, let us first see how God, Who is Spirit, could have a Son in the flesh. First of all, most people do not understand The Word, nor do they understand God and how He operates. They do not differentiate between the words "formed," "made," and "created," or "body," "soul," and "spirit." If we do not understand these truths, it is impossible to understand how a woman could conceive by the power of God and bring forth the Lord Jesus Christ. The most enlightening verse on the conception and the bringing forth of the Lord Jesus Christ is in Hebrews.

> Hebrews 2:14:
> Forasmuch then as the children are partakers of flesh and blood, he also himself likewise took part of the same; that through death he [Jesus Christ] might destroy him that had the power of death, that is, the devil.

Every child who is born in this world is a partaker

285

of the flesh and the blood* from his mother and father. Hebrews 2:14 says, "... He likewise took part." It does not say that Jesus Christ *partook*; He *took part* of the same.

Children partake of both flesh and blood, but Jesus Christ did not partake of flesh and blood; He only took part. According to the flesh, He was born of Mary; but according to the soul life that was in His blood, He was by divine conception. Thus Judas spoke a truth when he said, "I have betrayed the innocent blood."

God's Word says that Jesus was conceived by the Holy Spirit and born of Mary. He was conceived by God. That does not mean that God had intercourse with Mary. That is impossible because spirit is spirit; natural realm is natural realm. God created life within Mary's reproductive organs. God once again had to *create* — He had to create life in order to bridge the gap between His being Spirit and Mary's being flesh.

If He had wanted, God could have created soul life in any woman after Genesis 3:15. The question then is, why did God wait thousands of years after the fall to create life within a woman so that Christ could be born? Every woman from Eve to Mary was physically capable of bringing forth the Christ. The reason Mary was the one who brought forth the Messiah after

*"Blood" stands for life. It is the figure of speech *synedoche* — a part put for the whole.

thousands of years is that she was the first woman who ever literally and unreservedly believed what God said. It was she who said, "... be it unto me according to thy word ...." This is why Mary conceived and brought forth the Lord Jesus Christ. Jesus did not partake of the soul life of man, however; He only took part, the flesh. He was born of Mary, but the seed in Him was created by God.

The word "partake" in Hebrews 2:14 is *koinoneō* which means "to share fully." Children share fully in the flesh and blood of their mother and father. But where it says, "He also himself likewise took part of the same," the words "took part" in the Greek are the word *metechō* which means "to take only a portion." The part that He took was of the flesh; but the soul life in His blood was of God.

In the Christ Administration, it was Christ's flesh which manifested God to the senses man; but it is the blood of Jesus Christ that purifies, redeems and makes possible the abundant life for mankind. By His stripes we were healed and by His shed blood we have the remission of sins. According to the Word of God, when Jesus Christ was circumcised, we were circumcised* with Him; when He died on Calvary's cross, the Word of God says that we died with Him; when He

*Colossians 2:11: "In whom also ye are circumcised with the circumcision made without hands, in putting off the body of the sins of the flesh by the circumcision of Christ."

287

arose, we arose with Him; and when He ascended into heaven, we ascended with Him. The Word of God says in Ephesians 2:6, we are seated with Him in heavenly places while we are still here upon earth. What a tremendous testimony.

Chapter Nineteen
Born Again of Incorruptible Seed

Jesus Christ came to make the new birth available. Some people believe that the apostles were born again while Jesus was here; but if the apostles could have been born again while Jesus was on earth, Jesus Christ wouldn't have needed to die upon Calvary's cross; God wouldn't have needed to give the holy spirit. The problem with many Biblical teachers is that they do not consider the fact that one cannot have something until it is available, and the new birth was not available until Pentecost. No one, absolutely no one, was born again until the day of Pentecost. Everyone until that time was just body and soul, without eternal life.

What does it mean to be born the first time? To be born the first time one has to have seed planted. To be born again is to have the seed of God in Christ born within and this seed is spirit and life.

Genesis 3:15 records that immediately following the fall God "put enmity [strife] between thee [the serpent] and the woman, and between thy seed [the seed of the serpent] and her seed [the seed of the woman]." But woman has no seed; seed always comes from the male. Why then does Genesis say "her seed"? Because God knew that the redemptive seed would be born of woman when she conceived the Messiah by divine conception. "Her seed" was God's creation within woman. This is exactly what it says in Galatians.

> Galatians 3:16:
> Now to Abraham and his seed were the promises made. He saith not, And to seeds, as of many; but as of [to] one, And to thy seed, which [who] is Christ.

Who is the seed of the woman? She has no seed; but by God's creation the seed of the woman is Christ. To be born again is to have that seed of God in Christ in you.

I Peter gives a characteristic of Christ's seed which a person receives when he is born again.

> I Peter 1:23:
> Being born again, not of corruptible seed, but of incorruptible, by the word of God, which liveth and abideth forever.

The first time a person is born, he is born of corruptible seed; but when he is born again he is, according to I Peter 1:23, "born again, not of corruptible seed, but of incorruptible." The reason the word "seed" is not repeated is that this figure of speech puts emphasis upon the incorruptibility of the seed and not on the seed itself.

When it says *incorruptible,* it means *incorruptible.* One might now accuse me of believing in eternal security. I do not believe in eternal security; I believe in eternal life. Had God meant eternal security, He would have said eternal security. He does not mean eternal security, he means life — eternal life — because it is incorruptible and it is seed.

When we were born physically, we had seed in us. When we were born again, we received another seed. The difference is that with the second birth the seed is incorruptible.

How does the new birth occur? How do we have Christ's seed born within us? This original phenomenon occurred on Pentecost; and, since we are still living in that same administration, we are included in and affected by the greatness of that event. Let us study what happened on Pentecost when salvation, the new birth, first became available so we can understand its application to us.

The New Birth

> I John 3:9:
> Whosoever is born of God doth not commit sin;
> for his seed remaineth in him: and he cannot sin,
> because he is born of God.

When one is physically born, he has physical seed in him. Likewise, whoever is born of God must have the seed of God in Christ in him. The Word says, "Whosoever is born of God doth not commit sin." When the natural man is born again, in what part of his being does he not commit sin? In his body and soul he still commits sin; but in that seed of God which is incorruptible, he does not commit sin. Why? "For his seed [the seed of God in Christ] remaineth in him." If the born-again person could sin in that seed, the seed would not remain, it would be corruptible. But the Word says that this seed of God remains.

I John 3:9 states that a born-again person cannot sin because he is born of God. The first time I was born, I was born of my earthly father and mother. But when I was born again I was born of my heavenly Father, of God, and His seed remains in me and in it I cannot sin. That is why His seed is eternal life. It is eternal because God is eternal, and it is life because God is life.

Someone may say, "So you believe 'once saved, always saved.'" I have not read "once saved, always

292

saved" in the Word of God, any more than I have read "eternal security." All I have read in The Word is eternal life, and that I believe.

Eternal life becomes ours as body-and-soul men when we are born again of God's Spirit. What happens to bring this about?

Ephesians 2:5—9:
Even when we were dead in sins [dead because God's spirit is not within], hath quickened us together with Christ, (by grace ye are saved;)

And hath raised *us* up together, and made *us* sit together in heavenly *places* in Christ Jesus:

That in the ages to come he might shew the exceeding riches of his grace in *his* kindness toward us through Christ Jesus.

For by grace are ye saved through faith [the faith of Jesus Christ]; and that not of yourselves: *it is* the gift of God:

Not of works, lest any man should boast.

Salvation is of grace. If it were of works, one person could brag more than another because he had prayed longer or he had begged God more or he had

293

confessed more sins. Therefore one man would have a better salvation than another because he worked harder to get it. Fortunately salvation is not of works; it is by grace and grace alone.

> Ephesians 2:10:
> For we are his workmanship, created in Christ Jesus ....

The first time I was born, I was the workmanship of my father and my mother. When I was born again, I was God's workmanship, the product of my heavenly Father, not in the flesh but in the spirit. Do you think God is satisfied with His workmanship? I know what my earthly parents were able to do; and I am sure that my heavenly Father who created the heaven and the earth, can do better work than my earthly father and mother. "We are his workmanship, created in Christ Jesus." This is the new birth.

After Pentecost a man is still body and soul; he is spiritually dead. To whom does the man of body and soul legally belong? To the Devil. But when a natural man is born again of God's Spirit, he becomes the legal child of his Father Who is God. The Devil, the god of this world, has no legal right over a man when he is born again.

Most Eastern and some Western religions teach that

everybody has the spark of the Divine born in him. A spark of the Divine means that each person has a little bit of God in him and all one has to do is fan it, feed it, nurture it, and God will begin developing within him. The Bible says man is dead; and if a person is dead, he is dead. If there is a little bit of life, a man is not dead. God's Word says man is spiritually dead having only body and soul. Thus if man is to have spiritual life God must create. The word "create" is used because spiritual life has never before been in him.

Romans tells how it is possible for a man who is dead in trespasses and sins and without God and without hope to be made alive.

Romans 10:17:
So then faith *cometh* by hearing, and hearing by the word of God.

What faith? The faith of Jesus Christ. This faith comes when the man of body and soul hears the Word of God and believes.

Romans 10:9:
That if thou shalt confess with thy mouth the Lord Jesus, and shalt believe in thine heart that God hath raised him from the dead, thou shalt be saved.

295

The New Birth

What is it to "confess it with thy mouth"? It is to say it. Does one have to say it at an altar? Romans 10 does not say that. But, could one confess Jesus as his Lord at an altar? It does not say *where* one has to confess Jesus as Lord; the Bible simply says to confess. Does a person have to say it out loud? Romans 10 does not say so; it is possible to confess the Lord Jesus Christ silently without making an audible sound.

"Confess with thy mouth" does not say confess one's sins. If it had said "confess your sins," salvation would be of works; and we are not saved by works, but by grace. A man does not confess his sins; he confesses the Savior from sin, the Lord Jesus Christ.

I wonder how many thousands of people believe that they are born again of God's Spirit but are not. They may have a feeling on the inside that they are saved, but a feeling does not save them. A person is saved by being born again of God's Spirit. Feelings may come and go, but the Word of God lives and abides forever. I could go to the altar, cry out all my sins, and get a good feeling. But a person can get that same good feeling on a psychiatrist's couch. We are not saved by feeling, we are saved by doing what The Word says. It says, "confess with your mouth the Lord Jesus." That is, say, "Jesus, you are Lord in my life." Who has been lord as long as a person is just

296

body and soul? The person himself. But now that person is going to change lordships when he confesses with his mouth a new Lord — Jesus Christ.

That is what it says, but that is not all. Romans 10:9 further says, "and shalt believe in thine heart." The heart is the seat of the personal life; today we would say, "Believe with all your mind, all your strength, every ounce of your being." What is a person to believe? That Jesus Christ is the greatest prophet of all time? No. The Word says, "believe in thine heart that God hath raised him from the dead." One must confess with his mouth Jesus as Lord and believe in the innermost part of his being that God raised Him from the dead; then a man *shall* — absolutely, unquestionably — be saved. When? Not when he dies, but right when he confesses Jesus as Lord and believes that God raised Him from the dead.

Of all the great religious leaders there is only one who has been raised from the dead and that is Jesus Christ. This is the proof that He is God's only-begotten Son. Do you believe that God raised Jesus from the dead? Do you believe that He is your Lord? Have you confessed it with your mouth? The Word says that *you are saved.*

297

The New Birth

> Romans 10:10:
> For with the heart man believeth unto righteousness; and with the mouth confession is made unto salvation.

The moment I fulfill these two requirements, I am born again of God's Spirit. This is eternal life. This is such a tremendous truth that it is almost unbelievable; but I do believe it because God's Word is true and abides forever. Now I am His son for I have confessed with my mouth the Lord Jesus and I have believed that God raised Him from the dead.

The moment a person confesses with his mouth Jesus as Lord that person is converted, saved, born again. A man can be a natural man of body and soul one minute; but as he hears the Word of God and believes to the point that he says, "Jesus is Lord of my life and I know God raised Him from the dead," he is born again of God's Spirit. That person has instantly changed lords; he is now on the way to heaven and all hell cannot stop him from going because he is a son of God having Christ in him. He has eternal life. He is no longer a natural man because he has received the spirit from God.

Having had spirit created in him, the person again has a point of contact with God. Unlike Adam, who had spirit on a condition (as we read in Genesis 2), the born-again sons of God during the glorious

298

Church Administration have spirit born in them as seed. This spirit is given unconditionally.

When a child is physically born, all human potential is in that little package. With nurturing and feeding, the child develops into an adolescent, then into a youth, and finally into an adult. The new birth is like that. When a man is born again of God's Spirit, he has Christ in him. Everything that God is in Christ is in him. He has the love of God, he has the justification of God, the sanctification, the redemption, the righteousness, the faith of Jesus Christ. This is what one receives when he accepts the Lord Jesus Christ as his personal Lord and Saviour.

There is a lot of religion in so-called Christianity today, but true Christianity is not religion. Religion is what man does, what man makes. Christianity is what God wrought in Christ and in a believer when he is born again. Christianity is the work of God, not the work of man. Christianity is the way of a Father with His family. God is our Father and we are His children; He fathered us and we are born again of His seed.

When a man is born again of God's Spirit, this man of body and soul then has spirit. The man did not get rid of his body and soul when he was born again. He still has the five senses as media of learning. The added feature which comes with salvation is that the born-again person has spirit so that he can communicate with God. The believer can now receive information from God by spirit as well as through his senses.

The spirit within man is that which is eternal life.

Salvation is not earned; it is a gift of God.

Romans 6:23:
For the wages of sin *is* death; but the gift of God *is* eternal life through Jesus Christ our Lord.

I John 1:1,2:
That which was from the beginning, which we have heard, which we have seen with our eyes, which we have looked upon, and our hands have handled, of the Word of life;

(For the life was manifested, and we have seen *it*, and bear witness, and shew unto you that eternal life, which was with the Father, and was manifested unto us;)

I John 2:25:
And this is the promise that he hath promised us, *even* eternal life.

I John 5:11,12:
And this is the record, that God hath given to us
eternal life, and this life is in his Son.

He that hath the Son hath life; *and* he that hath
not the Son of God hath not life.

"He that hath the Son hath life." The spirit in him
is eternal life. But "he that hath not the Son" still has
no life. That man has natural life but he has no eternal life.

Verse 12 of I John 5 and several others like it have
caused problems because of the popular teaching that
everyone is heaven-bound and that it does not matter
whom one worships or what one believes because all
people are headed for the same place. The Word still
says that if a person has Christ, he has life; and if he
does not have Christ, he does not have life. If you
want to argue with The Word, go ahead and argue
with it. You must make up your own mind whether
you want to believe God's Word or men's words. This
Word of God and the words in it have stood for centuries. But the words of men whom I have known and
men whom you have known have not stood for
centuries. They come and they go; they are proved
right sometimes and wrong sometimes. I would rather
stake my eternal salvation on the accuracy of God
than listen to men, especially men who have a deroga-
tory attitude toward The Word. I would rather stake

301

my life on the integrity and accuracy of God's Word
than to stake it on what some man said and find out
later that he was wrong. Suppose the Bible is right,
suppose the accuracy of God's Word is true, and suppose that we do not believe it and, in the end, there
turns out to be a heaven. We would never quite make
it. We have everything to win by believing the Word
of God and nothing to lose. We have everything to
lose and nothing to win by believing what men say.
We who have the Son have life.

> I John 5:13—15:
> These things have I written unto you that [who]
> believe on the name of the Son of God; that ye
> may know that ye have eternal life, and that ye
> may believe on the name of the Son of God.
>
> And this is the confidence that we have in him,
> that, if we ask any thing according to his will, he
> heareth us:
>
> And if we know that he hear us, whatsoever we
> ask, we know that we have the petitions that we
> desired of him.
>
> I John 5:20:
> And we know that the Son of God is come, and
> hath given us an understanding, that we may
> know him that is true, and we are in him that is

true, *even* in his Son Jesus Christ. This is the true God, and [this is] eternal life.

The man of body and soul can so easily believe and receive eternal life, which is the greatest gift that God has ever given to man at any place, at any time.

Chapter Twenty
Remission and Forgiveness of Sin

Before going further, we need to clarify the difference between a believer's *standing* and his *state*. These words are most easily illustrated by looking at standing and state in an earthly family. In my earthly family I am a son of Mr. and Mrs. Ernst Wierwille. How long am I going to be a son in that family? As long as I live. That is my standing. What about my standing in my heavenly family? My standing in the family of God, as my standing in my earthly family, is one of a son. How long will I be a son? The spirit is eternal so my standing in the family of God is eternal.

Since my *standing* in my heavenly and earthly families is always one of a *son*, what is my state? My state in the Wierwille family sometimes fluctuated. When I misbehaved, I was still my earthly father's son because he had his seed in me. My *behavior* determined my *state* within the household.

When my father disapproved of my behavior and

305

my state needed uplifting, I would go to my father and say, "Dad, I'm sorry." Dad always accepted my apologetic gestures. My sonship had no bearing whatsoever upon what I did; but my state was directly affected by my actions.

What about a son of God? At the moment a person is born again, he is in perfect alignment and harmony with his heavenly Father. But, as a hypothetical situation let us say, after I was born again, since I had not been taught much about the Word of God, I continued to sin. When I was saved, all sins previously committed were wiped out; but soon I had some new ones. How could I get back into perfect fellowship with God? The same way I got back into my earthly father's graces. I said to my heavenly Father, "Father, I am sorry that I sinned and did not live according to your Word." Then I was in harmony with Father once more.

It is not enough for *God in Christ* to be *in you,* but *you* must be *in Him.* Christ in you is sonship (standing), but you in Christ is fellowship (state). I John points out how a person regains fellowship with his spiritual Father.

> I John 1:9:
> If we confess our sins, he is faithful and just to forgive us *our* sins, and to cleanse us from all unrighteousness.

This verse has nothing whatsoever to do with being saved or gaining sonship. This verse is telling of re-establishing fellowship after salvation. To confess one's sin is not salvation. (To confess the Savior is salvation.) "If we confess our sins, he is faithful and just to forgive us *our* sins, and to cleanse us from all unrighteousness." Which sins are we to confess? Those that we have committed after being saved. I can remember those because I have just committed them. I do not have to remember every one for the past ten or twenty years.

When I confess my sin, He cleanses me of all unrighteousness, sin committed after salvation. Every time we sin, we should confess our sin so that we remain in fellowship with our Father, so that our state with Him is in perfect harmony. The reason many people are not having their prayers answered is that they suffer from broken fellowship. When we have confessed our broken fellowship and are in good stead with God, we can pray and get our prayers answered. Then we can walk before God and the petitions we ask of Him will be fulfilled. Christ in us (salvation) and we in Christ (fellowship) determine the abundance of our Christian life.

Let us study *confession* in its accurate usage. There are two types of confession: unto salvation and to reestablish broken fellowship. The word "confess" in Romans 10:9 — is repentance unto salvation. After the Church was started on the day of Pentecost, Peter preached a tremendous sermon. He closed in Acts 2:38, "Then Peter said unto them, Repent ...." He didn't say repent of your sins. "To repent" is simply to confess the Lord Jesus and believe that God raised Him from the dead. Peter told them to repent "... and be baptized every one of you in the name of Jesus Christ for the remission of sins ...." When one repents, what happens? He receives remission of sins. When a person receives remission of sins, he becomes a son of God.

Repentance is for the unsaved sinner. He repents by confessing with his mouth the Lord Jesus Christ, the Savior from sin. How many times can a person repent? Let us read the definite answer from Hebrews.

> Hebrews 6:4—6:
> For *it is* impossible for those who were once enlightened, and have tasted of the heavenly gift, and were made partakers of the Holy Ghost,
>
> And have tasted the good word of God, and the powers of the world to come,
>
> If they shall fall away, to renew them again unto

repentance; seeing they crucify to themselves the Son of God afresh, and put *him* to an open shame.

These verses are used to teach just the opposite from what they say. People who wrongly divide The Word propound that if a person who once was saved becomes a sinner he can never get saved again. These verses do not even suggest such erroneous doctrine. What is impossible according to these verses? To renew the sinners again unto repentance. If a person could repent a second time, it would have to be a renewal. It says very plainly that it is impossible to renew a saved man again to repentance.

How many times can a man get saved? How many times can he repent? Once. How many times can a person be physically born? Nicodemus asked that question, can one enter a second time into his mother's womb and be born again? Likewise, it is impossible once a person is born again of God's Spirit to be renewed again unto repentance because he cannot become unsaved. It is impossible to be renewed unto repentance because repentance is a one-time event. The seed of Christ which is implanted at the moment of salvation is eternal.

After confessing the Savior from sin (repentance), confession of sin brings the saved person back into fellowship.

> II Corinthians 7:10:
> For godly sorrow worketh repentance to salva-
> tion not to be repented of ....

If one could be saved a second time, he would have
to be able to repent of having repented the first time.
How silly it becomes.

I used to demonstrate this in the classes with a
glass of water. The glass represented the body; the
water inside represented the soul. I put a little white
button on a string in the water and told my class that
this is now the seed of Christ, which the Bible says is
eternal life. Then I would illustrate what most people
think is eternal life: Today I confess with my mouth
all my sins. In goes the button, the seed of Christ.
Now I am saved. But tomorrow morning I have a bad
thought. Oops! God takes out the button, His spirit.
Then I am just body and soul, unsaved again. I feel
badly and I wait for the next revival to come. At the
next revival I go to the altar and I confess my sin and
in comes the spirit again. On and on it goes. My
earthly father did better than that. He put his seed in
me once and I am still his son. What about God
almighty?

It is devilish teaching to say that a person who is

born again of God's Spirit has the spirit removed with every evidence of human frailty. My heavenly Father did His part so well that I am His son as long as I live. As Victor Paul Wierwille I am not going to live forever; but as God's son, I have His life, which is eternal.

Repentance is one type of confession. The second type of confession is for mending broken fellowship. Sinning after salvation results in broken fellowship. We should not sin, but the good Lord knows that every man of body and soul will be tricked by the Devil and will sin. So God made a way out of sin, broken fellowship, for His sons. He made it possible that when we break fellowship, we can confess our sin of broken fellowship to Him and then He gives us forgiveness of sin.

I John speaks of fellowship and confession of broken fellowship.

I John 1:3—10:
That which we have seen and heard declare we unto you, that ye also may have fellowship with us: and truly our fellowship *is* with the Father, and with His Son Jesus Christ.

And these things write we unto you, that your

311

joy may be full. [Not half full, not two-thirds full, but full.]

This then is the message which we have heard of him, and declare unto you, that God is light, and in him is no darkness at all.

If we say that we have fellowship with him [God], and [we] walk in darkness, we lie, and do not the truth:

But if we walk in the light, as he [God] is ... the light, we [God and I] have fellowship one with another, and the blood of Jesus Christ his Son cleanseth us from all sin [broken fellowship].

If we say that we have no sin [broken fellowship], we deceive ourselves, and the truth is not in us.

If we confess our sins [broken fellowship], he [God] is faithful and just to forgive us *our* sins [broken fellowship], and to cleanse us from all unrighteousness.

If we say that we have not sinned [broken fellowship], we make him [God] a liar, and his word is not in us.

God said that everybody sins. Do we sin in the

spirit? No. But in body and soul we fall. God says that if any man claims not to sin, he is a liar, he makes God a liar, and God's Word is not in him.

I John 2:1:
My little children, these things write I unto you, that ye sin not [break fellowship]. And [but] if any man sin [break fellowship], we have an advocate [defender or mediator] with the Father, Jesus Christ [Who is our defender?] the righteous.

Remember the word "backsliding"? People are always saying, "Now be careful, brother, that you don't backslide." The word "backsliding" is never used in the New Testament. It is only used by un-instructed teachers, ministers and theologians who do not read The Word and consider to whom various parts of it are written. The word "backsliding" does not appear in the Epistles because we are sons of God, and a son cannot backslide. A son can get out of fellowship with God, a son can walk in darkness; but a son cannot backslide so far that he is no longer a son.

In the Old Testament Abraham was a servant of God. The Bible does not say that Abraham was a son of God; for in order to have a son, one must have seed and the seed was not available until Christ came.

313

The New Birth

This is the reason men in the Old Testament were not sons of God. Abraham was a servant of God and Moses was a servant of God because sonship was not yet available. A servant can backslide. In your household, a servant can slide back so far that you may fire him. But you cannot fire your son. He is still your son.

From time to time in the Old Testament, Israel is referred to as a son. But reading it carefully, one will see that Israel is not a son by birth but by adoption. If you adopt someone, he does not have your blood in him; he does not have your seed in him. Only through adoption did God take in Israel. Backsliding was possible during the Law Administration, but it is impossible during the administration of the Church.

Now we are sons of God because of birth.

Galatians 4:6,7:
And because ye are sons, God hath sent forth the Spirit of his Son into your hearts, crying, Abba, Father.

Wherefore thou art no more a servant, but a son; and if a son, then an heir of God through Christ.

We are not servants, but sons. We are in a much better position than a servant. Yet look at what Isaac and Jacob did as servants. What about you and me as

314

sons? Do we not have more ability, more rights in the household than servants? The Church is living so far below par that it is pitiful. Remember what some of the servants in the Old Testament did? How much more a son ought to be able to do.

Galatians 4:7 says that since we are sons, we are therefore heirs of God. A son of God is an inheritor of everything his Father has. How much does God have? We are heirs of God and joint-heirs with Christ, according to Romans 8:17. This is truly abundance.

315

Chapter Twenty-one
The Unforgivable Sin

In studying the new birth and fellowship with God, we should look at the accuracy of the Word of God on the related topic of the unforgivable sin. This subject is clearly defined in God's Word but still many people are in darkness.

The unforgivable sin is also called in the Word of God the sin or blasphemy against the Holy Ghost. All the Gospels have records of this sin.

Matthew 12:31,32:
Wherefore I say unto you [Jesus is speaking to the heads of the temple, the Pharisees], All manner of sin and blasphemy shall be forgiven unto men: but the blasphemy *against* the *Holy* Ghost shall not be forgiven unto men.

And whosoever speaketh a word against the Son of man, it shall be forgiven him: but whosoever speaketh against the Holy Ghost, it shall not be

317

forgiven him, neither in this world, neither in the *world* to come.

Mark 3:28,29:
Verily I say unto you [Pharisees and Sadducees], All sins shall be forgiven unto the sons of men, and blasphemies wherewith soever they shall blaspheme:

But he that shall blaspheme against the Holy Ghost hath never forgiveness, but is in danger of eternal damnation.

Luke 12:10:
And whosoever shall speak a word against the Son of man, it shall be forgiven him: but unto him that blasphemeth against the Holy Ghost it shall not be forgiven.

The men to whom Jesus was referring had committed the sin against the Holy Ghost, the unforgivable sin. To understand the unforgivable sin, we have to note that there are two seeds as told in Genesis.

Genesis 3:15:
And I will put enmity between thee and the woman, and between thy seed and her seed ....

Genesis 3:15 indicates two seeds — the seed of the serpent and the seed of the woman. Previously we

318

saw "her seed" to be the seed of Christ and "thy seed" to be the seed of the serpent. To see the result of these two seeds planted in man, let us take a hypothetical John Doe. He is born of body and soul, a natural man. He has no spiritual seed in him. When this man of body and soul confesses with his mouth the Lord Jesus and believes that God raised Him from the dead (Romans 10:9,10), he is born again with God's seed (Christ) in him. Having this seed in him, John Doe is body, soul and spirit with the love of God and eternal life.

However, there is another possibility for John. Rather than confessing Jesus as Lord, he believes the Devil is the true god. Then John Doe, a man of body and soul, is born again of the seed of the serpent. He is born again of seed, and seed cannot be removed. Because this seed cannot be removed, it is an unforgivable sin.

When John Doe accepts the Devil as god, he is born again of the seed of the serpent, the seed of the Devil. He then has the hate of the Devil, even as he who accepts the God and Father of the Lord Jesus Christ has the love of God. One man has eternal death, while the man born again of God's seed has eternal life. The households of the two gods are complete opposites. There are two seeds and two antithetical essences.

It is possible for a man of body and soul to go

319

through life and never accept either god. A person does not always make this choice. But if he does choose, he has only two alternatives. He can either accept the Lord Jesus Christ as his personal Lord or accept the Devil. If he accepts the Devil he is born again of the seed of the serpent, it is unforgivable (unrepentable) because a person cannot get rid of seed. It is permanent.

We have read accounts in Matthew, Mark, and Luke about blaspheming against the Holy Ghost. The fourth Gospel, John, also contains a record.

John 8:13—15:
The Pharisees therefore said unto him, Thou [Jesus] bearest record of thyself; thy record is not true.

Jesus answered and said unto them, Though I bear record of myself, *yet* my record is true: for I know whence I came, and whither I go; but ye cannot tell whence I come, and whither I go.

Ye judge after the flesh [according to the senses] ....

John 8:19:
Then said they [the Pharisees] unto him [Jesus], Where is thy Father? Jesus answered, Ye neither know me, nor my Father: if ye had

known me, ye should have known my Father also.

John 8:21—23:
Then said Jesus again unto them [the Pharisees], I go my way, and ye shall seek me, and shall die in your sins: whither I go, ye cannot come.

Then said the Jews, Will he kill himself? because he saith, Whither I go, ye cannot come.

And he said unto them, Ye are from beneath; I am from above: ye are of ["of" indicates the possessive case] this world.

Who is the god of this world? The Devil. John 8 says very plainly that they were *of* the Devil. If a person is *of* something, he has the seed within.

John 8:33:
They answered him, We be Abraham's seed, and were never in bondage to any man ....

John 8:37—44:
I [Jesus speaking] know that ye are Abraham's seed [Abraham's physical seed]; but ye seek to kill me, because my word hath no place in you.

I speak that which I have seen with my Father:

and ye do that which ye have seen with your father. [There are two fathers indicated here.]

They answered and said unto him, Abraham is our father. Jesus saith unto them, If ye were Abraham's children, ye would do the works of Abraham.

But now ye seek to kill me, a man that hath told you the truth, which I have heard of God: this did not Abraham.

Ye do the deeds of your father. Then said they to him, We be not born of fornication; we have one Father, *even* God. [They forgot to say which god.]

Jesus said unto them, If God were your Father, ye would love me: for I proceeded forth and came from God; neither came I of myself, but he sent me.

Why do ye not understand my speech? *even* because ye cannot hear my word. [Why?]

Ye are of *your* father the devil ....

"Ye are of *your* father the devil." They were born of the wrong seed. These Pharisees were born of the

322

seed of the serpent and that is the unforgivable sin.

When a man is born again of God's Spirit, he has the seed of God and cannot repent of it. When a man, on the other hand, chooses to be born of the seed of the serpent and confesses the Devil as his god, he is born of the seed of the serpent and he cannot repent of that either. A person can never undo the seed which is within.

One who is born again of God's seed has eternal life and the love of God. One who is born again of the seed of the Devil has eternal death and the hate of the Devil. Neither of these can be repented of. Once confession is made, the result is permanent.

The Word of God clearly defines the two spirit worlds. We who believe God need not err and wander about in darkness; we need to study God's Word to see its precise accuracy. The understanding of the new birth is basic to a believer's realization of what he is in Christ Jesus. This knowledge gives a believer assurance in his standing in the household of God and the confidence to keep his relationship with God in good stead. Being a son of God and having direct communication with God Almighty, every man should desire to manifest the more abundant life.

Part V

Power in Christ Jesus

Chapter Twenty-two
Renewing One's Mind

With the new birth, a man during the Church Administration is in a better position than Adam because Adam had spirit upon a condition. For those of us who received God's spirit after Pentecost, the spirit is given unconditionally. Adam, however, had one advantage: he started life with a perfectly renewed mind.

Now, under the Church Administration when a person is born again, he has the same mind he had before salvation. God works with spirit because that is His realm; man works with mind and flesh because that is his realm. After salvation, the mind of man must be renewed by the man himself if he is to release the spiritual power he received from God.

What does it mean to "renew one's mind"? It means "to hold The Word in mind and act accordingly." The Greek word for the renewed mind is literally translated "transfigured" or "transformed," *meta-*

morphoō. Believers are to get a new form, a new figure in mind. Romans 12 gives basic information on this topic.

> Romans 12:1,2:
> I beseech you therefore, brethren, by the mercies of God, that ye present your bodies a living sacrifice, holy, acceptable unto God, which is your reasonable [religious] service.
>
> And be not conformed to this world: but be ye transformed by the renewing of your mind, that ye may prove what *is* that good, and acceptable, and perfect, will of God.

How is a person to prove what is that good and acceptable and perfect will of God? By renewing his mind.

> Romans 13:14:
> But put ye on the Lord Jesus Christ ....

"Put ye on the Lord Jesus Christ." This is works. It cannot be referring to salvation because salvation comes by grace — "not of works, lest any man should boast." Where can a man put Him on? In the mind. Paul says, "Put ye on the Lord Jesus Christ" in the mind.

Ephesians 4:22, 23:
That ye put off concerning the former conversation the old man, which is corrupt according to the deceitful lusts;

And be renewed in the spirit [life] of your mind.

What is the "old man"? The old man is a figure of speech meaning the old ways which a person had before being born again. The old man is as old as the person himself.

Ephesians 4:24:
And that ye put on the new man, which after God is created in righteousness and true holiness.

The spirit is the new man. It is not as old as the man; this a person receives only when he is born again.

One renews his mind by putting in his mind that which God created in righteousness and then living it. When a person has done this, it is possible for him to walk by the power of God for now he has a mind coordinated and in harmony with his spirit.

Ephesians 4:25:
Wherefore putting away lying, speak every man

329

truth with his neighbour: for we are members one of another.

Ephesians 4:27—30:
Neither give place to the devil.

Let him that stole steal no more: but rather let him labour, working with *his* hands the thing which is good, that he may have to give to him that needeth.

Let no corrupt communication proceed out of your mouth, but that which is good to the use of edifying, that it may minister grace unto the hearers.

And grieve not the holy Spirit of God, whereby ye are sealed unto the day of redemption.

What is it to "grieve the holy Spirit of God"? What is the context? Ephesians is speaking of the renewed mind. To grieve the Holy Spirit of God is for a person not to renew his mind after being born again of God's Spirit — to keep the same *old* mind he had before — to continue stealing, lying, cheating and corruptly communicating.

Ephesians 4:31,32:
Let all bitterness, and wrath, and anger, and

clamour, and evil speaking, be put away from you, with all malice:

And be ye kind one to another, tenderhearted, forgiving one another, even as God for Christ's sake hath forgiven you.

Why is it that we sometimes find it difficult to forgive? Because we do not realize what God forgave us. This is part of the renewed mind.

All the Church Epistles refer again and again to the renewed mind.

Philippians 2:5:
Let this mind be in you, which was also in Christ Jesus.

That is the renewed mind. Christ always did the will of the Father. He always carried out His Word perfectly. When we let His mind be in us which was in Christ Jesus, we will have a perfectly renewed mind.

Colossians 3:5—11:
Mortify [make dead] therefore your members which are upon the earth; fornication, uncleanness, inordinate affection, evil concupiscence [lust], and covetousness, which is idolatry:

For which things' sake the wrath of God

331

cometh on the children of disobedience:

In the which ye also walked some time, when ye lived in them.

But now ye also put off all these; anger, [Quit being angry.], wrath, malice, blasphemy, filthy communication out of your mouth.

Lie not one to another, seeing that ye have put off the old man with his deeds;

And have put on the new *man*, which is renewed in knowledge after the image of him that created him:

Where there is neither Greek nor Jew, circumcision nor uncircumcision, Barbarian, Scythian, bond *nor* free: but Christ *is* all, and in all.

The power of God in Christ is also in a person who receives His spirit, the new birth. But for earthly practical purposes, one's power remains dormant until activated by his renewing the mind and acting with the renewed mind. Then the power becomes manifested in the senses realm.

Colossians 3:12–17:
Put on therefore, as the elect of God, holy and

beloved, bowels of mercies, kindness, humbleness of mind, meekness, longsuffering;

Forbearing one another, and forgiving one another, if any man have a quarrel against any: even as Christ forgave you, so also *do* ye.

And above all these things *put on* charity [the love of God in the renewed mind], which is the bond of perfectness.

And let the peace of God rule in your hearts, to the which also ye are called in one body; and be ye thankful.

Let the word of Christ dwell in you richly [in your mind] in all wisdom; teaching and admonishing one another in psalms and hymns and spiritual songs, singing with grace in your hearts to the Lord.

And whatsoever ye do in word or deed, *do* all in the name of the Lord Jesus, giving thanks to God and the Father by him.

To renew one's mind, a person must start at the beginning. First, he must confess the Lord Jesus Christ and believe that God raised Him from the dead. Then he must put God's thoughts in his mind as

333

Power in Christ Jesus

God expressed Himself in His Word. How is a person going to learn to walk with the greatness of the power of God unless he begins to put God's Word in his mind and tries to live by it? One learns to live this Word by simply walking by The Word.

A person must study the Word of God, not what people say around The Word or about The Word. What does *God* say? As I tell many of the people in my classes: get rid of your other reading material for a while and read the Word of God. If, for the next three months, you give your life primarily to reading and studying the Epistles that are addressed to you and then apply the principles by renewing your mind, three months from now you won't recognize yourself. You will be such a dynamic person. You will be manifesting the renewed mind and having your prayers answered. You will see signs, miracles and wonders.

Live The Word. To put it in your mind is not enough; you have to act upon it; you have to work at it. This process of building Christ in your mind is a deliberate process that you must do by your freedom of will. You determine that you are going to send the information from God's Word to your mind and that you are going to live it. To live by believing means to walk day by day and moment by moment by the revealed Word of God. The decision remains with you

334

whether you are going to walk by the senses or by the revealed Word of God. If you walk by the revealed Word of God, you will manifest the greatness of the power of God.

Chapter Twenty-three
Knowing One's Sonship Rights

No person is able to walk confidently in the renewed mind until he recognizes his legal position in
Christ. One has to know his sonship rights. I am a son
of God, born again of God's Spirit. What does this
sonship mean to me? To understand this I will have
to know what I received when I was redeemed, what I
got when God justified me. I must find out what is
righteousness, what is sanctification, and what is the
ministry of reconciliation. All these things I must
understand if I am going to walk with the greatness
and the power of God.

Previously we have studied redemption and sonship. We read that we are heirs of God and joint-heirs
with Jesus Christ. We know that with redemption we
have God's incorruptible seed born within and thus
have eternal life. Now, what about the other benefits?

Romans 5:19:
For as by one man's [Adam's] disobedience

many were made sinners, so by the obedience of
one [Jesus Christ] shall many be made
righteous.

If God through Jesus Christ makes a person righteous, then he is righteous.

I Corinthians 1:30:
But of him [God] are ye in Christ Jesus, who of
God is made unto us wisdom, and righteousness,
and sanctification, and redemption.

If God has given these things unto us, we have
Christ's wisdom, His righteousness, His sanctification,
and His redemption.

The word "sanctified" means "to be set apart."
Before a man is born again of God's Spirit, he is a
man of body and soul, that's all. But when he is born
again, he is set apart by God for heaven and all hell
can't stop him from going.

After being set apart for heaven, what comes with
justification, righteousness, and other sonship rights?

Philippians 3:9:
And be found in him, not having mine own
righteousness, which is of the law [If you keep
the Ten Commandments, you are not found in

338

Him, having your own righteousness of the law.], but that [righteousness] which is through the faith of Christ, the righteousness which is of God by faith.

How righteous is God? He is Righteous. Then spiritually a believer is as righteous — as free from sin — as God. That is what The Word says.

Romans speaks of justification or release from penalty of sin. The context concerns Jesus Christ.

Romans 4:25:
Who was delivered for our offences, and was raised again for our justification.

The "original" text reads, "Who was delivered for our offenses and was raised again when we were justified." We were completely released from the penalty of sin when God raised Him. Romans 3 tells that just as no man is made righteous by the law, neither is a man justified thereby.

Romans 3:20:
Therefore by the deeds of the law there shall no flesh be justified in his sight: for by the law *is* the knowledge of sin.

No flesh is justified in God's sight by the law. So

339

no matter how hard a man works at keeping the law, no matter how many times he gets down on his knees and prays till sunrise, he is not going to be justified by these sincere actions.

Romans 3:21—25:
But now the righteousness of God without the law is manifested, being witnessed by the law and the prophets;

Even the righteousness of God *which is* by [the] faith of Jesus Christ unto all and upon all them that believe: for there is no difference:

For all have sinned, and come short of the glory of God;

Being justified freely [not reluctantly or hesitantly] by his grace through the redemption that is in Christ Jesus:

Whom God hath set forth *to be* a propitiation through faith in his blood, to declare his righteousness for the remission of sins that are past, through the forbearance of God.

Romans 5:1:
Therefore being justified by faith, we have peace with God through our Lord Jesus Christ.

Being justified by the faith of Jesus Christ, we have peace. Peace is not something to be worked for; we get it when we receive Him. We are at peace with Him. If we renew our minds, we will be peaceful and act peaceably because we have the peace of God.

Romans 5:6—9:
For when we were yet without strength, in due time Christ died for the ungodly.

For scarcely for a righteous man will one die: yet peradventure for a good man some [men] would even dare to die.

But God commendeth his love toward us, in that, while we were yet sinners, Christ died for us.

Much more then, being now justified by his blood, we shall be saved from wrath through him.

How can people teach that Christians have to go through the tribulation as recorded in the book of Revelation? Romans pointedly states that we have been saved from the wrath to come.

Romans 5:10:
For if, when we were enemies, we were recon-

341

ciled to God by the death of His Son, much more, being reconciled, we shall be saved by his life.

Look at II Corinthians 5:17. "Therefore if any man *be* in Christ, *he is* a new creature." It does not say "Christ in you." Christ in a person is salvation; a person in Christ is the renewed mind, one's fellowship with Him.

II Corinthians 5:17,18:
Therefore if any man *be* in Christ, *he is* a new creature: old things [in one's mind] are passed away; behold, all things are become new [in a person's mind to the extent that he is in Christ, fellowship].

And all things *are* of God, who hath [past tense] reconciled us to himself by Jesus Christ, and hath given to us the ministry of reconciliation.

In the Gospels Jesus had the ministry of reconciling men to God. Jesus said, "I will build my church." In the Church Administration the born-again believers, you and I have this responsibility. If He gave us the ministry of reconciliation, we are responsible for its utilization, its operation, its working. We who have the ministry of reconciliation can sit down and do nothing. But unless others are told

342

about the new birth, about the holy spirit and its manifestations, unless they are told what their sonship rights are, they'll never know. Now you and I have this ministry.

II Corinthians 5:19:
To wit, that God was in Christ, reconciling the world unto himself, not imputing their trespasses unto them; and hath committed unto us the word of reconciliation.

What good is it for me to have the ministry of reconciling you to Christ unless I have The Word to tell you how to be reconciled, how to get saved, how to be filled with the holy spirit, how to operate the manifestations, how to believe to get your prayers answered, how to walk? Notice that God has not given the word of reconciliation to us; He has committed it to us. If He committed it, completely gave it over to us, God limited Himself in this administration to you and to me.

II Corinthians 5:20,21:
Now then [not when we die, but right *now*] we are ambassadors for Christ, as though God did beseech *you* by us: we pray *you* in Christ's stead, be ye reconciled to God.

For he [God] hath made him [Jesus] *to be* sin

343

for us, who knew no sin; that we might be made the righteousness of God in him.

Verse 20 says, "Now then we are ambassadors for Christ ...." Why not act like one? If the President of the United States called you to be an ambassador, you would go out and buy a new tuxedo and a black tie. You would get yourself a new umbrella and a new top hat, new luggage, and the other accessories. Why? Because you had been appointed to represent the best side of your nation.

When you are born again of God's Spirit, The Word says you are an ambassador for Christ. Do you know how the average Christian ambassador looks? He looks weighted down with all the sins of the world and completely whipped as he "bears his cross." He is unenthusiastic, glum and washed out. Do not be surprised when the rest of the world isn't standing around waiting to hear this ambassador's message. He couldn't entice a mouse to a garbage can let alone interest the secular world in their reconciliation with God. If it is such a hard job to be a Christian, not many people are going to be impressed by his emaciated example.

When are we going to believe our sonship rights? Why not walk down the streets in our communities, in our cities, in our towns, in our various sections of the country with our shoulders back and our head held high and say, "I am a son of God. I am an ambassador for the Lord Jesus Christ. How are you this morning? Well, *I* am wonderful!" We have become so accustomed to seeing the average Christian sullen and defeated that nobody projects the attitude of God's ambassador with sonship rights. You and I are what the Word of God says we are, we have what the Word of God says we have, and we will be what the Word of God says we will be. And *it* says that we are sons of God.

> I John 3:2:
> Beloved, now are we the sons of God, and it doth not yet appear what we shall be: but we know that, when he shall appear, we shall be like him; for we shall see him as he is.

Besides being ambassadors, we as believers also are called as messengers, witnesses, soldiers and workmen. As messengers we are, as Epaphroditus was, to minister to others' needs.

> Philippians 2:25:
> Yet I supposed it necessary to send to you Epaphroditus, my brother, and companion in labour, and fellowsoldier, but your messenger, and he that ministered to my wants.

As witnesses we are to tell others of Christ. Our

345

responsibility as witnesses is very extensive and challenging.

Acts 22:15:
For thou shalt be his witness unto all men of what thou hast seen and heard.

Acts 1:8:
But ye shall receive power, after that the Holy Ghost is come upon you: and ye shall be witnesses unto me both in Jerusalem, and in all Judea, and in Samaria, and unto the uttermost part of the earth.

As soldiers of Christ, we are not to become unduly involved in the trivia of this life, as II Timothy warns.

II Timothy 2:3,4:
Thou therefore endure hardness, as a good soldier of Jesus Christ.

No man that warreth entangleth himself with the affairs of *this* life; that he may please him who hath chosen him to be a soldier.

But we are to wage a good war as I Timothy admonishes.

I Timothy 6:12:
Fight the good fight of faith, lay hold on eternal life, whereunto thou art also called, and hast professed a good profession before many witnesses.

The figurative language of soldiers and soldiering is found throughout the Bible. Perhaps the most critical advice to us as warriors of Christ is given in Ephesians.

Ephesians 6:12:
For we wrestle not against flesh and blood, but against principalities, against powers, against the rulers of the darkness of this world, against spiritual wickedness in high *places.*

Ours is a spiritual, not a physical battle. Therefore we must equip ourselves with spiritual armor to fight evil powers.

Ephesians 6:13:
Wherefore take unto you the whole armour of God, that ye may be able to withstand in the evil day, and having done all, to stand.

As workmen we labor with God, as I Corinthians tells.

I Corinthians 3:9:
For we are labourers together with God: ye are

God's husbandry, *ye are* God's building.

We labor at many aspects of the Christian life; but our most fundamental responsibility as workmen is the basis of this book.

II Timothy 2:15:
Study to shew yourself approved unto God, a workman that needeth not to be ashamed, rightly dividing the word of truth.

Besides being ambassadors, messengers, witnesses, soldiers and workmen, we have been given the ministry of reconciliation and committed the word of reconciliation. When are we going to declare what The Word says without worrying about what the neighbors may say? We have to renew our minds to what The Word says, not to our neighbors.

This is why Christ died; this is why God gave His only-begotten Son. You and I ought to have the courage to declare what the Word of God says. Look at Colossians.

Colossians 2:6,7:
As ye have therefore received Christ Jesus the Lord, *so* walk ye in him:

Rooted and built up in him, and stablished in

348

the faith, as ye have been taught, abounding therein with thanksgiving.

Ephesians 1:17–23:
That the God of our Lord Jesus Christ, the Father of glory, may give unto you the spirit of wisdom and revelation in the knowledge of him:

The eyes of your understanding being enlightened; that ye may know what is the hope of his calling, and what the riches of the glory of his inheritance in the saints,

And what *is* the exceeding greatness of his power to us-ward who believe, according to the working of his mighty power,

Which he wrought in Christ, when he raised him from the dead, and set *him* at his own right hand in the heavenly *places,*

Far above all principality, and power, and might, and dominion, and every name that is named, not only in this world, but also in that which is to come:

And hath put all *things* under his feet, and gave him *to be* the head over all *things* to the church,

Which is his body, the fulness of him that filleth all in all.

Having the renewed mind while standing on our sonship rights is the exceeding greatness of His power to us who believe. When we put the mind of Christ in our minds and begin living His way, not only will our lives be abundant but the lives of others will be changed by our ministry of reconciliation.

Chapter Twenty-four
The Five Ministries in the Church

On the day of Pentecost the Church was established. To each member — to everyone who has believed, does believe, or will believe in Jesus Christ — has been committed the ministry of reconciling others to God. Besides this overall commitment which was made, God specifically designated gift ministries to the Church. The purpose of these ministries is to enable believers to walk with the power of God while adding new members to the Body and keeping the old members in fellowship. The five gift ministries are set forth in Ephesians 4. Before beginning to read, notice that verses 9 and 10 are in parentheses. A parenthesis is a figure of speech inserted as an explanation. So for the sake of clarity let us read verse 8 and skip to verse 11 to continue the direct point.

Ephesians 4:8 and 11:
Wherefore he saith, When he ascended up on high, he led captivity captive and gave gifts unto men.

351

Power in Christ Jesus

> And he [God in Christ] gave some, apostles; and
> some prophets; and some, evangelists; and some,
> pastors and teachers.

Some people contend that when the New Testament apostles died, there were no more apostles or prophets. This cannot be the case because God said that "When he [Christ] ascended up on high, he led captivity captive, and gave gifts" to the Church. We live during the Church Administration so these gifts must still be given to us. Ephesians says that He gave (1) apostles, (2) prophets, (3) evangelists, (4) pastors and (5) teachers. If there are any pastors left, there must be some apostles; if there are any teachers left, there must be some prophets; if there are any evangelists left, there´ must be some apostles, prophets, pastors and teachers.

Before we go any further, let me define the five gift ministries:

An *apostle* is one who brings new light to his generation. It may be old revelation, but it is new to the generation to whom he speaks.

A *prophet* is one who speaks for God to God's people. He is not an evangelist; he works within the body of believers. A prophet is a man who speaks to God's people to get them back to God's Word and

352

back to the fellowship which the Father ordained.

An *evangelist* is one who wins the lost, the unsaved, to Christ by teaching them the new birth and seeing them born again.

A *pastor* is one who cares for the individual needs within the Church. He cares for the flock.

A *teacher* expounds the accuracy of God's wonderful matchless Word to the believers.

Ephesians 4:11 says that God gave apostles, prophets, evangelists, pastors and teachers. Then verse 12 tells for what purpose He gave them.

> Ephesians 4:12:
> For the perfecting of the saints, for the work of the ministry, for the edifying of the body of Christ.

These ministries cannot be for the spiritual perfecting of the saints because spiritually the saints are perfect. As we learned before, saints have Christ within. But the ministries were given for the perfecting of the saints in their walk in the renewed mind. These ministries are for building and maintaining the body of Christ.

Verse 13 of Ephesians 4 tells how long these

353

Power in Christ Jesus

ministries will exist.

> Ephesians 4:13:
> Till we all come in the unity of the faith, and of the knowledge of the Son of God, unto a perfect man, unto the measure of the stature of the fulness of Christ.

When will this time be? I Corinthians 13 tells us that this will be when Christ returns. Then we shall see Him as He is and we shall be like Him for He has bought us and called us and gathered us. Until the time of the return, we have apostles, prophets, evangelists, pastors and teachers in the Church for the perfecting of the saints and the edifying of all believers.

> Ephesians 4:14—16:
> That we *henceforth* be no more children, tossed to and fro, and carried about with every wind of doctrine, by the sleight of men, *and* cunning craftiness, whereby they lie in wait to deceive;
>
> But speaking the truth in love, may grow up into him in all things, which is the head ... Christ:
>
> From whom the whole body fitly joined together and compacted by that which every joint supplieth, according to the effectual working in

354

the measure of every part, maketh increase of the body unto the edifying of itself in love.

"That we *henceforth* be no more children." We ought to grow up and not be babies that have to be nurtured on the bottle for a lifetime.

These are the reasons the ministries have been given to the Church. The Church is to be built up and not "... carried about with every wind of doctrine; by the sleight of men, *and* cunning craftiness, whereby they lie in wait to deceive." You and I as sons of God are to know what we have in Christ Jesus and be capable of walking with the efficacy and the power of God in our life. We have apostles, prophets, evangelists, pastors and teachers to help us in our abundant life in Christ Jesus.

> Hebrews 4:16:
> Let us therefore come boldly [not hesitantly] unto the throne of grace, that we may obtain mercy, and find grace to help in time of need.

We go boldly to our Father and we say, "Father, you know my need, and I thank you for its fulfillment even at this present moment." We must learn to stand firmly on our legal rights as sons of God. Romans 8:17 tells us that we are "heirs of God, and joint-heirs with Christ." If the Church shares fully in

355

everything which Christ has inherited, we as members of the Church have tremendous wealth. The Aramaic text in Colossians 2:10 says, "We are completely completely absolutely complete in Him." How then can we be lacking anything?

Chapter Twenty-five
The Holy Spirit and Fruit of the Spirit

The last preparation which Jesus Christ made before His ascension was to instruct His apostles about the coming of what we call Pentecost, the day on which the Church was founded. With the establishment of the Church, the promise of the Father was given. Acts 1 states these events.

Acts 1:4,5 and 8:
And, being assembled together with *them*, commanded them that they should not depart from Jerusalem, but wait for the promise of the Father, which, *saith he*, ye have heard of me.

For John truly baptized with water; but ye shall be baptized with the Holy Ghost not many days hence.

But ye shall receive power, after that the Holy Ghost is come upon you: and ye shall be witnesses unto me both in Jerusalem, and in all

357

Judea, and in Samaria, and unto the uttermost part of the earth.

The Church was given great ability with the coming of the inherent power of the holy spirit. Before studying the Word of God to see what is meant by the holy spirit, let us first clarify the difference between the Giver, Holy Spirit, and the gift, holy spirit.

At this point a law is involved. God cannot give mashed potatoes and gravy or books or houses. God can only give that which He is. Since God is Holy Spirit, He must give this as His gift. On Pentecost He gave holy spirit. The same words are used in the critical Greek text and in the Aramaic; and these texts have not differentiated between the Giver and His gift. That is where the confusion has come in. God is Holy Spirit with a capital *H* and a capital *S*; His gift which was given on the day of Pentecost was *pneuma hagion* which is holy spirit and should always be translated with a lower case *h* and a lower case *s*. God gave what He is – Holy and Spirit; His gift is the power from on high, holy spirit.

Since this gift is spirit, it cannot be seen, heard, smelled, tasted or touched. How then can I know by my senses what I received when God put His spirit in me and made me a being of body, soul and spirit? From God's Word. God's Word tells me what I have

358

received and then I deliberately put it in my mind and begin to act on the knowledge of His Word. As I act, I see the manifestations of the spirit in the senses world.

The Holy Spirit gives one gift to a receiving believer, but this one gift has nine parts or manifestations. There are no more and no less than nine manifestations of the spirit. These are set forth in I Corinthians 12.

> I Corinthians 12:7—10:
> But the manifestation of the Spirit is given to every man to profit withal.
>
> For to one is given by the Spirit the word of wisdom; to another the word of knowledge by the same Spirit;
>
> To another faith by the same Spirit; to another the gifts of healing by the same Spirit;
>
> To another the working of miracles; to another prophecy; to another discerning of spirits; to another *divers* [different] kinds of tongues; to another the interpretation of tongues.

The gift from the Holy Spirit was given on Pentecost and is as readily available in our times as it was

359

to the apostles for we all belong to the Church of
God. The gift comes with an individual's acceptance
of Christ as his Lord according to Romans 10:9. The
book of Acts and the Pauline Epistles are constantly
making reference to the power of the holy spirit or
else demonstrating the power which those men of
God knew they had. The reason we see so little (if
any at all) manifesting of the spirit today is that we
have never been taught. We have the gift, holy spirit,
but the manifestations must be operated by us; and
this most believers know nothing about.

The manifestations are divided by their usage into
three groups: (1) inspirational manifestations; (2) informative manifestations; (3) power impartation manifestations. The characteristics of the manifestations
suggest the names. The following will be a brief
definition of what the nine manifestations do for
those who operate them.

I. Utterance, Speaking, Worship, Inspirational
    Manifestations

    1. Speaking in tongues — bringing forth a mes-
       sage from God in a language unknown to the
       speaker which will edify the spirit. Speaking
       in tongues is to be used in private prayer life
       unless the message is interpreted in a believ-
       ers' meeting.

2. Interpretation of tongues — interpreting the speaking in tongues in a believers' meeting. It edifies, exhorts and comforts the body present as God gives the utterance to the speaker and the speaker brings it forth.

3. Prophecy — bringing forth in a believers' meeting a message from God in the language of the people present, a message that will edify, exhort and comfort them.

II. Revelation, Information, Instructional, Knowing Manifestions

1. Word of knowledge — receiving information from God concerning any given situation about which the believer by his five senses cannot know.

2. Word of wisdom — receiving instruction by the believer on what to do with the information which he has received through word of knowledge.

3. Discerning of spirits — receiving information by a believer concerning the presence, non-presence, and identity of spirits; if the spirits be evil, they can then be cast out in the name of Jesus Christ.

Power in Christ Jesus

III. Action, Power, Impartation Manifestations

1. Faith (believing) — manifesting the faith of Jesus Christ which makes it possible for a believer to bring to pass the impossible at the believer's command according to the revelation of word of knowledge, word of wisdom, and/or discerning of spirits.

2. Miracles — bringing about in the name of Jesus Christ phenomena which exceed the natural law.

3. Healing — ministering healing in the name of Jesus Christ to restore, to cure, to make sound or whole, or to physically reconcile. This manifestation is not prayer for the sick.

It is urgent, if we are going to have the power which Jesus Christ made available, that we study God's Word and begin evidencing the nine manifestions of the holy spirit.

The gift, holy spirit, is not the fruit of the spirit spoken of in Galatians 5, just as fruit is not a manifestion or a gift. Fruit is the result of the manifestion of the spirit. First a person has to receive spirit and then he has to manifest the power of the spirit in the senses world that finally the fruit will be produced.

362

The Holy Spirit and Fruit of the Spirit

Galatians 5:22, 23:
But the fruit of the Spirit is love, joy, peace, longsuffering, gentleness, goodness, faith.

Meekness, temperance: against such there is no law.

If we have been born again and are manifesting the gift of the holy spirit, we are producing love, joy, peace, longsuffering, gentleness, goodness, faith, meekness and temperance. Our evidencing the fruit of the spirit indicates the quality of our Christian walk.

With the knowledge of our sonship rights and having the renewed mind combined with the operation of the manifestations of the holy spirit producing fruit of the spirit, we are certainly more than victorious.* We certainly can be powerhouses! We need not wait any longer for we have the power to manifest the more abundant life now.

*Wierwille, Victor Paul, *Receiving the Holy Spirit Today* (American Christian Press, New Knoxville, Ohio).

Epilogue

As a final word to students of The Word, notice that the Pauline Epistles have a pattern in their message to the Church. The first revelation to the Church is the book of Romans. The next record is Corinthians. Corinthians was written to correct the practical error that crept into the Church because they failed to adhere to the revelation in the book of Romans. Once a person moves away from the truth of a revelation, he begins practicing error; after practicing error for a while, the error becomes his doctrine. The book of Galatians corrects the doctrinal error that had crept into the Church because they had practiced error as noted by Corinthians.

After Romans, Corinthians and Galatians comes Ephesians. Ephesians is a great revelation to the Church. Philippians, like Corinthians, corrects the practical error that crept into the Church due to its failure to adhere to the revelation given in the book of Ephesians. Then Colossians corrects the doctrinal error which crept into the Church due to the wrong

365

Power for Abundant Living

practice of Ephesians.

I and II Thessalonians stand by themselves because they speak about the return of Christ and the gathering together. Read the Epistles in the light which I have just shared and new vistas of understanding will become apparent to you.

Ephesians advises in chapter 6, "Finally, my brethren, be strong in the Lord ..." It does not tell us to be strong in what a theologian may say or in what a Bible teacher may say. If the theologian says what The Word says, if the teacher says what The Word says, then you have to be strong in what they say because of The Word, not because of the men.

Ephesians 6:10:
Finally, my brethren, be strong in the Lord, and [be strong] in the power of his might.

Verse 11 then begins by admonishing the believer to put on the whole armor of God. Never be satisfied with just being a minimal Christian. Be clothed with the whole armor. You are going to have to speak in tongues frequently in your private prayer life; you are going to have to speak in tongues and interpret in believers' meetings; you are going to have to bring forth words of prophecy in a believers' meeting; you are going to have to learn how to receive word of

366

knowledge, word of wisdom and discerning of spirits, so that you can carry out faith (believing), miracles and healing in your day-by-day living.

> Ephesians 6:11, 12:
> [You] Put on the whole armour of God, that ye may be able to stand against the wiles [trickery] of the devil,
>
> For we wrestle not against flesh and blood, but against principalities, against powers, against the rulers of the darkness of this world, against spiritual wickedness in high *places* [from on high].

Our fight, our battle, is not with John Doe or our neighbor or the minister. Our fight is always a spiritual one encountering spiritual powers, wickedness and evil spirits, who are trying to counterfeit God. "We wrestle not against flesh and blood, but against spiritual powers."

> Ephesians 6:13:
> Wherefore take unto you the whole armour of God, that ye may be able to withstand in the evil day, and having done all ... stand.

Remain steadfast on God's Word, for God's Word is God's Will and it means what it says and says what it means. God has a purpose for everything He says,

367

where He says it, why He says it, how He says it, and to whom He says it. Stake your knowledge and trust in God for He alone is your solid foundation.

Ephesians 3 is my prayer and benediction for you as you walk in the abundant life of God's powerful Word.

Ephesians 3:16–21:
That he [God] would grant you, according to the riches of his glory, to be strengthened with might by his Spirit in the inner man;

That Christ may dwell in your hearts by faith; that ye, being rooted and grounded in love,

May be able to comprehend with all saints what *is* the breadth, and length, and depth, and height;

And to know the love of Christ, which passeth knowledge, that ye might be filled with all the fulness of God.

Now unto him that is able to do exceeding abundantly above all that we ask or think, according to the power that worketh in us,

Unto him *be* glory in the church by Christ Jesus throughout all ages, world without end. Amen.

About the Author

Victor Paul Wierwille has spent a lifetime, over forty years, searching out the truths of God's Word. As part of his search he consulted and worked with many outstanding individuals in Christian studies for keys to power-filled, victorious living. Such men as Karl Barth, Joseph Bauer, Glenn Clark, Karl J. Ernst, Josiah Friedli, Louis C. Hessert, Elmer G. Homrighausen, E. Stanley Jones, George M. Lamsa, Richard and Reinhold Niebuhr, K.C. Pillai, Paul Tillich, Ernst Traeger, and many others, aided Dr. Wierwille in his quest to find the truths of the Word of God.

Dr. Wierwille's academic career includes Bachelor of Arts and Bachelor of Theology degrees from Mission House (Lakeland) College and Seminary, graduate studies at the University of Chicago and at Princeton Theological Seminary, where he earned the Master of Theology degree in Practical Theology. Later he completed his work for the Doctor of Theology degree.

For over forty years, Dr. Wierwille has devoted his major energies to intensive research and teaching of the accuracy of God's Word. Since 1953 he has taught Biblical research and teaching classes on Power

369

for Abundant Living. He is the founder and first president of The Way International, a nonsectarian, nondenominational Biblical research, teaching, and fellowship ministry. He is noted as founder and first president of several colleges and learning centers, including The Way College of Biblical Research, Indiana Campus; Camp Gunnison, The Way Family Ranch; and LEAD Outdoor Academy International. He is also past president of The Way College of Emporia.

As Dr. Wierwille perseveres in his research of the Word of God, he continues to write more research works and to develop further classes in Biblical studies, including The University of Life outreach courses, an international Biblical studies correspondence school. As a dynamic teacher and lecturer, he travels worldwide to hold forth the greatness of God's Word.

The Way International reaches out with the accuracy of God's Word to all parts of the United States and the world—helping people to receive power for abundant living.

HANDY HINTS

A FAMILY HANDYMAN BOOK

Copyright © 2024 Home Service Publications, Inc.,
a subsidiary of Trusted Media Brands, Inc.
1610 N. 2nd St., Suite 102, Milwaukee, WI 53212-3906

ISBN: 979-8-88977-000-8
Component number: 119100116H

Content Director: Mark Hagen
Creative Director: Raeann Thompson
Senior Editor: Julie Kuczynski
Editors: Christine Campbell, Sara Strauss
Associate Creative Director: Kristen Stecklein
Art Director: Anna Jo Beck
Deputy Editor, Copy Desk: Dulcie Shoener
Copy Editor: Suchismita Ukil
Associate Assigning Editor: Mary Flanagan

We are committed to both the quality of our products and the service we provide
to our customers. We value your comments, so please feel free to contact us at
TMBBookTeam@TrustedMediaBrands.com.

Text, photography and illustrations for *Family Handyman Handy Hints* are
based on articles previously published in *Family Handyman* magazine
(familyhandyman.com).

PHOTOGRAPHY AND ILLUSTRATION CREDITS
47-49, 128-131 Steve Bjorkman; **83** Tina Sargeant; **102** Rick Oddo; **138** Scott
Thompson; **157** Mike Peterson; **170** *tr, cr, br,* **172** Jeff Gorton; **209** Michael Winter;
Chapter openers/hexagon pattern carduus/Getty Images

All other photographs by Trusted Media Brands, Inc.

A NOTE TO OUR READERS
All do-it-yourself activities involve a degree of risk. Skills, materials, tools
and site conditions vary widely. Although the editors have made every effort
to ensure accuracy, the reader remains responsible for the selection and
use of tools, materials and methods. Always obey local codes and laws,
follow manufacturer instructions and observe safety precautions.

PRINTED IN CHINA
1 3 5 7 9 10 8 6 4 2

SAFETY FIRST—ALWAYS!

Tackling home improvement projects and repairs can be endlessly rewarding. But as most of us know, with the rewards come risks. DIYers use chain saws, climb ladders and tear into walls that can contain big and hazardous surprises.

The good news: Armed with the right knowledge, tools and procedures, homeowners can minimize risk. As you go about your projects and repairs, stay alert for these hazards:

ALUMINUM WIRING

Aluminum wiring, installed in millions of homes between 1965 and 1973, requires special techniques and materials to make safe connections. This wiring is dull gray, not the dull orange characteristic of copper. Hire a licensed electrician certified to work with it. For more information, go to *cpsc.gov* and search for "aluminum wiring."

SPONTANEOUS COMBUSTION

Rags saturated with oil finishes like Danish oil and linseed oil, and oil-based paints and stains can spontaneously combust if left bunched up. Always dry them outdoors, spread out loosely. When the oil has thoroughly dried, you can safely throw them in the trash.

VISION AND HEARING PROTECTION

You should wear safety glasses or goggles whenever working on DIY projects that involve chemicals, dust, or anything that could shatter or chip off and hit your eye. Sounds louder than 80 decibels (dB) are considered potentially dangerous. Sound levels from a lawn mower can be 90 dB, and shop tools and chain saws can be 90 to 100 dB.

LEAD PAINT

If your home was built before 1979, it may contain lead paint, which is a serious health hazard, especially for children age 6 and under. Take precautions when you scrape or remove it. Contact your public health department for detailed safety information or call 800-424-LEAD (5323) to receive an information pamphlet. Or visit *epa.gov/lead*.

BURIED UTILITIES

A few days before you dig in your yard, have your underground water, gas and electrical lines marked. Just call 811 or go to *call811.com*.

SMOKE AND CARBON MONOXIDE (CO) ALARMS

The risk of dying in reported home structure fires is cut in half in homes with working smoke alarms. Test your smoke alarms every month, replace batteries as necessary and replace units that are more than 10 years old. As you make your home more energy-efficient and airtight, existing ducts and chimneys can't always successfully vent combustion gases, including potentially deadly carbon monoxide (CO). Install a UL-listed CO detector, and test your CO and smoke alarms at the same time.

FIVE-GALLON BUCKETS AND WINDOW-COVERING CORDS

Anywhere from 10 to 40 children a year drown in 5-gallon buckets, according to the U.S. Consumer Products Safety Commission. Always store them upside-down and store those containing liquid with the covers securely snapped.

According to Parents for Window Blind Safety, hundreds of children in the United States are injured every year after becoming entangled in looped window treatment cords. For more information, visit *pfwbs.org*.

WORKING UP HIGH

If you have to get up on your roof to do a repair or an installation, always install roof brackets and wear a roof harness.

ASBESTOS

Texture sprayed on ceilings before 1978, adhesives and tiles for vinyl and asphalt floors before 1980, and vermiculite insulation (with gray granules) all may contain asbestos. Other building materials made between 1940 and 1980 could also contain asbestos. If you suspect that materials you're removing or working around contain asbestos, contact your health department or visit *epa.gov/asbestos* for information.

CONTENTS

CHAPTER 1

CLEANING

TRASH BAG DISPENSER

You can build a simple dispenser for trash bags using ½-in. pipe and a few fittings. Screw a floor flange to the cabinet, thread a 3-in.-long pipe nipple into the flange and then thread a 90-degree elbow onto the nipple. Next, cut a vertical pipe to be a bit longer than the width of the roll of bags. Thread the vertical piece into the elbow and slip on the roll.

Under-Cabinet Cleanup

When the floor of your sink cabinet needs a refresh, lay down squares of self-adhesive vinyl tile. The inexpensive squares are available at home centers and provide an easy-to-wipe-clean surface.

Peel-and-stick tile

Damaged cabinet bottom

Countertop Gap Filler

If crumbs, papers or even flatware pieces fall into the gap between your countertop and refrigerator, fill the void with nearly invisible plastic tubing. Clear tubing is available at home centers in several widths, starting at 1/8 in.

SCUFF MARK ERASER

Clean shoe scuff marks from vinyl flooring with a clean, dry tennis ball. Just a light rub erases heel marks.

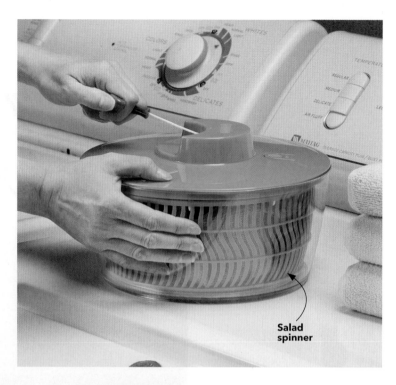

Salad spinner

Hand-Spin Laundry

For hand-washed clothing that shouldn't go in the dryer, you can remove excess water with a salad spinner. Then either lay the clothing flat or hang it on a rack to dry.

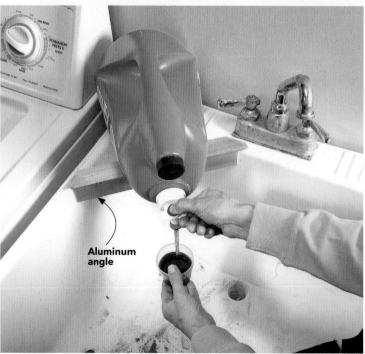

Aluminum angle

Minimize Liquid Detergent Mess

"Dripless" liquid detergent containers always drip just a little. Keep the mess under control with a special shelf on the corner of the laundry tub. Cut a 1½-in. aluminum angle long enough to support the front edge of the container, then glue the angle to the tub with silicone caulk. Rest the container on the ledge so drips just fall into the laundry tub instead of creating a gooey mess somewhere else.

BLEACH AWAY STAINS

Remove stubborn stains from marble, cultured marble or plastic laminate with a bleach-soaked paper towel. Cover the towel with a cup to contain the bleach odor and leave it in place overnight. If the stain has faded but not disappeared, just repeat the process. Test this trick in a hidden area first; it could discolor the surface.

Pressure

SPRAY BOTTLE SOLUTION

It's frustrating when you have to pump 20 times to get a spray bottle to start spraying! If no spray comes out after a few pumps, try squeezing the bottle while pumping. This forces the liquid up the draw tube and primes the pump right away.

Marker Cleanup

When a permanent marker has ended up in the wrong hands, vegetable oil can clean it off lots of surfaces—even skin! Wipe the area with a damp cloth afterward and then you're done.

Long-Reach Vacuum

A PVC pipe connected to a vacuum hose lets you reach high spots or narrow crevices so you can suck up cobwebs around skylights or dust bunnies behind radiators. In the plumbing aisle, pick up a 10-ft. piece of PVC pipe as well as PVC and rubber reducer couplings that will allow you to connect your vacuum hose to a different-size pipe.

SQUEAKY-CLEAN VASES

It's difficult to clean out the cloudy residue left in slim flower vases. But you can make any vase sparkle by adding warm water and a denture cleaning tablet. Let it fizz for a few minutes and then rinse the vase well.

FLASHLIGHT GLASS FINDER

Cleaning up broken glass is a real pain, but it's nothing compared with a glass shard in the foot. Get a flashlight and turn off the overhead lights. Scan the floor with the flashlight from a low angle and the shards will glisten—even the littlest pieces will stand out.

Easy Pill Removal

Keep your sweaters looking new by shaving off pills with a standard electric razor—just make sure it's on the lowest setting.

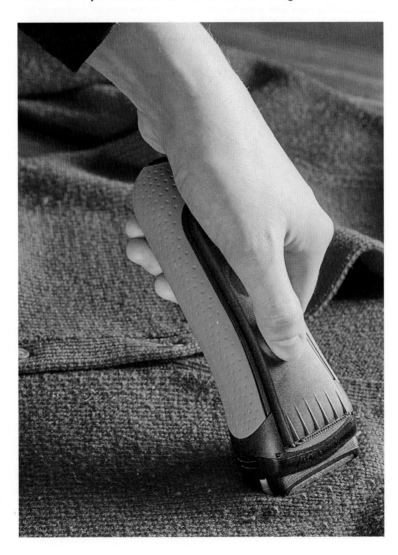

Dust Catcher

Hanging lots of paintings and photos means drilling lots of holes for wall anchors, which in turn means lots of dust on the floor. You can catch all that dust with a sticky note folded in the middle and stuck to the wall just under where you plan to drill. The paper will keep all the dust off the floor and off any furniture below.

Duct tape

Anything that hardens

EASY TOOL CLEANUP

Wrap your putty knife or trowel with duct tape when you're mixing grout, thin-set or anything else that hardens. The duct tape makes cleanup a breeze— just tear it off before the compound gets crusty. A little WD-40 will clean away any adhesive residue.

GARBAGE BAG HOLDER-UPPER

Tired of the garbage bag slipping down into the trash can? Cut out the middle of the lid with a utility knife and just snap the outer rim over the bag to keep it in place. This works well for recycling, but it's not so great for stinky stuff!

Trash Can Cleanup

Try using a liquid toilet bowl cleaner to wash the inside of a dirty trash can. The liquid will cling to the sides for better cleaning. Then use a toilet brush to reach down inside. Be sure to rinse the can well.

No-Mess Epoxy Mixer

For quick, thorough mixing of two-part epoxy, put the components into a plastic bag and knead them together with your fingers. Punch a small hole in the bag to make a neat dispenser.

GET THE GUNK OFF DRILL BITS

The heat produced during drilling causes resin to build up on drill bits. Resin-coated bits cut poorly, heat up and get dull faster. To remove resin, spray a bit with oven cleaner and let it soak for a couple of minutes. Then scrub it with a toothbrush and rinse it with water.

Oven cleaner

Drill bit

OVERHEAD RAG STORAGE

If your shop happens to be in a basement, you can store all sorts of things in the ceiling—the handiest may be a box of paper shop towels. A box of 200 towels can fit neatly between the floor joists above a workbench. Just reach up and pull one down to wipe up errant glue or stain.

Furniture Stripping Helper

When stripping old paint or varnish, how do you get rid of the stuff once it's on your putty knife? Cut a semicircular opening in the side of an empty gallon jug, then clean the loaded scraper on the flat edge of the hole. When you're done, upend the jug and use the neck of the jug as a funnel to pour the stripper into another container. The stripper will be ready for reuse.

Hose
to shop
vacuum

Less-Mess Tile Cutting

If you're cutting tile using a grinder, build yourself a vacuum bucket. Drill a hole the same size as your vacuum's hose into the side of the bucket, near the bottom. As you're cutting tile over the bucket, the vacuum will capture most of the dust.

BETTER METAL SHAVINGS COLLECTION

You can easily collect metal fragments by putting a magnet next to a drill bit. But the shavings can be difficult to remove from the magnet when you're done. Here's an easy way to solve the problem: Put the magnet in a plastic bag. When you've collected all the shavings, stand over a trash can and remove the magnet from the bag. All the shavings will fall into the trash and the magnet will be clean.

OUTDOOR SANDING STATION

To keep the fine dust out of your garage when sanding, build an outdoor sanding station. This sturdy plywood shelf has threaded hooks on the back edge that clip into eye bolts screwed into garage wall studs. The front of the shelf is suspended by chains (or cords) that are attached to eye bolts at the front corners and then snapped into eye bolts placed high on the garage wall. You can position the shelf at a comfortable height for your back. The temporary sanding station goes up and down quickly, and it keeps the dust outside.

Weed-Whacking Chaps

String trimmers leave your yard looking great—and your work pants and boots stained something fierce. Here's a slick solution: Cut the legs off a pair of old sweatpants, then slide them upside down over your work pants. The elastic bands will hold them up over your knees. Measure carefully before snipping your sweats so they drape nicely over your shoes. You'll be the fashion setter for all the other weed whackers on the block.

No-Spill Fluid Jugs

To avoid getting more windshield washer fluid on the tank than in it, store washer fluid in an empty laundry detergent bottle with a built-in funnel. Not only will you get a cleaner pour, but the detergent bottle is much sturdier than the flimsy one the fluid comes in and it won't leak in your trunk.

Bumper Sticker Release

The heat from a hair dryer softens adhesive, making bumper stickers, price tags and other labels easy to pull off. Start at one corner and pull slowly, allowing the heat to loosen the sticker.

CARGO LINER

Always carry a tarp in your car to protect against messy cargo (or occupants). To make the tarp stay put, use self-adhesive hook-and-loop fasteners such as Velcro. Apply the hook part of the fastener to the tarp—the hook side will cling to most car interiors, so it isn't necessary to use the loop side.

MESS-FREE PAINTING AND EASY CLEANUP

Simple tricks make painting jobs a breeze

Pre-Paint Lotion

Coat your face and arms with lotion before a painting project, and the spatter will easily wash off your skin.

WET YOUR BRUSH FOR NO-FUSS CLEANUP

Built-up dried paint near the ferrule is tough to clean off. To prevent this, wet the bristles with water before you paint and dab off the excess on a paper towel. For oil-based paints, use paint thinner.

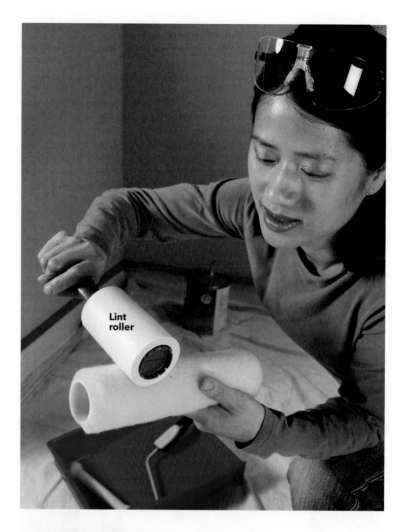

Lint roller

LINT-FREE PAINT ROLLER

The cheapest paint rollers shed all over the paint as you roll it on, but you can treat these rollers as if they're disposable, which means no cleanup! Before using a cheap roller, swipe it with a self-adhesive lint roller to remove all the loose fuzz—no more picking fuzz off a wet wall.

Coffee Can Drip Control

Coffee cans are great for dispensing paint if you cut a small section from the plastic lid and press it on the rim. Use the cut edge of the lid to scrape off excess paint from the brush so it won't drip.

Mess-Proof Painting

A plastic-wrapped case that holds 24 bottles of water is a perfectly sealed tray for your paint cans, brushes and trays. When you're opening the water bottle package, cut the plastic about 5 in. higher than the top of the box and then fold it in. Sloshed or dripped paint will spill into the tray instead of onto the dropcloth, so it won't be tracked all over the house.

Bottled water cases

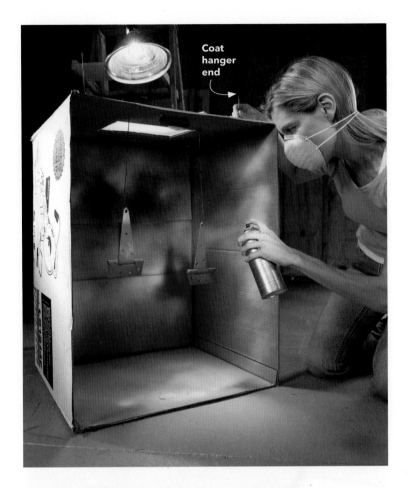

Coat hanger end

CARDBOARD SPRAY BOOTH

Prevent paint overspray with this clever spray booth made from a cardboard box. To illuminate your project, cut a hole in the top of the box, cover the opening with plastic wrap, and position a shop light above the box.

You can use coat hangers, poked through the cardboard, to hold and rotate the objects as you're painting them. Not only will your shop be neater, but your paint projects will now be thumbprint free.

PERFECT PAINT SHIELD

Aluminum roof flashing makes for a great paint shield. It's rigid, so you can actually get it under the baseboard and completely isolate your carpet from the baseboard. It comes in 10-ft. lengths at home centers, and you can cut it to any length you want. Plus, it is bendable, keeps its shape and is reusable. For safety, tape the sharp edges.

Don't Fill the Rim

Pouring paint from a can always results in paint filling the rim. Then when you tap the lid back on, paint splatters everywhere. To prevent this, just put a strip of painter's tape across the rim of the can before you pour.

Roller Spinner

To spin-dry a mini roller, chuck a ¼-in. bit into your drill. Slip the roller onto the bit and pull the trigger. Centrifugal force whips the water right out. Do this in a bucket, in a utility sink or outdoors.

A PET COMB FOR PAINTBRUSHES

If you're looking for a good-quality paintbrush comb, go to a local pet store and purchase a steel pet comb. They're inexpensive and really strong, and they do a great job of cleaning brushes.

SAVE A PAINTBRUSH

If you've fossilized a paintbrush by forgetting to clean it, don't throw it out. Quality paintbrushes aren't cheap, so try to rescue it first.

Pick up a quart of brush cleaner at a paint or hardware store, and pour some into a glass or metal container. Drill a ⅛-in. hole through the brush so you can suspend it by a stiff wire. The brush cleaner gives off nasty, flammable vapors, so cover the container with a plastic bag and set it in the garage or outside, out of reach of children and pets.

After the brush has soaked for a day or two, most of the paint will have come off. Now, pour fresh brush cleaner into another container and slosh the brush around to wash out the remaining paint. Let both containers sit overnight. The paint will settle to the bottom as sludge, so you can pour most of the brush cleaner back into the can, ready to rescue another brush. This method works on oil- or water-based finishes of any type.

Stiff wire

⅛" hole

Unclog a Nozzle

When a spray nozzle is clogged—or partially clogged so the paint just sputters out—soak it in a jar of acetone or nail polish remover. Use a glass jar since these strong solvents will destroy some types of plastic. Cap the jar and let the solvent work for a few hours.

Simple Paint Tray Cleanup

Here's the lazy way to clean a paint tray: Finish painting and let the wet paint tray dry overnight. The next day, start in one corner of the tray and just peel off the dried paint in a single sheet. This works best with a new plastic paint tray and when there's a reasonable layer of paint left in the tray. The method saves water and elbow grease!

Utility Sink Shelf

To make paint cleanup easier, cut a section of leftover wire shelving and set it over the front of your utility sink. It's the perfect place to dry sponges, foam brushes and roller covers. Just hang the paintbrushes from S-hooks so they can drip right into the sink. When you're done with the shelf, hang it over the side of the tub so it's ready for the next painting project.

GREAT GOOFS

Enjoy (and learn from) these reader-submitted stories

"AIR" ON THE SIDE OF CLEAN

During a hot spell, I finally decided to install the window air conditioner that had been sitting unused in my garage for five years. My wife suggested I clean it thoroughly before installing it. But since it had been wrapped up in the garage, I figured a light surface cleanup would be enough. After straining and sweating to install the unit in the window, I turned it on, expecting a delicious blast of cold air. I got the cold air all right. But the mouse droppings, dead bugs and spiderwebs weren't exactly "delicious." **–Harry Kashuck**

Turn Off the Bubble Machine!

While waiting for our new house to be built, my wife and I moved in with my in-laws. Not being familiar with their garage, I grabbed a blue bottle of what looked like windshield washing fluid to fill the empty reservoir in my car. It was a particularly cold day, and when I hit the washer button, nothing happened. I assumed the stuff had frozen. The next day was considerably warmer, so when the windshield got dirty, I hit the washer button again. Bubbles squirted all over my car and drifted onto the surrounding cars as I sped down the interstate. When I returned home, I grabbed the bottle and read closely. I had filled the reservoir with car wash concentrate! **–Dave McDaniel**

DUST DEVIL

I was feeling like Johnny-on-the-spot to be so promptly vacuuming up dust from the drywall that I'd sanded in the morning—until my sister started shouting, "Turn it off!" I turned to see a huge cloud of dust in the air. After earlier taking care of a water spill with the wet/dry vacuum, I'd forgotten to reinstall the dust filter.
–Michael Drefchinski

"I DID WHAT YOU SAID, DAD"

My bathroom sink stopped up and I had to take off the trap to pull out a clog of gunk. I removed the trap and caught the scummy, soapy, toothpaste goobery, hairy water in a bucket. I then positioned myself under the pipe to look up and make sure that all the gunk was out of the drain. I handed the bucket of water up to my 4-year-old son and asked him to get rid of it. He did what seemed perfectly natural to him—he poured it down the sink! All of the slimy water came right back in my face with a vengeance.
–Lindsay Gerard

Panel Remover

While I was enjoying a Sunday nap, my overly ambitious girlfriend removed the kitchen cabinet doors, took them out back and lined them up against the fence. I awoke to the sound of my 3,000-psi pressure washer's engine. I reached the backyard just as she squeezed the trigger and almost instantly blasted the panels out of a few doors. I just laughed—hard! Those doors were ugly anyway. **–Larry Dullock**

CHAPTER 2

ORGANIZATION

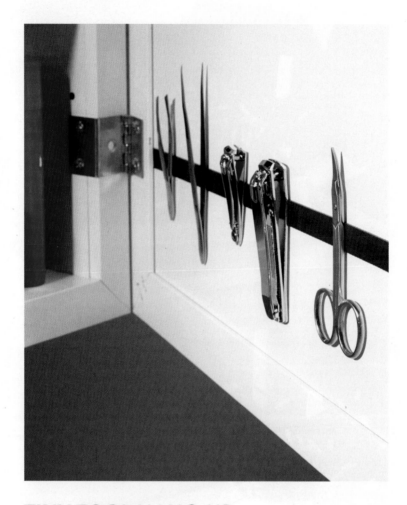

TINY TOOL HANG-UP

If you have a pedestal sink in your bathroom, you may not have any drawers available for storing small grooming tools such as tweezers, nail clippers and manicure scissors. Try this handy solution for your medicine cabinet. Purchase a strip of magnetic tape at the hardware store. It sticks to smooth surfaces, and the magnet can hold small metal items. When you need more gripping power, use two parallel strips!

His-and-Hers Shower Shelves

If you need more than shampoo and a bar of soap in the shower, here's how to provide space for all your vital beauty potions: Get a couple of those shelves that are designed to hang from a shower arm and hang them on cabinet knobs. Use No. 8-32 hanger bolts to screw the knobs into studs or drywall anchors.

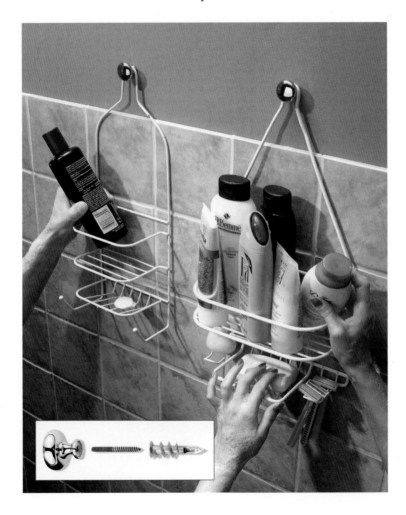

Make Your Own Lazy Susan

Lazy Susans can be very useful, but they can also be expensive, and sometimes those available in stores are too large for a cabinet anyway. Make your own lazy Susan with two matching pie tins and marbles. Just spread a single layer of marbles in the bottom tin and set the other tin on top. It spins just like the store-bought variety does!

Marbles

OVER-THE-SINK
PAPER TOWEL HOLDER

In a cramped laundry area, sometimes it is hard
to keep the roll of paper towels on the shelf from
falling into the sink. Solve this problem by slipping
a bungee cord through the roll and hanging it
from a nearby wire shelf. It works great!

TOOL APRON STORAGE

Tool aprons can be modified to store nearly any household item. First, sew a variety of pocket widths in the aprons. Then drive screws through a wood strip placed at the top of each apron and right into a door for easy access. For hollow-core doors, use hollow anchor fasteners to hold the screws firmly to the door.

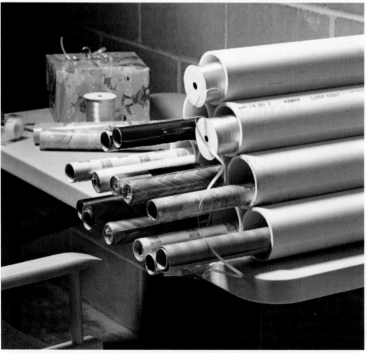

GIFT WRAP RACK

Wrapping lots of gifts can leave you with lots of clutter. To corral all your stray rolls of gift wrap and ribbon, make a rack by gluing together 30-in.-long pieces of 3-in. PVC waste pipe with all-purpose PVC glue. Leave the rack set up on a table in a craft room or the basement.

S-Hook Hang-Up

Turn any closet into a useful hang-up storage space by adding S-hooks to wire shelving. The hooks provide tidy storage for dustpans, brooms and other cleaning tools.

S-hook

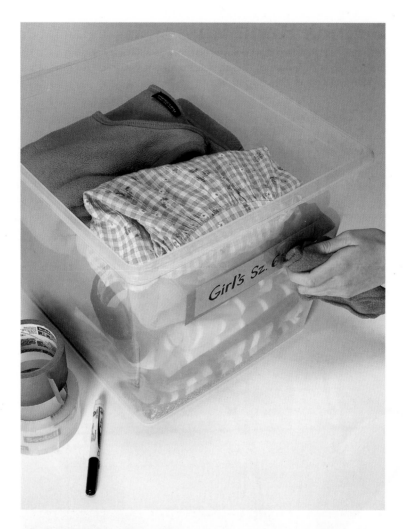

Erasable Tape

When you need to continually update labels on items such as storage boxes, create erasable labels. Put a piece of clear tape over masking tape and write on it using a dry-erase marker. The ink will wipe off easily, so be careful not to smear it.

TUCKED-AWAY IRONING BOARD

Ordinary coat hooks on the back of a closet door keep your ironing board out of the way but close at hand.

HOLIDAY LIGHT STANDS

Storing dozens of holiday light strings each year without wrecking them is tough. But here is a winning method. Just screw a dowel to each end of a wooden base cut to the size of a large plastic bin. Then wrap your lights around the dowels in a figure eight and place the stand in the bin. You'll be amazed how many light strings you can wrap around the stands without tangles or damage.

Perfect Paint Storage

Use a wide-mouthed laundry detergent bottle to store paint instead of the original paint can. Each bottle has a convenient handle and a no-drip pour spout, and the cap seals tight. The next time you need the paint, just shake the bottle well and you're ready to go.

Bread bag tag

Modem

Identify Cables with Bread Tags

The little plastic tags used to close bread bags are handy for identifying the cables on your computer components. Write the name of the device on the tag and slip it around the cable. No more wondering which cable belongs to which device.

Cord Control

Tame that cord jungle under your desk with a length of ½-in. foam pipe insulation. Paint it the color of your wall, and it will virtually disappear.

CHALKBOARD PAINT

Chalkboard paint is fantastic for creating reusable labels on metal bins, jars, drawers and a ton of other things. When you change the contents, just wipe off the chalk and rewrite the label.

You can apply chalkboard paint directly to most nonporous surfaces. Or make your own adhesive and magnetic labels by covering mailing labels and refrigerator magnets with the paint.

Chalkboard paint is available in spray-on and brush-on versions at home centers and hardware stores.

Rebar

Plumbing straps

EASY-ACCESS TARPS

Storing tarps can be a hassle. Big tarps are heavy, and smaller tarps get wedged behind or underneath things. A simple solution is to store them between your garage rafters or basement floor joists. Cut two rebar sections and cover them with plastic conduit cut short enough to roll freely between the joists. Mount the rebar to the framing using plumbing straps. The rolling conduit lets you slide your folded tarps easily into the joist cavity and down again whenever you need them.

Simple Gutter Shelving

Vinyl rain gutters make perfect storage shelves for long, thin items
such as molding pieces, light lumber boards, pipes and certain tools.
Simply screw a wraparound support bracket to each wall stud and
snap each gutter into place.

Double-Duty Shelf Brackets

Shelf brackets designed to support clothes hanger rods aren't just for closets. The rod-holding hook on each bracket comes in handy in the garage and workshop too. You can bend each hook to suit long tools or cords. The shelf brackets are available at home centers and hardware stores.

SIMPLE SPIRAL HOSE STORAGE

Here's a handy tip for storing your spiral hose next winter so you won't end up with a tangled mess in the spring. Just wrap your hose around the handle of a rake or shovel that you won't be using during the winter. Your long-handled tool will do double duty by keeping your hose tangle-free.

PRESERVE YOUR LAWN PRODUCTS

When a bag of fertilizer or weed killer is left open for a long time, the product will absorb moisture from the air and won't be able to go through a spreader. Even grass seed could use an extra layer of protection from a moisture-wicking concrete floor. Place opened bags of lawn products in large resealable plastic bags. The products will be free of clumps or pests and ready to go when you need them.

1

Better Extension Cord Storage

If you're one of those people who wraps cords around your hand and elbow, knock it off! It permanently twists the cords and makes for a tightly wound pile of spaghetti that's bound to be tangled when you go to unwind it. Here's how to wind up extension cords so they hang easily and don't get tangled: **1.** Wind the cord in big loops and plug the ends together. **2.** Drop one of the outside loops. **3.** Wind the dropped loop a few times around the loops you're holding. **4.** Stick the rest of that loop through the middle of the coil, give it a tug and hang the cord by its built-in hanging loop.

2

3

4

Drill-Powered Cord Storage

Built with a 5-gal. bucket, plywood scraps, a 12-in. length of 4-in. PVC pipe and a furniture leg dolly, this cord reel can easily roll up and store long extension cords. Cut two plywood discs to fit inside the bucket and two to fit inside the pipe. Glue the small discs in the center of each large disc. Slip on the pipe and secure it with a few screws. Attach the dolly to the bottom, set the reel in the bucket and cut a hole on the side of the bucket. To reel in the cord, drive a lag screw in the top of the reel and let your drill do the work.

Cord end hole

4" PVC

Furniture leg dolly

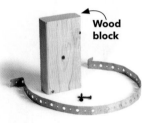

Wood
block

GARAGE STORAGE

Cardboard concrete-forming tubes are inexpensive at home centers and provide a great place to store baseball bats, long-handled tools and rolls of just about anything. Rest the tubes on pieces of 2x4 to keep them high and dry. Secure each tube to a garage stud with a plumbing strap.

Wood
block

SHOP VACUUM ORGANIZER

A PVC tee makes the perfect holder for shop vacuum attachments. Take one of your attachments to the home center and find a PVC tee that fits it. Drill a hole in the tee to fit a screwdriver, put a plywood spacer behind the tee and screw it to the wall.

PVC tee

Hole for mounting screw

Save Your Containers

Before heading out to a home center, raid your recycling bin for free and convenient workshop storage containers. Glass jars can be used to hold all sorts of liquids. Old tin cans are great for cleaning brushes. Sour cream or cottage cheese containers work well for fasteners and other small parts. Be sure to label your containers with a permanent marker.

Soap Box Nail Holder

Use a travel soap holder to store screws, nails and fasteners, and to protect them from rust. Tape the description from the original box onto the plastic container so you'll have all the information on a long-lasting package.

Shop-Made Parts Boxes

Have you priced those plastic parts bins? Too expensive! Try making your own out of scrap. The trick is to keep them modular. Make the front, back and bottom from ¾- or ½-in. material and the sides from ¼-in. plywood. Nailed and glued together, these will be plenty tough. The ones shown are 12 in. front to back (to fit in old kitchen upper cabinets), 3 in. tall, and either 3½ in. or 7 in. wide. Save up some scrap and you can make a couple dozen in an hour or so.

SPRING CLAMP ROOST

Spring clamps are convenient to use—but inconvenient to store. The solution: Use a cheap towel bar.

Large vinyl-clad storage hook

DRILL HANGOUT

Those big hooks that are often used to hang bikes also make slick drill hangers. Find the bargain hooks at any home center.

Travel-Friendly Drill Storage

Use industrial-strength hook-and-loop tape (such as Velcro) to attach your drill bit case to your drill case. Then the drill and the bits will always be together and travel easily to job sites.

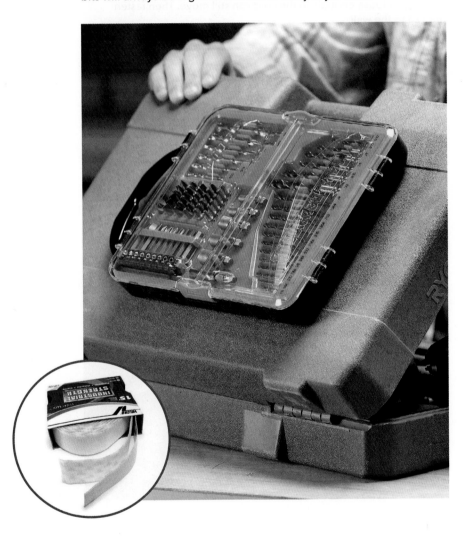

Elastic-Cord Tool Holder

Use an elastic cord to make a convenient tool organizer for chisels and other hand tools. Fasten one end of the cord to a 1x8 with an electrical staple and lay the cord straight without stretching it, then staple the other end. Add staples every 3 in. to create holders, leaving the staples just loose enough so the cord can still move. Then fasten the 1x8 to the wall.

Elastic cord

INSTANT TOOL HOLDER

Store files, large drill bits, screwdrivers and other long tools so they're easy to see and close at hand. Just cut off the top of a clear 2-liter plastic soft drink bottle, leaving a flap for hanging. Smaller bottles can hold smaller tools and common household items.

PIE PLATE POCKETS

Screw cut-in-half pie tins and heavy-duty paper plates to a shop wall and you've got space-saving storage for sanding discs, circular saw blades and abrasive discs that usually hide in a drawer. Be sure to tape the sharp edges on the cut pie tins to protect your fingers!

Bucket Lid Blade Holder

Tired of extra saw blades banging around in your drawer every time you open it? Attach the blades to a 5-gallon bucket lid with a bolt and a thumbscrew. Now they'll stay put, and the lid will protect your hands when you're digging around for other stuff.

5-gallon
bucket lid

¼"
carriage
bolt

Trunk Organizer

Make an inexpensive trunk organizer with file crates or plastic bins. Use self-adhesive hook-and-loop tape (such as Velcro) to secure each bin to the fabric lining of your trunk. It's a great area to store car items and to place bags of groceries without them toppling over.

Hook-and-loop tape

ONE-DAY STORAGE BENCH

Elegant outside, enormous space inside!

WHILE LOOKING FOR patio bench ideas, one of our editors found a sleek modern design with tons of storage inside. The price tag—over $1,000—wasn't a problem since he knew he could build his own version—in just a day. And so can you! It's really just a plywood box dressed up with solid wood slats.

FIGURE A
DECK BENCH
Overall Dimensions:
60" L x 23½" W
x 19½" H

FIGURE B
CLEAT LOCATION

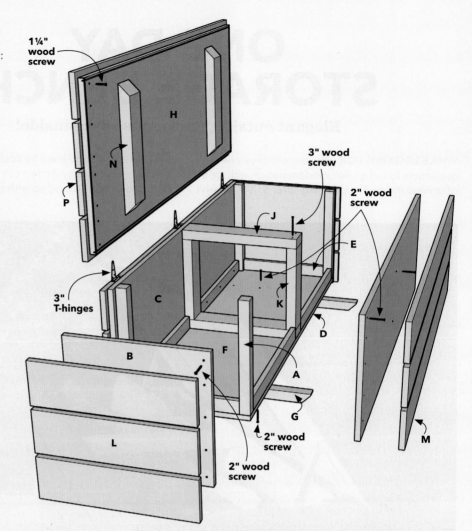

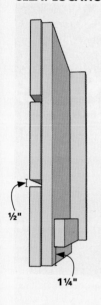

1¼" wood screw

3" wood screw

2" wood screw

3" T-hinges

2" wood screw

2" wood screw

½"

1¼"

CUTTING LIST

KEY	QTY.	SIZE & DESCRIPTION
A	4	1½" x 1½" x 16¼" (Box corner posts)
B	2	¾" x 17½" x 18" treated plywood (Box ends)
C	2	¾" x 17½" x 56" treated plywood (Box sides)
D	4	¾" x 2" x 24" treated plywood (Box long cleats)
E	2	¾" x 2" x 15" treated plywood (Box short cleats)
F	1	¾" x 54½" x 18" treated plywood (Box bottom)
G	2	1½" x 1½" x 18" (Feet)
H	1	¾" x 22" x 58½" treated plywood (Lid)
J	2	1½" x 3½" x 18" (Frame rails)
K	2	1½" x 3½" x 13" (Frame stiles)
L	6	¾" x 5½" x 19½" thermally modified (End slats)
M	6	¾" x 5½" x 57½" thermally modified (Side slats)
N	2	1½" x 3½" x 17½" (Lid battens)
P	4	¾" x 5½" x 60" thermally modified (Lid slats)

MATERIALS LIST

ITEM	QTY.
¾" x 4' x 8' sheets treated plywood	2
2x2 x 8' treated pine	2
2x4 x 10' treated pine	1
70 linear ft. of 1x6 lumber	
Wood glue	
Construction adhesive	
Exterior latex paint and primer	
3" exterior wood screws	
2" exterior wood screws	
1¼" exterior wood screws	
Tee hinges	3
Douper 200N/44lb Heavy Duty Gas Springs Lid Support Hinge	1 pr.

MATERIALS AND MONEY

This bench is mostly treated plywood, which stands up to the elements but can be unfriendly to work with. It's often slightly damp, if not soaking wet, so let it dry in your shop for a week or two before cutting. Store it flat to minimize warping as it dries. **Caution:** Warped boards are dangerous to cut on a table saw. A circular saw with a cutting guide is a safer option.

The bench's exterior was built using TMW (see "Thermally Modified Wood," below), which drove up the cost. Building the bench with cedar decking, which is rot-resistant, would be a less expensive option. The least expensive choice is construction-grade pine, which would give the bench a more rustic look.

1 Assemble the box sides. Attach the corner posts (A) flush with the long edges and tops of the box ends (B). Glue and screw the box sides (C) and ends together. Use a waterproof glue.

2 Install the box bottom. Glue and screw the bottom cleats (D and E) around the inside of the box (see **Figures A** and **B**). Apply glue to the undersides of the cleats, drop the box bottom (F) into place and fasten it with screws. Glue and screw the feet (G) to the box bottom.

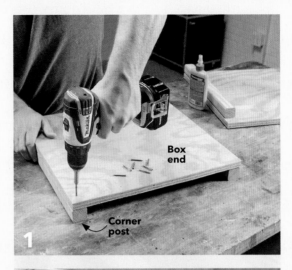

Box end

Corner post

1

Cleat

2

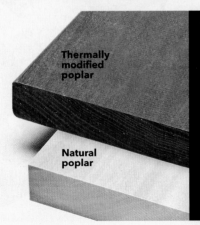

Thermally modified poplar

Natural poplar

Thermally Modified Wood

This bench was made with thermally modified poplar. Normally, poplar would be a poor choice for an outdoor project, but thermal modification changes the rules. Thermally modified wood (TMW) has essentially been cooked, removing the organic compounds. The chemical-free process makes wood more stable and resistant to decay and insects.

This process naturally darkens the wood. Left unfinished, it will weather gray like any other wood.

The price of TMW varies. Pine is the least expensive per linear foot, followed by poplar, and ash is the most expensive. To find TMW, ask a local hardwood lumberyard or search online.

3 Cut a drip groove. A kerf all the way around the underside of the lid (H) will help rainwater drip off the lid instead of clinging to it and running into the box. Apply exterior latex to the outer faces and visible edges of the lid and box.

Drip groove

3

4 Install the frame. Fasten the center frame (J and K) inside the box using glue and screws. The frame gives the box rigidity and helps flatten any warping in the plywood.

Frame

4

5 Attach the first slat. Attach a bottom end slat (L) flush with the box's bottom edge using exterior construction adhesive and driving screws from inside the box. Apply a bead of exterior caulk along the top edge of the slat so water can't seep behind the slat.

6 Attach remaining slats. Fasten the remaining end slats, using spacers and caulking the top edges as you go. Attach the side slats (M) using the same method. These short (1¼-in.) screws don't have a lot of pulling power, so maximize their use by pre-drilling and countersinking clearance holes through the plywood before driving the screws.

5

Spacer

6

7 Fasten the lid battens. Tack the lid battens (N) to the underside of the lid using glue and screws. Flip the lid right side up and secure the battens with longer screws. The battens help keep the lid flat.

8 Assemble the lid. Clamp the lid slats (P) together, placing ½-in. spacers between each pair of slats. Apply construction adhesive to the slats, and then center the lid on the slats. Drive screws through the lid into the slats. Again, pre-drill the screw holes for maximum pulling power.

9 Install the hinges. Attach the hinges to the lid, centering the hinge barrels ½ in. from the lid's edge. Then prop the lid in position near the box edge. Mark the hinge mortise locations on the top slat. The mortise depths are equal to the hinge barrel's diameter.

10 Cut hinge mortises. There are many ways to do so. You can use an oscillating multi-tool with a square, flush-cutting blade. It's well suited to the task, acting as both chisel and saw. Once all the mortises are cut, attach the lid.

11 Install the lid stays. The lid here is held open by pneumatic props, which also add a little assistance in lifting the heavy lid. Replace with less expensive lid supports if you like. Also, apply the exterior finish of your choice. This bench has an exterior penetrating oil stain.

Lid

Lid batten

7

Spacer

Lid slat

8

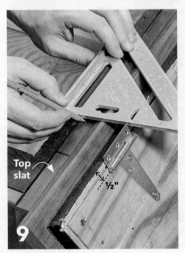

Top slat

½"

9

Hinge cutout

10

11

HOW TO ORGANIZE YOUR REFRIGERATOR– AND KEEP IT THAT WAY

Follow our pro-approved guidance to optimize your food storage and find a system that works for you

ORGANIZING YOUR REFRIGERATOR requires a relatively small amount of effort in the grand scheme of things, but it results in big payoffs. For starters, in an organized refrigerator you can easily see all the food you have. This not only helps when it comes time to meal prep and plan your grocery list, but it also reduces the amount of food you waste. And when food is stored in the right containers and at the correct temperatures, it lasts longer without spoiling, which saves you money. Finally, if you keep good-for-you choices at eye level, you can even improve your diet. Read on to get started.

BEFORE

WHAT YOU'LL NEED:
- Cooler or cooler bag
- Clear bins
- Glass food storage containers
- A turntable

Step 1: Clear Out the Fridge

Before you can ably tackle organizing your fridge, you need to clear out and declutter, according to Regina Ragone, a culinary nutritionist based in Long Island, New York, with two decades of experience leading test kitchens at national magazines. Ragone suggests taking out all the food items from your refrigerator so you can evaluate each and determine its fate. Check the sell-by dates, get rid of wilted or moldy produce, and make a decision about what's to become of last week's leftovers. As you sift through the fridge contents, place all items that you are keeping in a cooler or cooler bag until it's time to return them to the fridge.

Step 2: Clean the Fridge

Now that your refrigerator is empty, it's time to deep-clean it from top to bottom. Here's the three-step process:
- Thoroughly wipe all walls, shelves, drawers and compartments with a

AFTER

soft cloth dampened with warm water and mild dish soap.

- For caked-on gunk, such as jelly, syrup, ketchup or mustard, Ragone suggests using warm water and a scrubby pad rated safe for nonstick pans.
- Close the doors to allow your refrigerator's interior to get back to the right temperature (37 to 40 degrees for the refrigerator and 0 degrees for the freezer) before you begin replacing the contents according to your new organization plan.

Step 3: Organize the Fridge

Experts agree that the best refrigerator organization plan doesn't have to be complicated. In fact, a simpler system is generally better, because you are more likely to consistently maintain it. Most refrigerators have a variety of shelves, drawers and compartments to simplify the logistics of fruit and vegetable storage. Organizing the fridge with bins is another option.

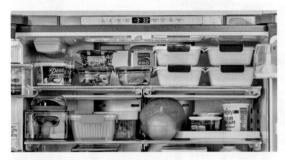

Start with the Shelves ▲

A typical fridge has top, middle and bottom shelves. To find out what should go where, we checked in with Sally Kuzemchak, RD, a consultant to national food brands and trade organizations, the creator of the *Real Mom Nutrition* blog, and the primary "restocker" of a refrigerator and freezer for herself, her husband and her two sons.

Because warm air rises in your fridge—just as it does everywhere else in your house—store items that need to be kept coldest, including most dairy

products and raw meat, on the lower shelves. The rear part of your fridge that's farthest away from the door is colder than the front, so keep that in mind when storing food as well.

TOP SHELF
- Prepared/ready-to-eat foods
- Leftovers. Store in leakproof, clear containers so contents are visible. (You're more likely to eat what you see.)
- Prepared dips and salsa
- Pies and cakes that need to be refrigerated

MIDDLE SHELF
- Eggs. Keep them in the original container or store them loose in an organizer. (Note: If your fridge has egg cups in one of the doors, don't use them. The door is too warm for eggs!)
- Whole melons
- Hard cheeses (such as cheddar, Swiss and Muenster). Keep them in the store wrapping until opened, then wrap them in waxed paper or, for a sustainable option, beeswax food wrap.
- Crisper containers of ready-to-eat fruits and veggies, such as sliced peppers, baby carrots, grapes, etc.
- Sour cream, cottage cheese and ricotta. Place on a turntable for easy access.

BOTTOM SHELF ▲
- Milk
- Cans of seltzer or other sodas in a drink organizer
- Snacks such as string cheese, yogurt and

TIPS ON FRIDGE ORGANIZATION

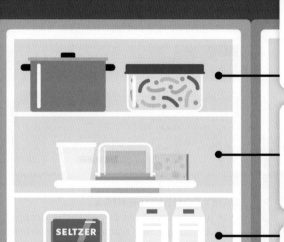

TOP SHELF
Best for: Leftovers and prepared foods you need to eat ASAP
- Since this food sits closest to eye level, you won't forget about it.

MIDDLE SHELF
Best for: Dairy products with a longer shelf life, such as hard cheeses, sour cream and cottage cheese
- Adding a turntable makes it easy to find what you're looking for.

BOTTOM SHELF
Best for: Milk and snacks
- Corral canned beverages in a drink organizer and grab-and-go snacks in clear bins.

SHALLOW DRAWER
Best for: Uncooked meats
- One of the coldest spots in the fridge, a shallow drawer keeps meat fresh longer.

CRISPER DRAWERS
Best for: Produce
- Set veggies to high humidity and fruits to low humidity. Keep them separate.

DOOR
Best for: Condiments
- More stable than other foods, condiments are OK in the warmest part of the fridge.

individual hummus or guacamole containers. Corral these in organizers for a neater look.

- Tender herbs (such as basil, parsley, mint, cilantro, dill and tarragon). To store fresh herbs, snip the bottoms, then stand them in a Mason jar with an inch or so of water in the bottom, or invest in an herb saver.

Move On to the Drawers ▲

Newer refrigerator models often have settings for drawers. The shallow drawer should be set to "meat," the crisper drawer designated for fruit should be on the lowest humidity setting and the one for veggies should be on the highest.

SHALLOW DRAWER

- Deli meat, such as roast beef, ham and turkey, in the original deli packaging
- Fresh meat, fish and poultry. Leave them in the store wrapping until ready to prepare. If the packaging isn't airtight, position a plate or tray underneath to catch drippings.

CRISPER DRAWER FOR FRUIT

- Whole apples (loose and unwashed)
- Oranges
- Whole berries in a berry container

CRISPER DRAWER FOR VEGGIES

- Whole heads of cauliflower, broccoli and lettuce. Leave unwashed in the original packaging or keep loose.
- Whole peppers
- Whole carrots

Finish with the Doors

The doors are the warmest parts of the fridge. They're also subjected to the most temperature fluctuations, since you and your family members open and close them repeatedly.

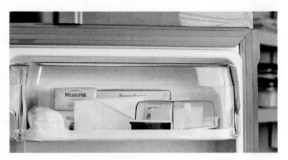

DAIRY COMPARTMENTS ▲

- Butter. Leave unopened in the wrapper. Once opened, place it in a butter dish.
- Soft cheeses, Brie, cream cheese, etc. If opened, neatly wrap them in parchment.

DOOR COMPARTMENTS ▲

- Orange juice
- Oat milk and other alternative milks
- Condiments, such as ketchup, mayonnaise, Sriracha, mustard, salad dressings and pickles
- Jams and jellies
- Sesame and walnut oils. Note: Only sesame and walnut oils need to be refrigerated; olive and vegetable oils belong in the pantry.

Step 4: Organize the Freezer ▲

Organizing the freezer is as simple as following the same basic method outlined for organizing the fridge. Evaluate all contents and toss anything with freezer burn. Kuzemchak suggests creating zones and grouping like with like, such as all veggies together and all cold packs in one place. Create another dedicated zone for breakfast foods, such as frozen waffles, bagels or breakfast sandwiches. Store any leftovers in well-labeled, clear glass containers. (Yes, you can put glass in the freezer!) Kuzemchak's top tip: Do what makes the most sense for your family and lifestyle. Make it easy for people to see and grab what they want so they don't have to root around, which makes a mess.

More Tips for Organizing Your Fridge

Knowing what belongs on the upper, middle and lower shelves is important, but the following tips will take your fridge organization to the next level.

- **Stack where you can.** Pile items in neat stacks, in clear bins if needed, to take advantage of vertical space and maximize square inches.

- **Add a turntable.** Positioning a turntable on a shelf makes for maximum storage and accessibility. Just spin to grab what you need.
- **Keep food visible.** Use glass storage containers for leftovers. Your family being able to see the food increases the chance that it will actually get eaten, which is the point of saving those leftovers or buying those berries in the first place.
- **Avoid mixing fruits and vegetables.** Keep fruits and veggies in separate drawers, not mixed. They emit gases at different rates, so storing them together can speed up spoiling. If you have strawberries, rinse them with a vinegar fruit wash before storing to fight the dreaded mold.
- **Pop in an open box of baking soda.** Your mom was right! Baking soda does absorb odors to help keep your fridge smelling fresh.
- **Leave the top of the fridge clear.** For better energy efficiency, forgo storing cookbooks or platters on top of your fridge. Doing so can cause your fridge to work harder, running up your electricity bill.

CHAPTER 3

MAINTENANCE

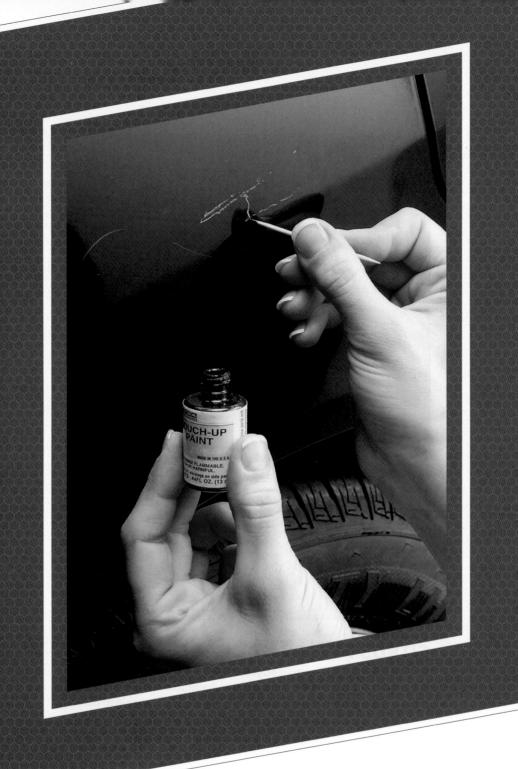

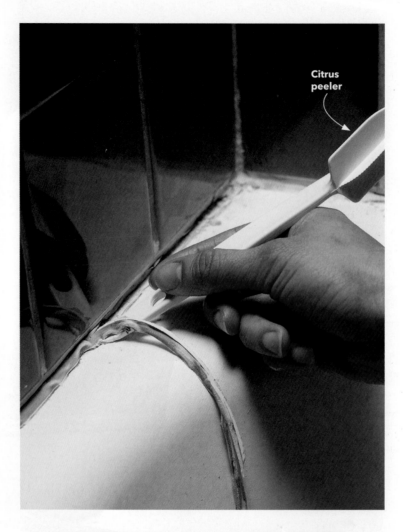

Citrus
peeler

CITRUS PEELER CAULK REMOVER

The flexible head and cutting edges of a citrus peeler make for a great tool to remove old caulk from around the bathtub or windows. Wedge the tip under the caulking, and with some luck, you'll be able to pull the whole bead out without scratching countertops and fixtures.

Caulk-Gun Sight

When caulking, the long end of the angled tip of the caulk tube can sometimes rotate a bit and mess up the job. To make sure you stay on track, grab a black marker and make a mark on the long end of the tip. Now, whenever the tube rotates, you can see it and correct the position of the tip to maintain a smooth caulk bead.

Power Snake

If you don't seem to have much luck augering toilets with those crooked, S-shaped handles that come with plumbing snakes, try this souped-up alternative. Cut your snake down to 6 ft. and make an adapter you can hook up to a cordless drill. Cut the head off a long lag bolt that'll thread inside the snake. Chuck the bolt into a cordless drill, and on the slow setting screw the lag bolt into the snake. The power auger will bust through the worst clogs. You can go easy on the trigger; it doesn't have to spin fast.

Plumber's Gloves

Gardening gloves with a rubbery coating are great for plumbing projects: They grip pipe like a vise and keep that nasty acid flux off your hands. But don't wear them while soldering; some coatings are flammable.

EMPTY THE TRAP

Before you remove a sink trap, give the drain a few plunges with a toilet plunger. This will push most of the water out of the trap, lessening the mess when you pull the trap. If you have a double sink, be sure to plug the other drain to contain the air pressure. If the strainer isn't a screw-down style, you'll have to hold it down while you plunge the drain.

SIPHON BEFORE SOLDERING

Before soldering a water pipe that you can't drain, use aquarium tubing to siphon the excess water out of a vertical copper pipe between the plumbing shutoff valve and the faucet. Once the water is out, you can solder the joint with ease.

Aquarium tubing

Silicone grease

No-Seize Faucet Handles

Corrosion can weld faucet handles onto valve stems, making any future repairs a headache. A dab of plumber's silicone grease will prevent this.

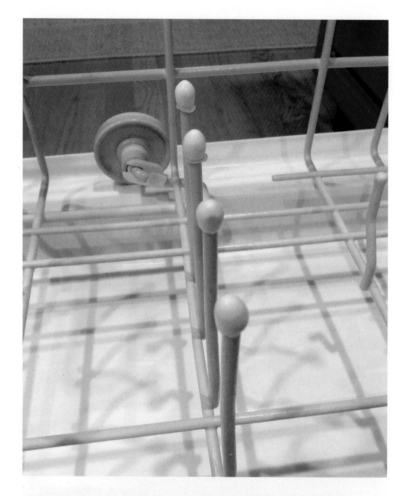

Simple Dishwasher Rack Fix

As dishwashers age, the plastic coating on the rack posts wears off and the exposed metal begins to rust and stain dishes. Here's an easy, quick and inexpensive fix: Get some of the plastic end cap covers that are used for wire shelving and glue them over the posts. (We used polyurethane glue.) No specialty kits or expensive dish rack replacement necessary.

SLICK REFRIGERATOR DRAWERS

If your refrigerator drawers are running rough, take them out and let them warm to room temperature. Coat the sliding parts with car wax, and your drawers will slide in smoothly again.

POP BOTTLE PILLOW

There's no need to strain your neck or get your hair dirty when you're working on your back under a sink or car. Take along an empty 2-liter plastic pop bottle for a pillow. You can let out air to adjust the comfort level, and even recycle it when you're done.

SOUPED-UP TROUBLE LIGHT

The hook on a trouble light works great, provided there's something to hang it from. But add a spring clamp to the back and you've got a light that you can use just about anywhere. Drill 3/16-in. holes through the metal cage and the clamp handle, then join them with a No. 8 x 1/2-in. machine bolt. Use two nuts or a locknut so that you can swivel the light without having it loosen.

Easy-Pull Furnace Filters

Regularly checking and replacing your furnace filter is a must-do for home maintenance, especially when your furnace is being heavily used in the summer and winter. To make it easier to remove the filter, attach a masking tape tab to the edge.

Plumbing Tape for Loose Screws

There are probably a few screws and bolts around your house that just won't keep tight. To solve the problem, wrap a bit of plumbing tape (polytetrafluoroethylene) around the threads and screw the fasteners back in. So long, wobbly chair legs and spinning drawer pulls!

NO-SCRATCH TOOLBOX

Cut and glue a piece of carpet to the bottom of your toolbox to protect surfaces such as floors and countertops from scratches. The carpet also makes it easy to slide the toolbox around rather than having to pick it up just to move it a little way.

EASY-READ PANEL

Make the circuit numbers stamped onto your electrical panel box easy to read by marking over each one with a black permanent marker. Lightly wipe away any excess ink with a rag dipped in a solvent such as denatured alcohol.

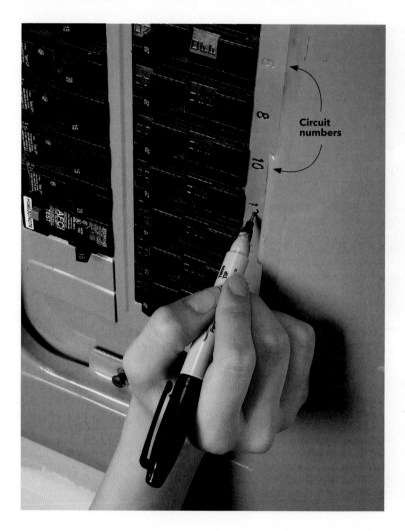

Circuit numbers

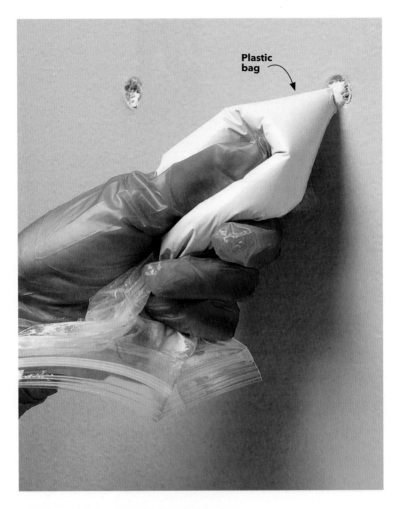

Plastic bag

Squeasy Spackling

Removing wall anchors can leave behind deep holes to fill. Instead of using a putty knife and going back to the can each time, put the spackling compound in a plastic bag. Then just cut a notch in one corner and squeeze the compound into the hole. If it's too thick, add a bit of water and knead the bag to mix it in.

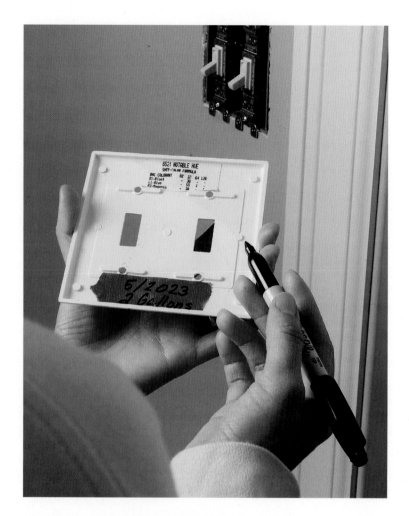

Painter's Reminder

When you're finishing a painting project, write on a piece of masking tape the date and how many gallons of paint were needed for the job. Stick the tape to the back of the light switch plate. To get the exact shade next time, also include the color formula sticker peeled off the paint can. When the room's due for a fresh coat, you'll be ready to go.

STAIN DABBER

For a quick touch-up, pour some stain into a condiment bottle. Leave the cap off and cover the top with multiple layers of cheesecloth or cotton, and secure them with a rubber band. When you tip the bottle, the stain flows through the pad. The thicker the pad, the easier it is to control the flow.

Cheesecloth pad

THREE-RING TOOL & APPLIANCE FILE

Store your appliance and tool manuals in three-ring binders so you can find them when you need them. Insert labeled dividers to organize them for quick reference.

Ladder Balance

Paint a stripe at the center balance point of your extension ladder. That way, you always know where to pick it up.

5" ferrule

7" galvanized spike

Gutter Reinforcement

Do you damage your gutters every time you lean a ladder against them? Then try this:

In the areas where you'll place your ladder, drill two $\frac{3}{16}$-in. holes and drive two 7-in. galvanized spikes with 5-in. ferrules into the gutters behind where each ladder leg rests. The ferrules, instead of the gutter, support the ladder's weight. Most home centers sell standard gutter spikes and ferrules.

A BETTER GRIP FOR LONG TOOLS

To save your back when raking mulch or shoveling heaps of dirt, add a second handle to your long-handle tools. A section of PVC pipe with a T-fitting and cap works perfectly. Add a screw through the T-fitting and into the handle for won't-budge stability.

PVC pipe and cap fitting

PVC T-fitting

Conduit strap

EASY WATERING

Stop dragging your garden hose all over the yard by attaching it to your fence with conduit straps (available in the electrical section of home centers). Then just hook up the hose at the spigot end and whatever sprinkler you want at the other end, and open the valve. It will make watering the back forty an easy task.

Summertime Sled

A plastic sled is a cheap and useful form of transportation for landscaping stuff. And since the sled is at ground level, heavy cargo is easy to load up too.

Downspout Blowout

Here's a way to unplug a downspout without climbing a ladder: Wait a day or two after rain to let all the water seep past the clog and out of the downspout. Then blast out the clog with your leaf blower. Be prepared for a mucky shower of gutter sludge. If you have an electric leaf blower, don't use this trick unless you're sure that all the water has drained out of the downspout, and always use a GFCI-protected outlet.

Pool noodle

MORE COMFORTABLE MOWING

The vibration in the handle of some push-style lawn mowers can be uncomfortable after a long time out in the yard, even aggravating arthritic hands. To make mowing more comfortable, tape a piece of a pool noodle over the handle. Your hands won't ache as much when the task is done.

Stay-put cleat

PORTABLE POTTING

Cut a piece of plywood roughly to the shape of your wheelbarrow's back end and screw a few wood cleats along the sides to keep it from slipping off while you wheel. Now you'll have both soil and a potting surface right at hand when you take the wheelbarrow to the garden.

NO-SLIP TOOLS

When you're working on the roof, wrap rubber bands around tools to help them stay put. The rubber will grip on roofs with up to a 6/12 slope.

Easy Mulch Spreading

Mulching around flowers and bushes in tight quarters is easier if
the mulch is in a small container. So place buckets and pails in your
wheelbarrow and fill them with mulch. It doesn't matter if the mulch
misses the bucket and lands in the wheelbarrow. Once you've emptied
the buckets, dump the mulch left in the wheelbarrow in an open area
and spread it out.

Use two ropes for heavy loads

Easy Brush Unloading

You may spend all afternoon loading your trailer with weeds and other yard debris, so here's a trick for speedy unloading. Before loading, lay some rope down the center of the trailer, leaving plenty of slack in front, and secure the other end to the back of the trailer. Then load the trailer right on top of the rope. When you're ready to dump the brush, flip the front end of the rope over the pile, and pull the yard waste out of the trailer. Even if it doesn't all come out, at least you can break the middle out and make short work of it from there.

SCRATCH TOUCH-UP

Sometimes the small brushes that come with vehicle touch-up paint slop the paint on and make the repair look worse than the scratch. Try using a toothpick: The tip of the toothpick fills the scratch with just the right amount of paint.

SERVICE RECORD STORAGE

For easy access to car and tool manuals and service records, screw a closing accordion file onto a board mounted to a garage wall. Keep a pencil with it to quickly track routine maintenance chores.

Drip Detector

Lay a couple of white cardboard boxes end-to-end on your garage
floor where you park your car. Not only will doing so protect your floor
from stains, but you'll be able to identify which fluid is leaking by its
color and location on the white surface.

UNCLOG A TUB DRAIN IN FIVE MINUTES— *WITHOUT* CHEMICALS

Don't flush money down the drain—a DIY fix is simple

About 80% of the time, you can fix slow-draining or clogged tub drains without chemicals and without a pricey plumber visit. The problem is usually just a sticky wad of hair that collects on the crossbars, a few inches under the stopper. All you need to do is figure out how to remove the stopper and fish out the gunk. Bend a little hook on the end of a stiff wire or a coat hanger with needle-nose pliers, and shove it through the clog—you'll nearly always extract the entire ugly mess. If hair is wrapped around the crossbars, slice through it with a utility knife and then grab it with the wire. Read on to determine which type of stopper you have and how to remove it.

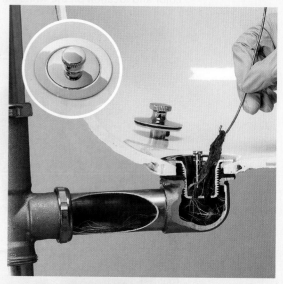

DROP STOPPERS

The most common type, a drop stopper, has a knob that you lift and turn to open the drain. It often has a setscrew under the cap. To remove a drop stopper, loosen the setscrew and slide off the stopper.

Setscrew

Crossbars

Lift the stopper and loosen the screw on the shaft slightly. Slide the stopper off the shaft.

PUSH/LOCK DRAIN STOPPERS

These stoppers lock and seal when you press them down and release when you push down a second time. The way to remove them isn't so obvious. In most cases, you have to hold the stem while unscrewing the cap as shown. With the cap off, you can sometimes fish out the hair from the crossbars. Otherwise simply remove the entire shaft by unscrewing it. You may have to adjust the screw tension on the stem when you reinstall everything to get a good seal.

Hold the stopper stem tightly with a finger and unscrew the top.

LEVERED STOPPERS

Many tubs, certainly most older ones, have a stopper located inside the drain and overflow tube. Most of these have a lever on the overflow plate and a screen over the drain. The screen keeps most hair out of the drain, but some get through and eventually form a clog at the crossbars. Simply unscrew the screen for easy access to this clog and remove it as before. If the drain has an internal stopper, unscrew the overflow plate and pull the linkage and stopper up and out. Then clean the linkage and stopper and run water down the drain to flush it out.

Occasionally, the linkage is out of adjustment and the stopper doesn't open far enough from its seat to allow a good flow. Adjust it, reinsert it, and test it. Run water into the tub. If it leaks out, lengthen the stopper linkage to seal the drain better. If the drain doesn't open to let the water out, shorten the stopper linkage.

First, remove the screen and clean the crossbars. Then unscrew the overflow plate, pull out the linkage, clean the stopper and linkage, and rinse the drainpipes. Readjust the linkage if necessary. Reinstall the assembly.

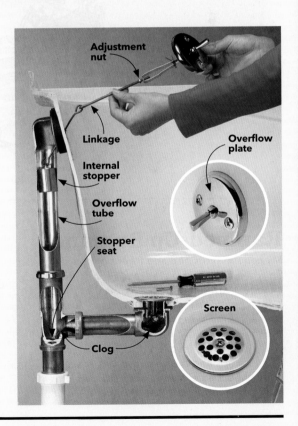

GREAT GOOFS

Enjoy (and learn from) these reader-submitted stories

HOW MANY DIYERS DOES IT TAKE ... ?

I walked into the laundry room the other day and turned on the light switch—and nothing happened. The circuit breaker hadn't tripped, so I thought it must be the switch or the ballast in the fluorescent fixture. I got my tester and checked the two wires on the switch. My tester didn't light up, so I thought it must be bad. After installing the new switch, the light still didn't work. Next I bought a new ballast for the fixture, installed it and still nothing. Then it dawned on me that it must be the simplest solution of all—a burned-out fluorescent bulb. Sure enough, once I replaced the bulb, it worked perfectly. Next time I'll start with the most obvious! —**Gail N. Shultz**

Ramped-Up Romance

My college girlfriend and I were on the skids. So when her new car was ready for its first oil change, I saw my chance to show that I was both a gentleman and a handyman. I brought my car ramps over to her place and inched up the ramps carefully. But not carefully enough. Clunk! The wheels rolled right off the ends of the ramps and the car was stuck there like a beached whale. Needless to say, this did not rekindle our romance. –**Kenneth Power**

Stuck on a Project

My brother called me one Sunday and told me the vinyl tile floor he'd just laid was peeling up. Being somewhat of a home improvement expert, I told him I'd be right over. When I saw the floor, I could tell he hadn't used enough adhesive. I got right to work lifting tiles several rows at a time, troweling on more adhesive. I laid down a large area of adhesive, placed some tiles in the middle of it and then stood on them to reach the corner. The tiles slipped and I fell face first into the adhesive, sticking helplessly to the tacky floor. I yelled for help and they struggled to set me free, causing the other tiles to slide. Finally, we got all the rows straightened, and I spent a few more hours peeling the adhesive off my arms and face! **–Melissa Wright**

WISE GEYSER

We moved into an older home that needed lots of TLC. At the top of my list was fixing the leaky hot water faucet in the kitchen. I asked around for advice and a co-worker told me all I needed to do was replace a washer. This sounded so easy that I got right to work. I grabbed my adjustable pliers and started to remove the faucet head. Just then my wife (a second-generation do-it-yourselfer) asked if I'd shut off the water. I confidently told her, "If it leaks, I'll shut off the water." Seconds later, the faucet handle flew toward the ceiling. I instinctively tried to cover the faucet with my hand, only to get scalded. We finally got the water shut off and then mopped up the lake in the kitchen. And yes, I humbly fixed the faucet with a bandaged hand! **–Gene Kannenberg**

Sewer Intruder

I'm a maintenance supervisor for a large apartment complex. One day we got a call to clean out a drain in one of the units. We proceeded to snake the waste line to unclog the pipe. When we tried to remove the snake, it wouldn't budge. About this time I was paged and told that a woman in a nearby apartment was hysterical. She claimed that something had come up her shower drain, grabbed the rug and was trying to pull it down. It clicked immediately in our minds, so we went to her apartment to assure her that it was our plumbing tool and not some sewer beast devouring her bathroom rug. **–Dennis DiCarlo**

TANGLED UP IN SNOW

Last fall I got a brand-new snowblower and couldn't wait for it to snow. When the white stuff finally arrived, I started up the snowblower and quickly finished my own driveway and walk. So I decided to be neighborly and do the driveway and walk for the nice old lady next door. Everything was fine until I suddenly hit her garden hose and got it royally tangled in my snowblower. I spent an hour picking out stuck bits and pieces of the hose. Later that evening, the phone rang and the lady next door said her basement was all wet. I discovered that the jarring of the hose had caused a leak inside the house behind the hose bib. I now only snow-blow my own place! **–Emil Gaverluk**

THE BATHROOM IS OCCUPIED

To save a few bucks, I decided to cut down one of our trees myself. I easily removed all the lower branches with my pole saw, and then I had the brilliant idea of taking the saw upstairs and hanging out of the second-story bathroom window to remove the upper branches. All went well until the last (pretty large) remaining limb. I planned the cut so the branch would fall into the "safe and open space" in the yard. Unfortunately, the nearly 12-ft. limb had other ideas. I narrowly avoided being skewered as it crashed through the window opening and came to rest a few inches from the door. People do a variety of things in their bathrooms—but how many have cut firewood while standing in the bathtub?
–Greg Ruvolo

Fillet O' Boat

A friend of mine rounded up a group to make some much-needed repairs on his storage shed. We each picked out tasks and got to work. The sawhorses were in use, so I suggested we do our cutting on the flat bottom of his 16-ft. johnboat. We had only sawed a few boards when we discovered a long saw cut through the bottom of the boat. Needless to say, our fishing trip that summer was canceled. I wonder if he'll call me for future projects.
–C. Noel Frugate

CHAPTER 4

EVERYDAY SOLUTIONS

Vent deflector

ICE CUBE CATCHER

Refrigerator ice dispensers sometimes send cubes flying. To corral the ones that slip by your glass, turn a magnetic vent deflector upside down and use it as a catch basin. Deflectors are available at home centers. If the magnets won't stick, use hot glue. You can easily remove the deflector without damaging the finish on your fridge.

Adjustable Drawer Divider

If you have a removable utensil tray in your kitchen drawer, you may have experienced it sliding around or even spilling flatware. Here's an easy fix: Fit a piece of ¼-in. plywood between two strips of adhesive-backed foam—one at the back of the drawer and one at the front. The tray stays put, and the divider makes another usable space for long utensils. The divider is easy to move as needed.

½" foam tape

½" foam tape

Easy-Glide Appliances

Stick self-adhesive chair pads to the underside of your kitchen appliances. They'll glide easier over your countertops without scratching the surface.

REFRESH A FRIDGE
WITH COFFEE GROUNDS

Eliminate refrigerator and freezer smells with a bowl of ground coffee. Place the bowl inside, close the door and don't open it until morning. If odors still linger, refill the bowl with fresh coffee and repeat.

RESTORE DENTED CARPET

Old furniture depressions in carpets can be really ugly. Lay a wet, wrung-out towel over the carpet "dent" and iron with a hot clothes iron for about a minute. The steam will release crushed fibers and make them pliable. Lift the towel, hand-fluff and presto—no more mark!

MILK JUG FURNITURE MOVERS

When you have to move heavy furniture on carpeting, don't just drag it around. That's hard on the carpet, and you could end up damaging the furniture legs. Make the job easier with these homemade moving pads. Cut the bottoms off four plastic water or milk jugs with a utility knife and rest each furniture leg on its own slider. The rounded, slippery bottoms make them perfect for moving furniture. Yes, you can buy fancier versions at the store, but these work just as well, and best of all, they're free!

Milk jug bottom

No-Slip Seat Cushions

The rubber mesh designed to keep rugs from sliding around can also make seat cushions stay put. Get the mesh at a home center or discount store and cut it to fit. This trick works on wooden chairs and upholstered furniture too.

No-Show Wreath Hanger

Want to hang your wreath on your door this holiday season without an ugly hanger? Stick a removable hook upside down on the inside of the door and hang your wreath over the top.

ZIP-TIE YOUR DECORATIONS

Zip ties are a simple and inexpensive way to string holiday lights on banisters and fences without marring the railing with nail marks. You'll find them in the electrical supplies aisle of your local home center. After the holidays, snip off the ties with scissors.

FREE PACKING MATERIAL

Line your packages with the recycled "shreddies" from your paper shredder. The material cushions your parcels' contents, and with all the junk mail these days, you'll have a never-ending supply.

Charger Helper

When you plug in a cellphone charger, there's a 50% chance you'll insert the USB cable upside down. To save time and fuss, put two triangles cut from electrical tape on the cable and the charger. If the triangles match, you're plugging in the cable the right way.

Pet Repellent for Furniture

To train your pets to stay off furniture, place plastic carpet protectors—prickly side up—on their favorite perch. Available in office supply stores and the carpet/flooring department of home centers, the protectors can be cut to the size you need with a pair of scissors or a utility knife. The plastic teeth will train your pet to associate the couch with "uncomfortable." Soon they will seek cozier spots to relax on and leave the easy chair to you. Just remember to remove the protector before you sit down!

The Big-Dog Diner

Large dogs sometimes have to strain to reach low-profile food bowls. You can buy elevated dog bowls at pet stores, but you'll pay a premium. Instead, make your own out of a couple of cheap 2-gallon plastic buckets from a discount store. Just flip them upside down, cut holes in the bottoms with a jigsaw and set a couple of 2-qt. stainless steel bowls into the openings.

PVC DRYING RACK

This PVC mitten/glove dryer uses heat from the floor vent. Make the racks with a 6-in. section of 2-in. PVC pipe, a 4-in. to 2-in. bushing fitting, a wire hanger and duct tape.

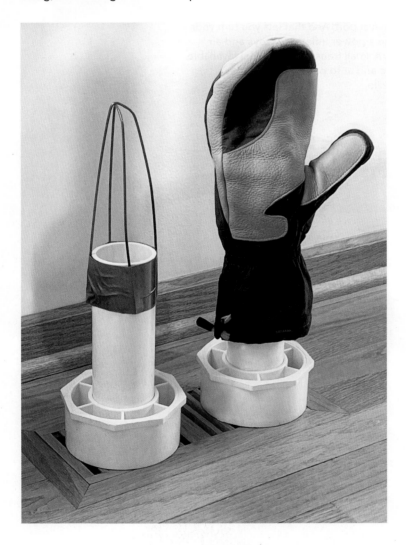

RAPID INFLATION

On many shop vacuums, you can plug the hose into the exhaust port. And that lets you turn your vacuum into a power inflator for toys and air mattresses. A small transmission funnel (available at hardware and auto parts stores) makes a perfect nozzle.

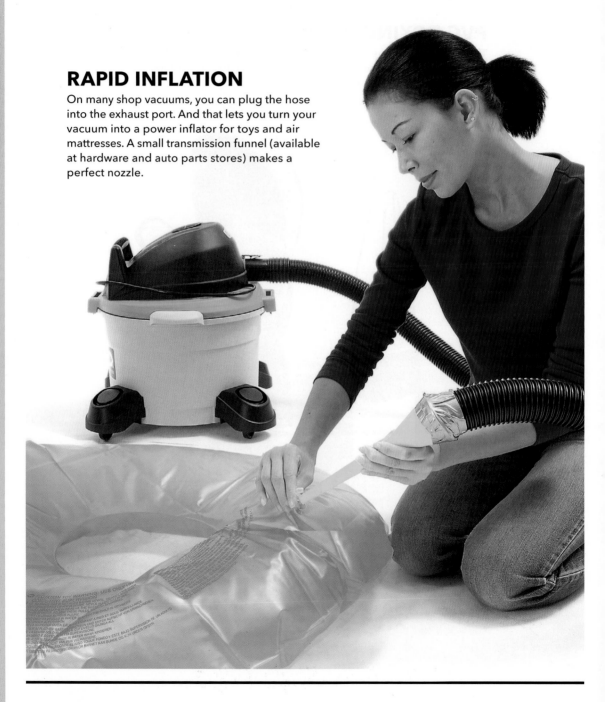

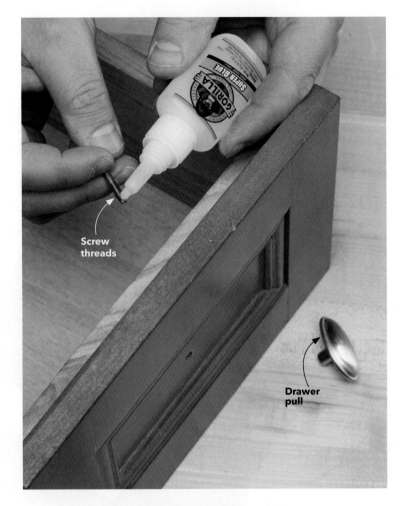

Screw
threads

Drawer
pull

A Sure Fix for Loose Screws

To secure a machine screw that keeps coming loose, add a few drops
of super glue to the screw's threads. Put the screw back in quickly;
you have only a few seconds before the glue sets. Note: If you may
want to remove the screw someday, use a removable thread-locking
product such as Loctite Threadlocker Blue 242 instead.

Quick-Draw Tape Dispenser

Quick-draw your masking tape for all those painting prep jobs. Hang a key chain carabiner—the larger, the better—on a belt loop and slide on a roll of tape. Now you can dispense the tape on the go and never waste time searching for the lost roll. This tip works great for electrical taping jobs as well.

DRYWALL INSPECTION LIGHT

Here's a handy way to find and fix imperfections while sanding drywall. Wear a hiker's headlamp and peer down the wall to spot divots and bulges. The headlamp is better than a trouble light or flashlight because it keeps your hands free. Head lamps are available at camping and discount stores.

NO-ROLL PENCILS

Carpenter's pencils are handy because they don't roll off your workbench or countertop. But some people prefer regular pencils for precise marking. To keep them from rolling off the workbench, put a tape "flag" around the end.

Keep Extension Cords Up and Out of the Way

Look down at the floor in any working shop, and you'll probably see a tangle of extension cords snaking across the floor, waiting to be tripped over. Get them out from under foot by hanging them from hooks running across the ceiling. Leave a cord or two hanging down over the workbench, then just plug in and go. Keeping cords up high also keeps power tool plug prongs from getting stepped on and bent.

Glue "Preserves"

It's frustrating to reach for a previously opened can of PVC cement or tube of silicone sealer only to find that the products have solidified or become an unusable gooey mess. To preserve the life of opened products, store them in a glass jar with a good seal (such as a Mason jar). You'll be surprised by how long your products can really last.

NO-WAIT GLUE

No one likes waiting for the glue to reach the bottle's tip when they're in the middle of a big glue-up. To make sure the glue is ready to flow immediately when you pick up the bottle, just turn the bottle upside down in a can and leave it on your workbench.

EARPLUG TETHER

Earplugs never seem to be around when you need them, and too often people go without rather than search for them. Why not tether your earplugs to your cap? That way, there's no longer an excuse for skipping the hearing protection.

Pocket Magnet

Sure, it's not a lot of trouble to use a tape measure's clip to keep it handy in the shop, but having the tape measure stuck to your pocket is even easier. A rare earth magnet gets the job done.

Keep a few magnets stuck to your tape measure's clip so you don't lose them. Note: This won't work with a 25-ft. tape; it's just too heavy. And don't put the magnets in the same pocket as your phone or credit cards.

Long-Reach Magnet

Here's a simple tool that will save your back whenever you drop screws, nuts or bolts on your workshop floor. Just glue a magnet onto the end of a stick and use that to pick them up.

Easy-to-Move Deck Umbrellas

Does your deck umbrella always seem to be in the wrong spot to shade you from the sun? Mount several sets of galvanized plumbing pipe straps on your deck posts or railing in key places. Use straps with a slightly larger diameter than the umbrella pole. Then pick a spot and slip the umbrella pole through the straps until the bottom of the pole rests on the deck. You'll get shade right where you need it.

STAND-UP SHOVEL

If you live in a snowy area, it's very convenient to step out of your patio door and have a snow shovel ready to go. However, if you just prop the shovel against the side of the house or the deck railing, you're likely to find it face down covered by snow. Solve this problem by buying a broom clip at the hardware store and installing it on the deck railing. No more digging for your shovel after a storm.

5-GALLON SQUIRREL SOLUTION

Determined squirrels can usually figure out a way to have a banquet at your bird feeder even if it's a squirrel-proof model. But you can defeat them by cutting off the bottom of an empty 5-gal. plastic water bottle with a jigsaw. Drill a hole through the neck of the bottle, slide the bottle over the pole and hang it from the feeder with a short length of coat hanger. You're in business (and the squirrels are out of luck). They'll try to get around it, but they can't.

Windproof Dog Dishes

How many times have you gone outside to fill your dog's food or water dish only to find that it's blown halfway across the yard? Really heavy pet dishes are expensive, but here's a cheap dog dish that won't blow away. Fill a plastic ice cream bucket with a couple of inches of sand, then put a second container the same size inside it. Use the inside bucket as your dog's dish, and it'll stay right where you put it.

Double Potting

Ever wish you could reorganize your garden in the middle of the growing season? Here's a clever way to do it. You'll need a bunch of pots of similar sizes. Put your plants in doubled pots, and then bury them up to their rims. Whenever you want a change, lift out the top pot and put in a different one. This method is also really slick for bringing plants indoors over the winter.

MUNCH-PROOF YOUR FLOWER BULBS

Keep hungry critters from snacking on your freshly planted flower bulbs by staking poultry netting over the bed. You can either remove the cloth in the early spring or let plants grow through the holes and leave it throughout the growing season.

Tent stakes

Poultry netting

STAY-PUT SOLAR LIGHTS

Many people use solar lights along their driveway, but most of them come with flimsy plastic stakes that are impossible to pound into gravel or clay-packed areas. Replace the stakes with sections of copper tubing that have a diameter matching the bottom of the light heads. The tubes are much easier to pound into hard-packed soil, and they're less likely to be kicked over in high-traffic areas.

Fence-Post Holder

Keeping a fence post plumb while you pour concrete into the hole can be a real challenge when working alone. A Workmate workbench can save the day. Here's the system: Position the workbench over the hole, clamp the post in place in the workbench and plumb it, then pour the concrete. By the time you have dug the next hole, the concrete will be firm enough to gently lift the workbench off the post.

Trunk Lid Tie-Down

When you're hauling oversize items in your car trunk, there often isn't a good place to tie a rope to the trunk lid. Make one by manually engaging your trunk's upper lock latch: Just move it over with your finger until it clicks into place.

Insert a 2-in. ring or a small carabiner (available at home centers) into the latch and run a rope through it and the trunk's bottom hasp for a handy tie-down. To release the ring, pull the "trunk release" lever in your car.

Hatchback Protector

Have you ever tried the juggling act of loading and unloading a hatchback while keeping the hatch from banging against the metal rib of the open garage door? To protect your car's finish, glue foam pipe insulation to the metal garage door rib with rubber cement. The hatch will rest damage-free against the foam.

LOAD SUPPORT

Next time you head to the home center to pick up long, floppy materials such as trim, plastic pipe or vinyl siding, take your extension ladder. It provides a stiff support for your flimsy load. Include some heavy weights to hold down the end of your cargo and plenty of elastic cords to strap your load to the ladder. Also tie down the ladder so it doesn't slide from side to side.

GET A GRIP

If you're in a region that gets freezing rain or snow, keep a milk jug filled with sand in a winter emergency kit in the trunk of your car. If you get stuck on ice, just sprinkle some sand under your tires to give your car the grip it needs.

No-Chip Tip

Protect your car doors and garage walls with a plush carpet remnant. Mount the carpet to your garage wall with adhesive-backed hook-and-loop fasteners such as Velcro.

Car-Care File in the Trunk

Keep your car's maintenance records in the car itself, and you'll never have to ransack your house looking for them. Just put them in a locking plastic bag and slip them under the carpet in the trunk.

LAUNDRY ROOM PEDESTAL

Save your back without spending an arm and a leg

FRONT-LOADING APPLIANCES have a lot of great features, but being easy on your back isn't one of them. That's why manufacturers offer matching pedestals that raise the machines to a comfortable height. But these pedestals can cost hundreds of dollars each, and you still won't have a place to stash laundry baskets. With our plan, you can build your own unit for a fraction of the cost and get a functional pedestal that will look great in any laundry room. You can choose from the three versions we show here—contemporary, Craftsman and classic. They differ only in the amount of trim and moldings that you add on to the basic plywood carcass.

Space for baskets

Stock moldings

Standard boards over plywood

Choose Your Style

Build it basic or deck it out with moldings.

CONTEMPORARY

Leave off the trim, and you have a sleek and functional pedestal. This version doesn't require any miters, so even a beginner can build it.

CRAFTSMAN

Adding trim on the face and sides transforms the pedestal with minimal additional cost and work. Most of the trim cuts are simple right angles, so even this version is easy.

CLASSIC

If you prefer a traditional look, add moldings. You'll need to cut a few miters to fit the moldings where they meet at the corners, so this version requires slightly more skill.

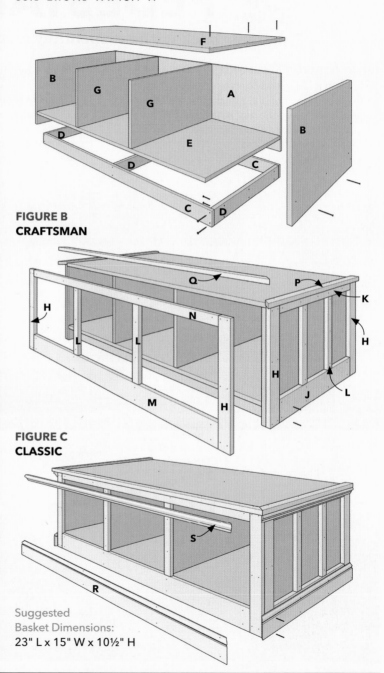

FIGURE A
CONTEMPORARY
Overall Dimensions:
58½" L x 31½" W x 18¼" H

FIGURE B
CRAFTSMAN

FIGURE C
CLASSIC

Suggested
Basket Dimensions:
23" L x 15" W x 10½" H

¾" plywood

Saw guide

1 CUT THE PLYWOOD PARTS. Get straight cuts with a circular saw and guide. To see how to make a guide, go to *familyhandyman.com* and search for "saw guide."

SKILL, TIME AND MATERIALS

The skill required goes up as the versions get fancier. Including painting, expect to spend a weekend on this project. In addition to standard DIY tools, you'll need a circular saw and a straightedge guide or table saw to cut the plywood. A miter saw would make cutting the trim for the Craftsman version easier and is necessary if you want to add the moldings. A finish nail gun would simplify all the trim work.

The pedestal requires two sheets of plywood, and some trim boards and moldings if you want to add them. You'll find all these at any home center or lumberyard. Remember, you can always ask to have the plywood cut into smaller pieces to fit in your vehicle. See the Materials List on p. 172.

GET STARTED BY CUTTING THE PARTS

The first step is cutting the plywood parts to the right size. Follow the Cutting List and Cutting

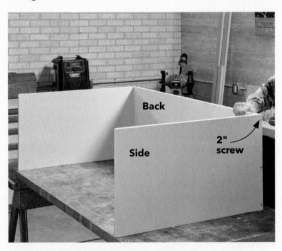

Back

Side

2" screw

2 SCREW THE SIDES TO THE BACK. Drill ³/₃₂-in. pilot holes through the sides into the back. Then drive 2-in. screws to connect the sides to the back.

FIGURE D
DIVIDER LOCATIONS

PEDESTAL TOP

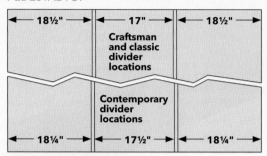

PEDESTAL BOTTOM

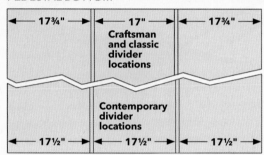

FIGURE E
PLYWOOD CUTTING DIAGRAM

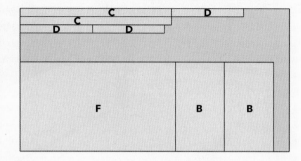

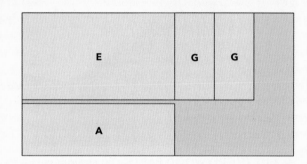

CUTTING LIST

KEY	QTY.	MATERIAL, DIMENSIONS (PART)
A	1	¾" plywood, ¾" x 54" x 17½" (Back)
B	2	¾" plywood, ¾" x 30" x 17½" (Sides)
C	2	¾" plywood, ¾" x 54" x 2¾" (Toe space frame front and back)
D	3	¾" plywood, ¾" x 25¾" x 2¾" (Toe space frame sides and middle)
E	1	¾" plywood, ¾" x 54" x 29¼" (Bottom)
F	1	¾" plywood, ¾" x 55½" x 30" (Top)
G	2	¾" plywood, ¾" x 14" x 29¼" (Dividers)

Add trim for the Craftsman version

H	6	1x3 board, ¾" x 2½" x 17⅞" (End stiles)
J	2	1x4 board, ¾" x 3½" x 25" (Bottom end rails*)
K	2	1x2 board, ¾" x 1½" x 25" (Top end rails*)
L	6	1x2 board, ¾" x 1½" x 12⅞" (Interior stiles*)
M	1	1x4 board, ¾" x 3½" x 52" (Bottom front rail*)
N	1	1x2 board, ¾" x 1½" x 52" (Top front rail*)
P	2	1x2 board, ¾" x 1½" x 31½" (End nosings*)
Q	1	1x2 board, ¾" x 1½" x 58½" (Front nosing*)

* Cut to fit

Add moldings for the classic version

| R | 3 | Baseboard molding, cut to fit (Trim at base) |
| S | 3 | Base cap molding, cut to fit (Trim under cap) |

MATERIALS LIST (for all 3 versions)

ITEM	QTY.
4' x 8' x ¾" plywood	2
2" screws	50
1¼" screws	10
Wood glue	
Paint	
Edge banding or wood filler	
Additions for the Craftsman version	
1x2 x 8' paint or stain grade board	4
1x3 x 9' paint or stain grade board	1
1x4 x 9' paint or stain grade board	1
1" brads	
1¼" brads	
Additions for the Craftsman version	
6' base cap molding	2
6' base molding	2

TIP
Tack plywood panels together with finish nails to hold them in place while you drill pilot holes and drive the screws.

Diagram on p. 172. You can get great results with nothing more than a circular saw and a straightedge guide. With a guide like this, you just make two marks on the plywood for the size of the part you're cutting. Then line up the guide with the marks and clamp it **(Photo 1)**. The only trick is to make sure the guide is on the side you want to keep. Then run the saw along the guide's fence to make the cut.

It's quicker and simpler to paint or finish the plywood parts before you assemble them. If you're building the contemporary version, you'll need to cover or fill the raw plywood edges that are exposed. You could apply veneer edge banding to the edges. But if you're going to paint the pedestal, it's easier to simply fill the edge grain with Zinsser Ready Patch or a similar product before painting. Use a small flexible putty knife to trowel the filler onto the edge of the plywood. Let the filler dry. If there are still recessed spots or holes, add a second coat. After the second coat dries, sand the filler smooth. Now you're ready to brush or roll on two coats of paint.

After the paint dries, you can assemble the carcass. Start by screwing the sides to the back **(Photo 2)**. Next, build the toe space frame from the four strips of 2¾-in.-wide plywood. The frame is sized to allow a 2-in. toe space at the front of the pedestal (contemporary version). Set the frame between the sides and snug it up to the back **(Photo 3)**. Drive 1¼-in. screws from the inside into the back and sides. Before you install the top and bottom, draw faint pencil lines on the inside faces to indicate the positions of the interior dividers **(Photo 4)**.

Since the divider locations are slightly different for the contemporary version, make sure to use the correct dimensions **(Figure D)**. On the outside face of the top and bottom, make faint center lines to indicate where screws should be driven. Set the bottom on the toe space frame and attach it with screws **(Photo 5)**. Then align the top and drive screws through the top into the sides and back **(Photo 6)**. Finish the carcass by lining up the two dividers with your light pencil lines and securing them with screws **(Photo 7)**. If you're building the contemporary version, you're done.

ADD A FACE FRAME AND DECORATIVE END PANELS

Adding ¾-in.-thick trim boards to the front and sides is all that's required to build the Craftsman

3 **ADD THE TOE SPACE FRAME.** Cut the parts to length from the plywood strips. Drill pilot holes and join the parts with 2-in. screws. Set the frame into place and connect it to the sides and back with 1¼-in. screws.

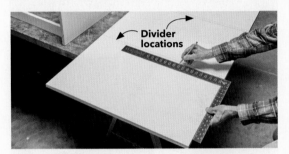

4 **MARK THE DIVIDER LOCATIONS.** Mark the positions of the two dividers on the top and bottom. Draw light pencil lines to indicate the edges of the panels. Turn the panels over and make a single line to indicate the center of the dividers. Use this line as a guide when you drill the screw holes. You can wash off these lines or paint over them after the pedestal is assembled.

5 **ADD THE BOTTOM.** Set the bottom in place and drill pilot holes for the screws. Attach the bottom to the toe space frame with 2-in. screws.

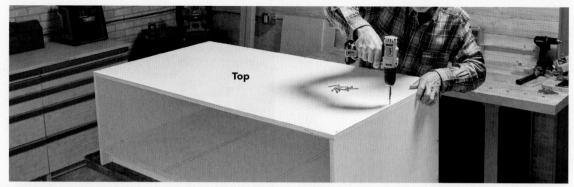

6 **ATTACH THE TOP.** Set the top in place. Drill pilot holes and drive screws through the top into the sides and back.

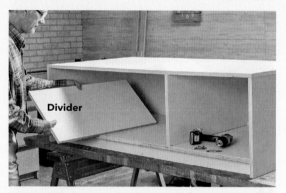

Divider

7 **INSTALL THE DIVIDERS.** Line up the dividers with the pencil lines (see Photo 4) and secure them by driving screws through the top and bottom into the dividers.

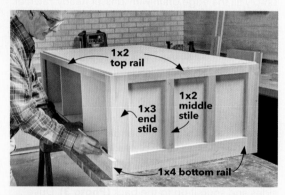

1x2 top rail

1x2 middle stile

1x3 end stile

1x4 bottom rail

8 **NAIL ON THE TRIM BOARDS.** Install the trim on the ends of the carcass, starting with the end stiles. Make sure that all the trim is ⅜ in. below the top surface of the pedestal. Finish by gluing and nailing the trim to the front.

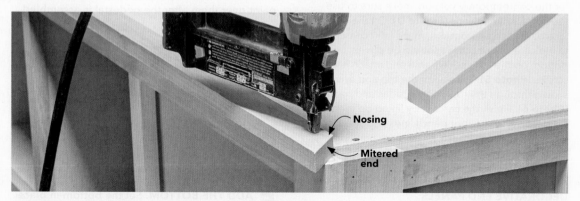

Nosing

Mitered end

9 **GLUE AND NAIL THE NOSING.** Cut and fit the 1x2 nosing that runs along the two sides and front of the pedestal. Miter the ends at the corners. Then glue and nail the nosing to the top of the trim.

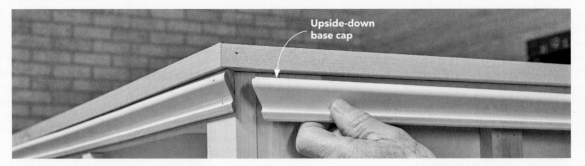

Upside-down base cap

10 **ADD MOLDINGS. Install the decorative trim that fits under the nosing. Miter the outside corners. Nail the trim to the pedestal.**

version. Set all the trim boards ⅜ in. below the top surface to create a ⅜-in. lip when the top nosing is applied. This lip will help ensure that your washer and dryer don't vibrate off the edge. Use glue and 1¼-in. brads to secure the ¾-in.-thick trim.

Start by installing the end stiles (vertical boards) on the sides. Add the rails (horizontal boards) next, and finish the sides with the two interior stiles. Follow the same sequence to install the front trim **(Photo 8)**. Finish this version by gluing and nailing on the 1½-in.-wide nosing **(Photo 9)**. We mitered the ends of the nosing, but you could also use square joints and simply fill and paint the exposed end grain.

ADD MOLDINGS FOR A CLASSIC LOOK

We chose a base cap molding for under the nosing, and matched the existing baseboard molding for the bottom trim. But you can choose any moldings to fit the style of your room. Miter the ends of the moldings and use 1-in. brads to attach them **(Photo 10)**. We wrapped the bottom of the pedestal with standard Princeton-style baseboard to match the baseboard in the room. **Photo 11** shows how you can cope your new molding to create a tight fit with an existing base molding. For more information on how to cope moldings, go to *familyhandyman.com* and search for "coping." If your baseboard isn't compatible or you don't care about creating a built-in look, then skip the coping step and just cut a square end on the baseboard.

When you're finished installing the trim and moldings, fill the nail holes. Let the filler dry and sand it smooth. Then brush another coat of paint on the trim and moldings to finish the project.

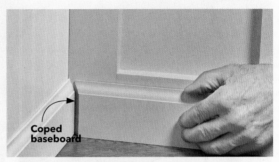

Coped baseboard

11 **COPE THE BASEBOARD. For a built-in look, cope the baseboard to fit against the existing base. To learn how to cope baseboard like a pro, go to *familyhandyman.com* and search for "coping."**

Dealing with the Dryer Duct

Raising your dryer also raises the position of the dryer's exhaust. And that may mean reworking the dryer's exhaust duct. If the current duct enters the wall at least 20 in. from the floor, there's no problem. But if the duct is lower than that, you'll have to raise it. Also, if you want to snug the dryer up to the wall as we did here, you'll need to recess the vent in a dryer vent box. For help with dryer ducting, go to *familyhandyman.com* and search for "dryer vent install."

Also take a look at the gas and/or electrical lines serving the dryer to make sure they'll accommodate a raised dryer.

VITAL SUPER GLUE TIPS

Clever techniques for sticky situations

IF YOU'VE BEEN DISCOURAGED by past attempts to fix stuff with cyanoacrylate-based adhesives—known as "CA" or "super glue"—it's time to take another look. New formulas have expanded its versatility, and a few simple tips can make the difference between success and failure.

In this article, we'll give you tips for selecting the right super glue for the job and offer advice on getting the strongest bond. We'll even show you a few unique uses for this remarkable glue.

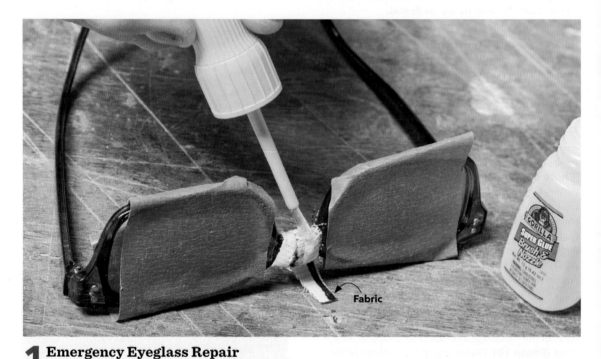

Fabric

1 Emergency Eyeglass Repair

If you wear eyeglasses, you've probably tried in vain at least once to repair a broken pair with glue and electrical tape. But here's a fix that really works. It's not pretty, and it's not a substitute for new glasses. But it'll work in a pinch. Start by tacking the parts together with super glue. Then cut a thin strip of fabric and tack one end to the glasses. Gingerly wrap the fabric around the broken section, applying a little super glue as you go. For this task, we used super glue that comes in a container with a brush. After the glue sets up, you can sand the fabric to smooth it slightly, and if you want, use a colored marker to blend the repair.

2 Buy Small Containers to Avoid Waste

If you don't use super glue often and find that larger containers have hardened when you go to use them again, buy economical small containers instead. You won't throw as much away.

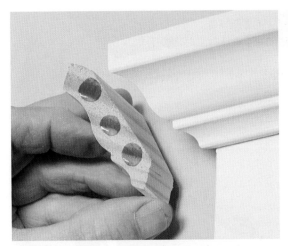

3 Attach Small Molding Pieces

Attaching small pieces of moldings with nails without splitting them is tricky. The next time you have to install molding, try attaching it with super glue. You need only a few dots of thick "gel" formula to hold moldings in place.

4 Be Your Own Cobbler

Super glue is great for shoe repairs because it works so fast. You can reattach loose soles or heels, fix detached welts or add pads to your high heels. Combining super glue with an accelerator will get you back on the road in a hurry.

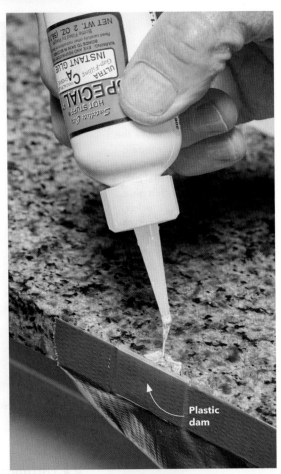

Plastic dam

5 Repair Stone Countertops

You may not get an invisible repair, but filling chips or gouges in stone countertops hides the flaw and can help prevent further damage. For this edge chip, we cut a small rectangle of polypropylene plastic from a plastic container lid and taped it to the side to form a dam. Fill any recess in layers until the super glue is slightly proud of the surface. After the super glue hardens, use a single-edge razor blade held at about an 80-degree angle to scrape the glue until it's level with the surface. On soft stone such as marble, use masking tape to protect the surrounding surface from scratches.

You can make the patch blend in somewhat by adding stone powder or plastic pigment to the super glue. But if you do add pigment, work fast, because the pigment can accelerate the hardening process.

6 Choose the Right Viscosity

Originally all super glue was thin and runny, almost like water. But then manufacturers discovered that thicker glue would be easier to use in some cases. Here are a few tips to help you choose the right thickness for your repair.

If your parts fit tightly together and the material isn't very porous, look for thin glue. If you don't see "gel," "thicker formula" or similar terms on the label, it's probably thin. Thin glue spreads out easier in a tight-fitting joint and leaves a less visible repair line because it takes up so little space. On the other hand, if you're joining porous materials and the pieces don't fit perfectly, thicker "gel" formulas will work better. Thicker glue can fill small gaps and still create a strong bond. Keep tubes of both thin and thick on hand so that you'll be prepared for any type of repair.

7 Reinforce Hairline Cracks

You can reinforce pesky hairline cracks in pottery by applying thin super glue and letting it wick in. Wipe the excess from the surface quickly, before it hardens.

8 Ultimate Glue-Saving Tip

If you're like most people, you've probably thrown away more super glue than you've actually used, because either the tip got clogged or the glue hardened. Modern caps are better than they used to be, eliminating some of the problem. But for an even greater chance of preserving your glue, store it in an airtight jar along with some desiccant packets. The desiccant absorbs moisture and will keep the air inside the jar dry, preventing the glue from hardening. You'll find desiccant packets in bottles of vitamins and medicine or electronics packaging.

Desiccant

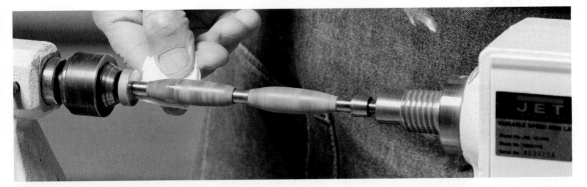

9 Finish Wood with Super Glue

While it's too expensive to use on large surfaces, super glue makes a great finish for small wood projects. Since it hardens so quickly, you can build up several coats in minutes. A super glue finish is durable and waterproof. On flat surfaces you can spread a thin layer with an old credit card or other flexible plastic spatula. Apply super glue to curved surfaces with small pieces of lint-free paper towel. Use a fresh piece of towel for each new coat. To speed up the process even more, spritz the surface with accelerator between coats. Thin- to medium-viscosity super glue works best for finishing. Note: To finish a pen with super glue as in the photo above, put a drop or two of the glue on a small pad of paper towel. Wipe it quickly onto the pen blank as it's turning on the lathe. Build up about 10 coats for a finish that can be polished to a glass-smooth surface.

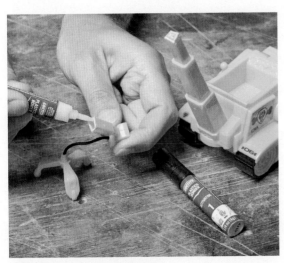

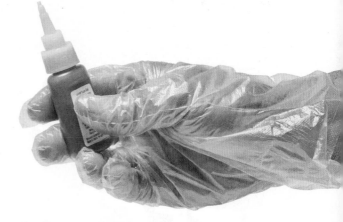

10 Match the Glue to Your Material

Regular super glue doesn't work well on glass, since glass is too smooth to achieve a good bond. And it doesn't work on plastics such as polyethylene and polypropylene. But some formulas will bond these materials. If you're repairing glass or plastic, make sure that material is specified on the label.

11 Poly Gloves Are Best

Super glue will stick to most vinyl and rubber gloves. And that means if you're wearing these types of gloves, you could get stuck to your repair job. To avoid this, buy a box of the thin poly gloves that food handlers use. The glue won't stick to these, and they're really cheap and easy to put on. If you can't find them in a store, you can order a lifetime's supply online or beg for a few pairs from your favorite restaurant or fast food joint.

CHAPTER 5

TOOLS & TECHNIQUES

HAMMER CUSHION

You can use a rubber chair-leg cap to instantly convert a hammer into a rubber mallet. And if you want to drive a nail without denting the surrounding wood, cut a hole in the rubber cap. Pound until the rubber strikes wood, then finish driving the nail with a nail set. A 1⅛-in. rubber cap—available at home centers and hardware stores—will fit tightly over most hammers.

Mark Straight Lines on Round Pipes

It's not easy to cut a straight line all the way around a pipe with tin snips or a hacksaw. To make the job a lot easier, mark a cutting line with a square piece of cardboard or stiff paper. Just align the edges of the cardboard and pull it tight around the pipe, then mark the edge all the way around. As long as you follow the line, your cut will be perfectly straight.

Wrap Teflon Tape in Tight Places

If there's not enough room to roll Teflon tape around a threaded fitting in a wall cavity, under sinks or along the ceiling, try this workaround. First, apply several wraps of tape around a pencil and tear it from the roll. Then position the pencil next to the fitting and start the wind. Hold the starting edge with your fingers and rotate the pencil so it unrolls the tape through the narrow clearance on the other side of the fitting. This technique allows you to keep the tape taut so it applies smoothly.

Popcorn
ceiling

TAPING SHORTCUT

When hanging drywall in inconspicuous places (like inside closets),
skip the taping step and instead use paintable caulk in the corners.
Smooth it out with a wet sponge or finger, let it dry and you're ready
to paint. This technique is especially useful if you have a textured
ceiling, where taping is all but impossible without scraping off the
texture. Then you have to respray. This little cheat saves hours of
taping and sanding, and it looks great.

STIR IT UP

Over time, paint pigments tend to settle to the bottom of the can, so a thorough mix is key for even coverage. To speed up the mixing process, use a paint can opener chucked into a drill. Cut and straighten the bent prying end and grind it flush with the shaft. Now whenever you have paint that needs mixing, simply tighten the modified opener in the drill chuck and stir away!

Easy Paint Seal

If you don't keep a roll of Press'n Seal with your painting supplies, you're missing out! The cling film is perfect for covering roller trays, paint pails, rollers and brushes in between coats. You can then keep all your painting tools covered and clean them just once, even after two or three coats. You can also use the film to cover coffee cans or other containers of leftover paint.

Scraper in a Pinch

If you ever need a scraper for a quick fix (such as scraping up paint drips on a countertop), clamp a utility blade in a pair of locking pliers and scrape away.

Locking pliers

EASIER DOOR WORK

Before removing a door that will be reinstalled, snug a wooden wedge underneath it at the hinge side and duct tape the wedge to the floor. This makes reinstalling the door much easier because you'll get the height right on the first try.

DENT PREVENTER

Prevent dings in finished surfaces by cutting a kerf into a shim and then slipping the shim around the nail as you hammer it in. The shim shields the surface against errant hammer blows.

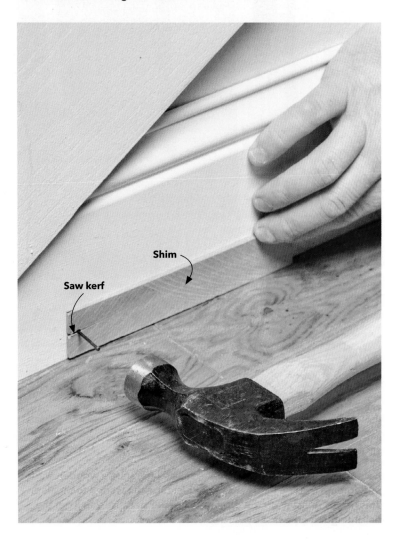

Shim

Saw kerf

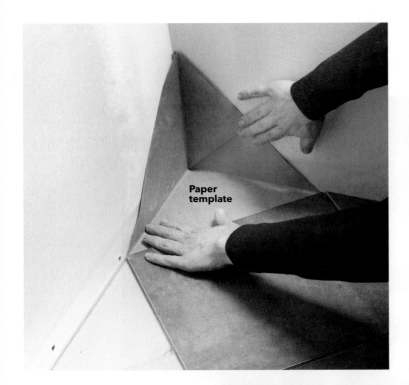

Paper template

Precise Tile Measuring

When you're tiling a floor and you need to cut odd edge pieces, try this. Lay the field tile first. When you get to the outside edges, get exact measurements by making a paper template. Cut a piece of sturdy paper the exact size of the tile you're using and set it in place. At the wall, crease the paper and fold it over at the correct angle. Then transfer the angle to the actual tile using a wax marker or heavy pencil. You'll get a much more accurate cut and fit.

Homemade Nut Loosener

Rusted bolts and nuts can be extremely tough to loosen. Luckily, you can make your own rust penetrant by mixing equal amounts of automatic transmission fluid and acetone in a metal oilcan. The solution really penetrates—after a few minutes, even the toughest bolts and nuts spin loose (with a little elbow grease, that is). Best yet, it's stuff you probably already have on the garage shelf.

Metal
file

Dedicated Nail Puller

Nippers are great for pulling brad nails, but the sharp edges often
cut the nail as you try to pull it out. Dull a pair of nippers slightly with
a metal file and mark it as your designated nail puller. Use a cheap
pair; higher-quality nippers with hardened cutting edges may not
file easily. Shoot a few nails into a test board to get it just right.

ON-DEMAND MAGNETIC SCREWDRIVER

Magnetic screwdrivers often tend to accumulate metal debris from screw heads, and it's tough to remove it all. To provide on-demand magnetism instead, try this trick: Stick a rare earth magnet on the screwdriver shank. Once you no longer need it, simply remove the magnet, and any metal debris will come off easily. This is especially helpful for assembling small parts with tiny screws!

Magnet

CUT STRIPS FAST

When you need to cut lightweight material into strips, here's a cutter you can make in seconds. Stick a razor blade or utility knife into a piece of scrap wood (we used plywood) at a slight angle and secure a fence in place. Then, while keeping the material held against the fence, pull it through the blade. This cutter can handle cardboard, light plastic, rubber, leather, textiles and tape.

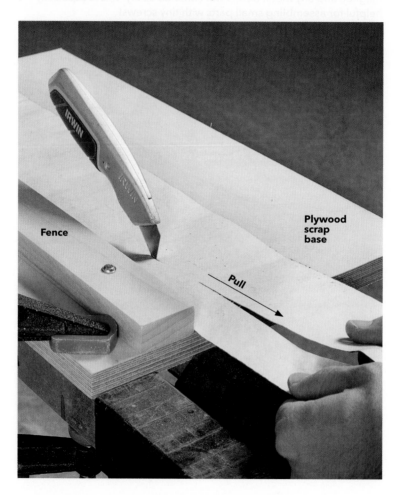

Fence

Plywood
scrap
base

Pull

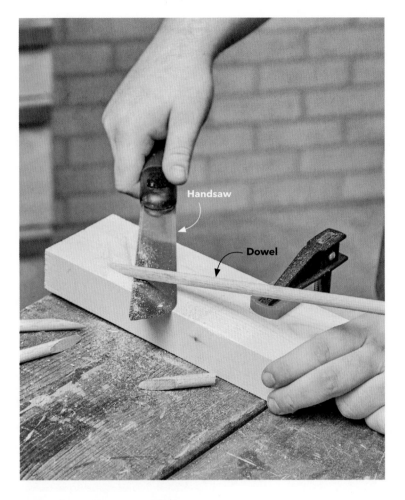

Handsaw

Dowel

Make Your Own Pocket-Hole Plugs

Instead of buying pocket-hole plugs, use this jig to make as many as you need. Drill a pocket hole into a 2x4. Then insert a ⅜-in. dowel and slice it off flush with the face of the 2x4. After making the angled cut, push the dowel through, cut the end at 90 degrees and repeat.

Blade-Height Gauge Block

Looking for a quick way to set the height of a table saw blade? Cut notches on the end of a 4x4 block at the blade heights you use most often—we chose ¼ in., ⅜ in., ½ in. and ¾ in. Then, to use the block, position the desired notch over the blade and raise the blade until its highest point just touches the block.

PENCIL TRICK FOR SANDING

When you're sanding an edge flush to the adjacent surface, first draw a squiggly pencil line across the joint. Use the marks as a guide to help you sand flat and avoid sanding through the plywood's veneer.

REPURPOSE A FOAM BRUSH

Don't throw out a foam brush when you're done with it. Cut away the foam, and you'll be left with a great flexible glue applicator!

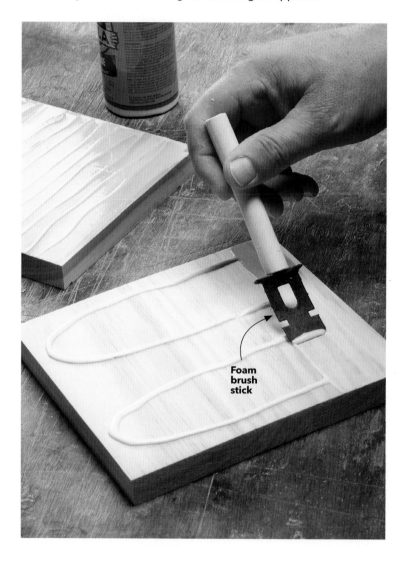

Foam brush stick

Stop block

1x4

A Stop Block for Long Cuts

Setting up a stop to make repeat cuts is definitely a timesaver. Here's one solution for cuts that extend beyond your saw's fence. Attach a long 1x4 to your saw fence and use a stop block made from a short piece of 1x4 and a ¼-in. plywood lip. Slide the stop block to where you need it, then clamp it into place.

Hole-Saw Depth Marker

The best way to avoid tear-out with a hole saw is to drill halfway through the wood and flip it to complete the hole. But how do you know when you've cut halfway? Easy—mark your saw with a line that's slightly more than halfway. With ¾-in. stock, mark the saw at just past ⅜-in. Use a pencil so you can wipe off the line and mark a different depth as needed. This tip also makes it easier to remove the plug; more of it extends past the saw teeth so you can grab it to pull it free.

FINISHING STANDS

When you're finishing table legs or other furniture parts, cut square ¼-in. plywood "stands" and screw them onto each end. The table legs stay put as you apply your finish, making the job much easier than it would be if the parts were hung on a hook. And you can stand them vertically to dry.

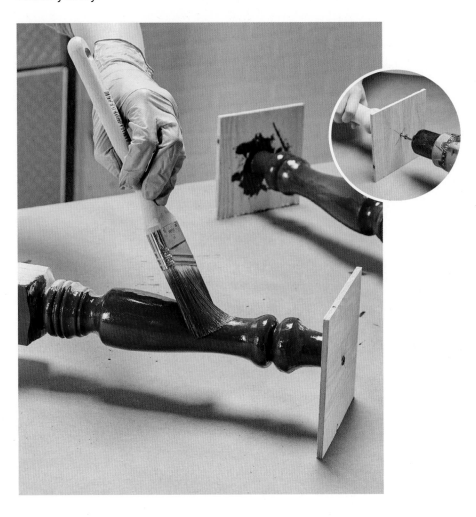

AROUND-THE-SHOP CURVE GUIDES

When you need to draw a curve on a project, instead of reaching for a ruler and a compass, start looking around your shop. There are dozens of round objects available for tracing a perfect curve or radius—anything from a 5-gallon bucket to a roll of tape to the dime in your pocket.

Marking Gauge with Pencil

This just might become one of your favorite and most-used tools: a marking gauge with a hole drilled in it to accept a pencil. You can use it when you want to align screws, drawer pulls or other hardware that doesn't require a high level of precision.

Floor Ruler

No need to scramble for a ruler every time you need to measure something big. Draw a ruler on your shop floor with a permanent marker. It won't be accurate enough for precise measurements, but for rough cutting it will save you time and effort. When the markings start to wear off, just redo them.

BOBBY PIN NAIL HOLDER

When you're hammering small nails or nails in tight quarters, keep your fingers out of the line of fire with a bobby pin. It will grip even the smallest nails.

QUICK MIXING SURFACE

Instead of using a container to mix a little epoxy, make a mixing surface on your workbench using painter's tape. Lay down several strips, overlapping the edges so the epoxy doesn't get on your bench. When you're done, peel off the tape and throw it away.

FOLD SANDPAPER INTO A PAD

For sanding edges and curves by hand, this sandpaper trick can't be beat. Take a quarter sheet of sandpaper and fold it in half, then fold it in half again. Tear halfway along the crease as shown, then fold one half inside the other. Voila! This method makes a firm but flexible pad, and the inner surfaces don't wear against each other. When the two outer surfaces have been used up, simply refold to expose the two inner surfaces.

DIY Edge-Band Clamps

You could buy clamps ready-made for gluing on edge banding, but there's a cheap and easy way to make them on your own. All you need are spring clamps and rubber bands. Poke a rubber band through the holes in the jaws of the spring clamp, then loop it around the ends of the clamp to hold it in place. It works great!

Rubber band

Garden Straightedge

If you need to pull up sod for a new garden or a flower bed, one good way to cut straight lines is to use an edger and a 2x6.

Bungee cord

VINYL SIDING HELPER

Long lengths of vinyl siding can be tough to install by yourself, so consider using this trick. Hang a bungee cord on the wall above the siding and use it to hold the siding in place while you nail it off. The elasticity of the bungee cord makes it easy to pull the siding down to snap it into place before nailing.

ROOT-CUTTING SHOVEL

For digging in root-filled soil, make a small "V" in the tip of your shovel or trowel with a file or grinder. Keep it sharp with a file. The "V" will trap and slice the roots as you dig.

PREPAINT NAIL HEADS

When you're installing pre-painted wood or engineered-wood siding, paint the tops of galvanized nail coils the color of the house before loading them into the gun. It's much faster than going back and painting them one at a time later. Use a foam brush and apply the paint sparingly so it doesn't drip over the edges of the nail heads. Let the paint dry completely before loading the coils into the nail gun.

Easier-to-Connect Irrigation Fittings

Connecting plastic irrigation tubing to barbed fittings can be tough on your hands. To make the job easier, use an electric teakettle to pour boiling water onto the tubing. This softens the tubing, making it easier to push onto the fittings.

Barbed
fittings

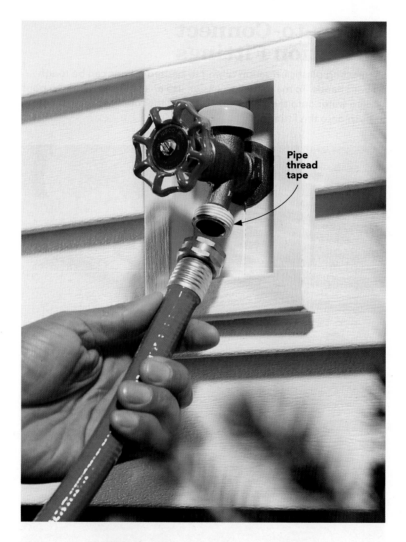

Pipe
thread
tape

Easy-Off Hose

A single wrap of pipe thread tape (available at hardware stores and home centers) on outdoor faucet threads makes it easier to thread the garden hose on and off.

REDISCOVER THE DOWEL JIG

Strong, simple joinery never goes out of style

IF YOU THINK pocket screws and biscuits have put dowel jigs out to pasture, think again. We love pocket screws and biscuits, but dowels offer a combination of strength, simplicity and accuracy that simply can't be beat. That's why most furniture pieces are still manufactured with dowels.

A self-centering jig can make joints as well as a machine, and we think it's a worthy addition to any home shop. All you need is a drill. Read on for our best tips for choosing and using a dowel jig.

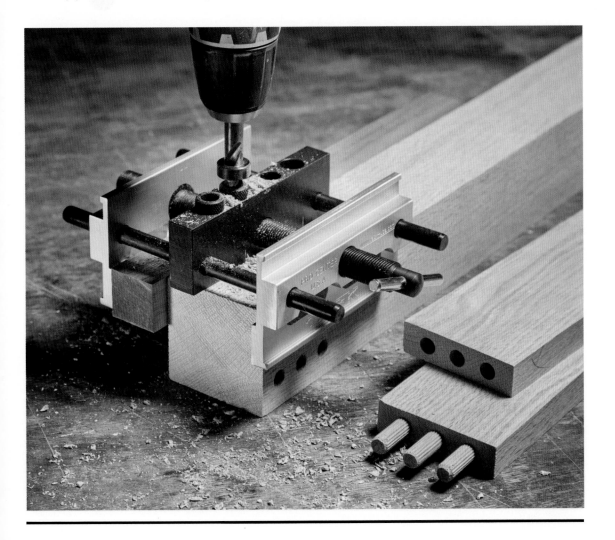

How It Works

The heart of the jig is a steel block with holes to guide your drill bit. On many models, the holes are threaded, which lets you install bushings for drill bits of various sizes. The holes are precisely perpendicular and located in the exact center of the block.

Center lines for each hole are scribed on the side of the block. They're visible through two windows.

A screw runs through the whole block. Turning the screw's handle moves both sides of the jig an equal amount as it clamps onto the wood. That's why the jig is "self-centering": Clamping the jig centers the holes on the wood automatically.

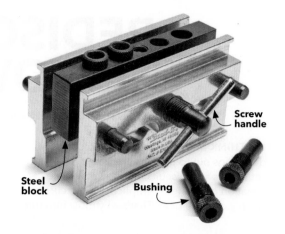

Screw handle

Steel block

Bushing

How to Make a Joint

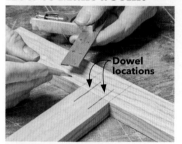

Dowel locations

Center line

1 MARK THE PARTS. Position the parts and mark the dowel locations with a pencil. We're showing a T-joint here, but most joints require the same steps.

2 MATCH UP THE LINES. Align your pencil lines with the center lines on the jig's block. Tighten the screw to clamp the jig into place. Drill the dowel holes.

3 PRESTO! Add dowels and glue for a fast, strong and perfectly aligned joint.

TIP: IMPROVE THE HANDLE

The short handle on a dowel jig can dig into your hand when you loosen or tighten the jig. One solution is to use a cheater pipe, but here's a better one: Screw on cheap round knobs from the hardware store. Cut threads on the handle using a ¼-in.-20 die.

Die cutter

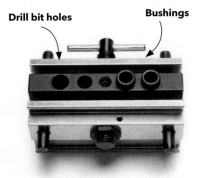

Drill bit holes   **Bushings**

Choosing a Jig

Various manufacturers make self-centering dowel jigs. At first glance, they all seem the same. But there are little differences that matter a lot.

PRO ADVICE You'll find dowel jigs in various styles, and some of them carry tempting price tags. But they are often flimsy, inaccurate or just hard to use. Every woodworker we talked to prefers the classic self-centering styles shown here.

SHOP ONLINE Woodworking stores and some home centers stock dowel jigs. But start your search online, where you'll find the widest selection.

THE BASIC MODEL

The most basic jigs have holes sized for various drill bits (no bushings). If you want to use more than one dowel in a joint, you have to move the jig. That can lead to alignment problems, so choose this type only if you're on a tight budget.

BUSHINGS ARE BETTER

Some jigs come with bushings of various sizes that screw into threaded holes. That lets you drill holes of the same size without moving the jig. This model has two bushing holes and two drill bit holes that don't accept bushings.

Additional bushing holes

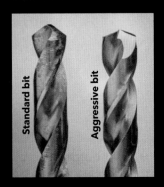

TIP: CHOOSE A STANDARD TWIST BIT
An aggressive twist bit is intended to cut rapidly, but that's not good for a dowel jig. An aggressive bit can grab the wood, pulling itself too hard and too deep, sometimes even causing the stop collar to slip. A standard twist bit is much better for a dowel jig. A brad point bit is OK too.

Standard bit   **Aggressive bit**

EVEN MORE BUSHING HOLES

This model has four threaded holes. That gives you more options for spacing between holes, and you could drill four holes without moving the jig. Extra bushings are sold separately.

EXTRA CAPACITY IS NICE

The other jigs shown here can clamp onto stock up to 2⅜ in. thick. That's almost always enough. But wide-capacity jigs handle stock of 6 in. or more separately.

Make a Vertical T-Joint

A self-centering jig isn't designed to make side-by-side holes in the face of a board (as shown in part A). But you can still do it. Here's how: Use the jig to make a guide block. The block itself will then act as a jig to position the holes. To start, measure how far your jig will open, and then cut a block of that length. Mark a center line on the block. The rest is shown here. Dowel the end of part B using your dowel jig.

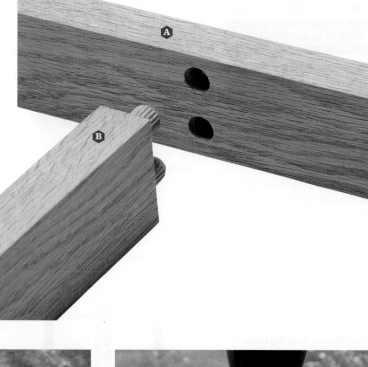

1 **MAKE A GUIDE BLOCK.** Drill two holes through a block, using the jig to position the holes perfectly.

2 **DRILL THROUGH THE BLOCK.** Align the block's center line with the joint's center line.

Make Better Edge Joints

Dowels are a big help when you're edge-gluing boards; they keep the boards aligned and flush. They also strengthen a joint that's not perfectly tight.

Stop collar

1 MARK THE DOWEL LOCATIONS. Cut the boards 1 in. extra long and butt them together. Mark dowel center lines 2 in. from each end and 8 to 12 in. apart in between.

2 DRILL THE DOWEL HOLES. Align the jig with the center lines and drill. Control the hole's depth using a stop collar. Glue dowels into one set of holes. Measure how far each one sticks out; cut any that are too long. Glue the boards together, then cut them to the final length.

TIP: FILE IF THE FIT IS TIGHT
The spacing between holes must be precise for two parts to fit together. If you find the spacing isn't quite right, file one side of a dowel pin to make it skinnier. Put a few layers of tape under the file so you don't mar the wood.

Make an L-Joint

Two boards joined as an "L" make a great table leg or box corner. Glue alone will make the joint plenty strong, but dowels provide perfect alignment.

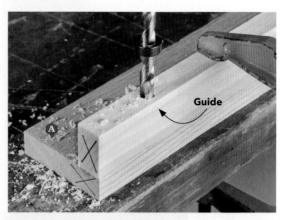

2 **DRILL THE FACE SIDE.** Clamp the guide to the face of part A and drill. Remember to align the "X" with the top of the part.

1 **MAKE A GUIDE.** Cut a scrap the same length as your workpieces and mark one end with an "X." Drill holes through the scrap using the dowel jig.

3 **DRILL ON THE EDGE.** Drill matching holes in the edge of part B, again aligning the "X" end with the top.

Make an Offset Joint

Usually, you want dowels in the center of a part, as in part A below. But sometimes you don't, as in part B. Well, you can fool your self-centering jig into making a joint that isn't centered. All you have to do is add a spacer block. Determining the precise width of the block is a little tricky, so test your setup on scraps before you drill the actual parts. You'll need an extra-wide jig if part B is more than 1½ in. thick.

1 ADD A SPACER BLOCK. Position dowel holes off-center by placing a block against the workpiece. Then drill the holes as usual.

TIP: SET A STOP COLLAR USING A BUSHING

When you buy a dowel jig, pick up a set of drill bit stop collars. A stop collar prevents you from drilling too deep, which can be a disaster.

The easiest way to position a stop collar is by using one of the bushings from your jig. Measure to the beginning of the bit's tip, not to the pointed end. Add ¹⁄₁₆ in. to allow space for glue at the bottom of the hole. This bit is set up to drill a hole 1¹⁄₁₆ in. deep, perfect for a 2-in. dowel.

8 EASY WAYS TO CUT METAL FAST

Select the best blades and tools for the job

THERE'S NOTHING WRONG with using a good old-fashioned hacksaw, but there are faster and easier ways to cut metal. In this article, we'll show you power tool tips and techniques for cutting the types and thicknesses of metal that DIYers handle the most.

1 Opt for a Diamond Blade

An angle grinder fitted with an abrasive metal-cutting disc works well to cut all kinds of metal, including bolts, angle iron, rebar and even sheet metal. But the discs wear down quickly, cut slowly and shrink in diameter as you use them. Instead, we recommend using a diamond blade that's rated to cut ferrous metal. These will last much longer, cut faster and cleaner, and wear down much slower than abrasive discs. You'll find ferrous-metal-cutting diamond blades at home centers, hardware stores and online.

2 Cut Metal with Your Circular Saw

It may not be an obvious choice, but fitted with the right blade, a circular saw is a great metal-cutting tool. You can cut mild steel up to about ⅜ in. thick using a ferrous-metal-cutting blade. Be careful, though! Hot metal chips will fly everywhere. Put on your safety gear, keep bystanders away and cover anything you don't want coated with metal chips. You'll find ferrous-metal-cutting blades at home centers, hardware stores and online. There are two types: inexpensive steel-tooth blades and carbide-tooth blades. Carbide-tooth blades are more expensive but will last longer.

Ferrous-metal blade

Metal roofing

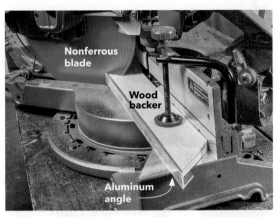

Nonferrous blade

Wood backer

Aluminum angle

3 Cut Aluminum with Your Miter Saw

Making accurate cuts on aluminum rods, tubes and angles is easy with a miter saw and a blade designed to cut nonferrous metal (check the label). If the motor housing on your saw is open and could collect metal chips, tape a piece of cloth over the openings to protect the motor windings and bearings while you cut the aluminum. (Remove it when the saw goes back into regular service, or the motor will overheat.) Trapping the aluminum with a wood backer as shown reduces the danger of flying metal shards and makes it easier to hold the metal in place for cutting. This tip is especially important when you're cutting thin-walled pieces. Without the backing board, the blade will often catch on the metal and distort it and make it unusable.

Tips for Cutting Metal Safely

Cutting or grinding metal sends tiny chips or shards of metal everywhere. And they can be hot and sharp. To avoid eye injuries, cuts, burns and other injuries from cutting metal, follow these rules:

- Read and observe the safety precautions printed on metal-cutting discs and blades.
- Wear safety glasses, a face shield and hearing protection.
- Cover all exposed skin with gloves, a long-sleeve shirt and pants.
- Allow freshly cut metal to cool before touching it.
- Wear gloves when handling metal that could have sharp edges.
- Securely clamp metal before cutting it.
- Never allow anyone near you while you're cutting metal unless they're wearing hearing and eye protection.

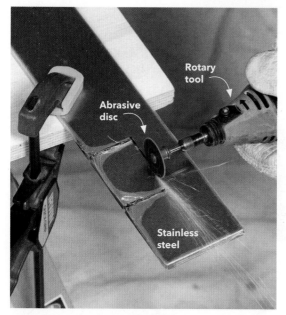

Rotary tool

Abrasive disc

Stainless steel

4 Cut Stainless Steel with an Abrasive Disc

There are many types of stainless steel, and some hard varieties are challenging to cut. For small jobs such as cutting stainless steel backsplash tiles, a rotary tool fitted with an abrasive metal-cutting disc works fine. For larger jobs, mount an abrasive disc in an angle grinder.

Steel stud

5 Simply Score and Snap

Siding contractors and roofers routinely score and snap aluminum siding and flashing to create straight, precise cuts. And you can use the same technique any time you need a straight cut on aluminum or other light-gauge sheet metal, even steel. Clamp or hold a straightedge or square along the cutting marks and score a line with the tip of a sharp utility knife blade. Then bend the sheet back and forth a few times to snap it. You can use the same trick to cut steel studs. Snip the two sides. Then score a line between the cuts and bend the stud to break it.

Metal-cutting blade

Oscillating tool

6 Get Into Tight Spots with an Oscillating Tool

When access is tight, or you need to make a flush cut, an oscillating tool fitted with a metal-cutting blade will solve the problem. Corroded mounting nuts on toilets and faucets are easy to cut off with an oscillating tool. You can also use an oscillating tool to cut plumbing pipes, automotive bolts, nails and other metal objects in places where a larger tool wouldn't fit. Just make sure the blade is intended to cut metal.

7 Cut Smarter: Use a Recip Saw

The next time you reach for your hacksaw, grab your reciprocating saw instead. Mount a metal-cutting blade in your recip saw, and you've got the ultimate power hacksaw for cutting bolts, rods, pipes and angle iron. A recip saw with a metal-cutting blade also works great for remodeling demolition when there are nails and pipes to cut off. Here are a few tips for cutting metal with a recip saw:

- Set your saw to straight rather than oscillating if there's an option for it.
- Extend blade life by keeping the saw's speed slow.
- Choose a blade with 20 to 24 TPI (teeth per inch) for thin metal, 10 to 18 TPI for medium-thickness metal and about 8 TPI for thick metal.
- Buy bimetal or carbide-tooth blades for longer blade life.

Metal-cutting blade

Match the Blade to the Metal

With the right blade or grinding disc, you can cut almost any kind of metal. The key is to match the blade to the material.

There are two types of metal: ferrous and nonferrous. (The term "ferrous" is derived from the Latin word "ferrum," which means iron.) Any metal that contains iron is a ferrous metal and requires a ferrous-metal-cutting blade. Steel angle iron, steel roofing, rebar and steel bolts are examples of ferrous-metal building materials. Most metal-cutting blades and discs are labeled for cutting either nonferrous or ferrous metal.

The two most common nonferrous metals DIYers need to cut are aluminum and copper. Nonferrous metals are usually softer and easier to cut than ferrous metals.

Metal lath

Diamond blade

8 Cut Metal Lath and Mesh with a Grinder

Metal lath and hardware cloth can be cut with tin snips, but there's an easier way. Mount a diamond blade in your angle grinder and use it like a saw to cut the mesh. We recommend using a diamond blade that's labeled as a ferrous-metal-cutting blade, but many tradespeople use a regular masonry diamond blade with good results.